DATE DUE
REMINDER

Please do not remove
this date due slip.

THE EAST-WEST CENTER—officially known as the Center for Cultural and Technical Interchange Between East and West—is a national educational institution established in Hawaii by the U.S. Congress in 1960 to promote better relations and understanding between the United States and the nations of Asia and the Pacific through cooperative study, training, and research. The Center is administered by a public, nonprofit corporation whose international Board of Governors consists of distinguished scholars, business leaders, and public servants.

Each year more than 1,500 men and women from many nations and cultures participate in Center programs that seek cooperative solutions to problems of mutual consequence to East and West. Working with the Center's multidisciplinary and multicultural staff, participants include visiting scholars and researchers; leaders and professionals from the academic, government, and business communities; and graduate degree students, most of whom are enrolled at the University of Hawaii. For each Center participant from the United States, two participants are sought from the Asian and Pacific area.

Center programs are conducted by institutes addressing problems of communication, culture learning, environment and policy, population, and resource systems. A limited number of "open" grants are available to degree scholars and research fellows whose academic interests are not encompassed by institute programs.

The U.S. Congress provides basic funding for Center programs and a variety of awards to participants. Because of the cooperative nature of Center programs, financial support and cost-sharing are also provided by Asian and Pacific governments, regional agencies, private enterprise and foundations. The Center is on land adjacent to and provided by the University of Hawaii.

East-West Center Books are published by The University Press of Hawaii to further the Center's aims and programs.

POPULAR MEDIA
IN CHINA

POPULAR MEDIA
in China
Shaping New
Cultural Patterns

Edited by GODWIN C. CHU

Foreword by A. DOAK BARNETT

𝓩 *An East-West Center Book*
from the East-West Communication Institute

Published for the East-West Center by
The University Press of Hawaii
Honolulu

Copyright © 1978 by East-West Center

Manufactured in the United States of America.

Library of Congress Cataloging in Publication Data
Main entry under title:

Popular media in China.

  Bibliography: p.
  Includes index.
    1. Mass media—China. 2. China—Popular culture.
I. Chu, Godwin C., 1927–
P92.C5P6   301.16'1'0951   78–13282
ISBN 0–8248–0622–0

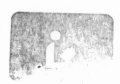

Contents

Foreword

The profound changes that have taken place in China during the past quarter century cannot be understood without knowledge of the structure and content of communication in the society. The leaders of the Chinese Communist Party have, from the start, recognized the great importance of developing new means to communicate to the Chinese people the ideas and values that they believe to be crucial to their revolutionary objectives. Since achieving power, they have rapidly developed a communication system that is far more extensive, and reaches the entire population far more effectively, than anything that existed in China in the past.

Modern mass media play a very basic role in the new communication system. As in other developing societies, the press and radio in particular are critically important as instruments for transmitting the leadership's views. Not surprisingly, much of the recent research on communication in China has focused on these familiar media.

Important as they are, however, modern media constitute only a part of China's new communication system. The Chinese have shown great imagination in adapting traditional media, including old forms of art and entertainment, to new uses. It is possible that, in a subtle fashion, these may have a greater impact on many ordinary Chinese than modern mass media do.

This volume is a collection of valuable studies of several of these "popular media": folk songs, opera, serial pictures ("comic" books), short stories, and wall newspapers. They throw important light both on how these channels of communication are used and on what the ideas and values that they attempt to communicate are.

The aim of Peking's leaders is ambitious: to create a new culture and transform the basic patterns of thought and behavior of the Chinese people. Some of the values they stress are rooted in tradition, but many are radically new. The mixture is a fascinating one, as several of these studies reveal.

It is significant that some of the popular media discussed in this volume are particularly important in relation to children, and others are ones that reach the mass of the population, including illiterates, in ways that modern media such as the press cannot. The Communists clearly are determined to do their best to change the thinking of all Chinese, not just those who belong to the country's new political elite, and they are attempting to ensure that the coming generation accepts the new values endorsed by the leadership.

Studies such as these, which focus on the structure and content of popular media, obviously do not measure the extent to which the thinking of Chinese has actually been remolded by the regime's far-reaching effort to create a new culture; intensive interviewing of large numbers of Chinese would be required to try to answer that question. The studies, however, illuminate the ideas and values Peking's leaders wish to communicate and the imaginative ways in which they are going about the task of creating a new culture.

The study of communication, a very fruitful approach to the understanding of any society, has only begun to be applied to China. This volume makes a valuable contribution and, hopefully, will encourage further work in the field.

A. DOAK BARNETT

Preface

Chinese culture has been a matter of puzzlement to many Westerners ever since the day Marco Polo brought back his tales of Cathay. This enigma seems to have deepened in almost three decades, a period during which China has been experiencing perhaps the most drastic cultural change in her long history. What are the Chinese cultural patterns of today?

Because of the increasingly visible roles China is expected to play in Asia, and because understanding her culture is a requisite for better relations with China, this matter of culture change has become a question having at once both academic interest and policy significance.

We hope this volume offers a partial answer. Through an analysis of some of the revolutionary popular media in the People's Republic of China, one can gain a glimpse of the new values, beliefs, and aspirations of the Chinese today. These popular media are important because they represent a fusion of the elite ideology of the Party and the input, admittedly fragmentary, of the common people. Even though the extent to which the revolutionary themes have penetrated traditional Chinese culture has yet to be ascertained, popular media do portend the direction in which Chinese culture is moving, albeit slowly.

The idea for this volume grew out of a series of discussions with Frederick T. C. Yu of Columbia University while he was a visiting scholar at the East-West Center in 1975. A. Doak Barnett, of the Brookings Institution, read and commented on the initial drafts of these studies during his tenure as a senior fellow at the East-West Communication Institute in 1976–1977. His many suggestions have been incorporated into the studies. Among other colleagues, Ai-li Chin and Chia-shih Hsu read the manuscript and made many helpful suggestions.

This volume was prepared with the support of the East-West Center. The views expressed, however, are those of the individual contributors and of the editor. We alone assume responsibility for errors in facts and interpretation.

CHAPTER 1   Popular Media:
A Glimpse of the
New Chinese Culture

Godwin C. Chu

COMMUNICATION AND CULTURE

The Chinese have an old saying: "When you are on a mountain, you do not see its true shape." Culture is like that also. Few of us can describe the culture in which we live. Often it takes an outsider—a traveler or an anthropologist—to describe it for us. The various studies assembled in this volume are initial attempts to catch sight of the true shape of a mountain—from a distance. The mountain in this case is the new Chinese culture. What we can see is, admittedly, a rather small part, for the new Chinese culture, like a mountain painted in a traditional Chinese landscape, is enshrouded in clouds and can only be discerned when the prevailing winds shift.

Part of the difficulty of understanding the new Chinese culture, aside from the scarcity of firsthand materials, lies in the ambiguities and diversities surrounding the concept of culture. Because of the varied applications of this term, American anthropologists, A. L. Kroeber and Clyde Kluckhohn surveyed the literature twenty years ago and, after reviewing hundreds of definitions, proposed the following:

> Culture consists of patterns, explicit and implicit, of and for behavior acquired and transmitted by symbols, constituting the distinctive achievement of human groups, including their embodiments in artifacts; the essential core of culture consists of traditional (i.e., historically derived and selected) ideas and especially their attached values. . . .[1]

To say that cultural patterns are acquired and transmitted by symbols suggests that culture and communication are inseparable. Indeed, this point is made clear by Edward Sapir when he says, "every cultural pattern and every single act of social behavior involve communication in either an explicit or implicit sense."[2]

Analyzing the communicative behavior of a people, including both its pattern and content, will therefore help us understand their culture. How do they communicate? What do they communicate about? From their overt and diverse communication it should be possible to identify some general, relatively uniform themes that constitute what Kroeber and Kluckhohn call the essential core of culture, or "core values," as they are sometimes referred to.[3] In comparing behavioral patterns in pre-Communist China and America, for instance, the anthropologist Francis Hsu has identified the cultural value of submission to authority for the Chinese in contrast to one of self-reliance for the Americans.[4] In other words, a good deal of the behavioral patterns of Chinese before 1949 can be understood in terms of their tendency to defer to authority figures. Conversely, we gain insight into the behavior of Americans when we fully appreciate their strong disposition to assert individual independence and to rely upon themselves.

We thus move from overt, diverse behavior to covert cognitions—ideas, values, and beliefs that exist in the minds of people and, to a large extent, guide and regulate their behavior. To study the cognitive components of any culture, several alternatives are available. A researcher can systematically observe the behavior of a people and make inferences about their ideas, values, and beliefs; he can seek verbal reports from the people themselves about their values and beliefs either by formal or informal interview, life history, or some form of projective testing; he can analyze popular verbal content for ideas about various aspects of their life, ideas that have been transmitted orally or in written form in folk tales, drama, and folk songs; or he can live in a culture for a good part of his life and form intuitive, subjective impressions. Each approach has its own merits and limitations that have been discussed elsewhere.[5]

In the case of China, because of limited opportunities for direct behavioral observation, interviews, psychological testing, or personal experience in the country, the examination of popular verbal content has become essential simply because it is one of the few methods available. We do not suggest that this is the only productive way of analyzing Chinese culture. Nor do we expect to gain a full understanding of current Chinese culture by this method alone. We do believe, however, that this method will provide glimpses of insight which will help us understand the values and beliefs of the Chinese.

ANALYSIS OF POPULAR VERBAL CONTENT

In using popular verbal content as a basis for making inferences about a culture, we may ask several questions. First, is the content of folk tales, drama, and folk songs a valid repertoire of social heritage that has gone through the processes of *spontaneous* selection and elimination? Do we have sufficient reason to believe that whatever has been retained represents what the people think, feel, and follow? In traditional China, for instance, when we analyze *Twenty-Four Legends of Filial Piety*, the assumption is that the model of behavior portrayed in the legends represents mores that were socially endorsed and spontaneously chosen over time from among numerous such stories. Second, are the values and beliefs espoused in the verbal content *representative* of the population as a whole? In that sense, the conclusions one draws from an analysis of classical literature, for instance, probably cannot be assumed to reflect the values and beliefs of the peasants. *Dream of the Red Chamber*, a well-known classic, is just such an example. Finally, when we analyze drama, fiction, folk tales, and folk songs, whether written in the historical past or the contemporary present, do the results provide valid indices for the *current* cultural patterns? These three questions measure spontaneity, general applicability, and currentness.

For folk media, we suggest that the answers to all three questions are positive. The originators of folk songs, popular drama, and folk tales are usually unknown. Out of the many songs and stories that gained circulation at one time or another, only those with broad appeal were spontaneously disseminated to the general audience and transmitted from generation to generation. If the folk songs are still being sung and the folk tales still told and enjoyed, this seems to reflect their current relevance and popular acceptance.

In China today, the traditional folk tales, popular drama, and folk songs have been replaced by a new set of media created by the Party—revolutionary opera, children's songs, picture books, and short stories. For the purpose of maintaining a distinction, we shall refer to these as *popular* media, rather than *folk* media—for these media are being popularly promoted, although they do not necessarily possess all the attributes of folk media. We shall briefly note the particular relevance of these popular media in the contemporary Chinese social context.

There is reason to believe that the content of the revolutionary opera, short stories, picture books, and children's songs reflect a model of *current* Chinese cultural patterns, as those are being actively propagated by the Party authorities. That is, the Chinese people are being urged to follow *now* the revolutionary models portrayed in these media.

Second, there is no question that the values and beliefs

reflected in the popular media are being advocated for the entire population of China, particularly the vast number of peasants and workers, although the techniques may vary for different age groups. The requirement of universal, general applicability appears to be met.

The question of spontaneity deserves special attention. Do these revolutionary stories, children's songs, and opera themes tell us what the Chinese people, in general, spontaneously aspire to and believe in? This question has no simple answer. On one hand, much of the popular media content has an elite origin, reflecting as it often does the ideological orientations of the Party. On the other hand, in the actual production there is considerable input from the grassroots level. For instance, peasants, workers, and soldiers contribute their ideas to revolutionary opera and write some of the short stories. Many revolutionary folk songs are composed by school children. The degree of spontaneity is thus difficult to assess because the popular media in China today are a fusion of what is designed and what is spontaneous. Although we suspect, however, that much of the old Chinese culture has survived, and that the Chinese culture today is an unascertained mixture of the old and the new, we have chosen to study the new popular media on the grounds that culture is an adaptive, ongoing social process. It has a tendency to adjust to a changing environment. The thrust of the programs of social transformation in China for the last twenty-nine years has been to move toward the future, not to hold on to the past. Eventually one would expect the influence of the old culture to diminish over time, and the grip of the new culture to gain more and more strength, albeit slowly. In that sense, the content of popular media can indicate the trend of cultural change. Although it may not tell us "what is," it does outline "what should be" and suggest, rather possibly, "what will be in future."

The significance of the popular media resides partly in the Chinese theory of psychology, particularly with regard to the role of perception in human behavior.[6] According to Marxist-Leninist epistemology, the external world, or "objective reality," is reflected in our consciousness, which differs largely according to our class backgrounds. The unfolding of objective reality is considered to be the ultimate source of social change. The Chinese Communist leaders have accepted this Marxist theory of consciousness but have given it a subtle Maoist interpretation. From the work Chinese psychologists did before the Cultural Revolution, primarily on the psychology of recognition, it seems that the Chinese do not unreservedly regard the development of proper consciousness to be the inevitable outcome of proletarian class background. If left alone, the proletariat—the masses—will not necessarily develop desirable consciousness according to the Communist doctrine, because their eyes may not see "objective reality." Rather, this process has to be aided by the *correct recognition* of objective reality.

In other words, objective reality has very much a social-perceptual component, and it is the Party's role to provide the ideal context in which the ideologically sound elements of reality will be correctly recognized. Only in this way will the right kind of consciousness develop among the mass of people. The popular media are thus employed by the Party as an instrument to aid the process of correct recognition, so that the Chinese will know what is desirable for them to know and see what is desirable for them to see. Correctness, in the thinking of the Party leaders, is more important than spontaneity.

In a sense, the mass media of newspapers, magazines, and radio share this role of aiding the correct recognition. We have chosen to analyze popular media not just because they are unconventional and relatively unknown to us[7] but, more importantly, because they differ from mass media in both content and style in a way that makes them more revealing of Chinese culture.

The content of Chinese mass media is largely informational and ideological, including reports on current events, struggle movements, and production campaigns. Only infrequently does it reveal the concrete behavioral patterns of the Chinese at the level of personal interaction. Popular media content also has a strong ideological orientation. Because drama and fiction seek to portray a behavioral reality, however, we can get beneath the ideological messages a glimpse of the specific human relations, values, and beliefs which are not manifest in the mass media, and which the ideologically inspired authors may or may not be conscious of. Sporadic and latent as they are, such glimpses can be highly revealing.

In terms of style, the mass media in China tend to be prescriptive and repetitive. The same message is often presented many times with slight variations in order to direct the audience in a particular way. Undoubtedly, there is some element of that in the popular media as well. Because the popular media are also intended to be entertaining, however, they are more emotive. The lessons they bring forth are more instructive than prescriptive. They present more varied details about the life of the Chinese, details that may not be essential to the major ideological themes. Such details are included as if to appeal to the basic emotions of the people— love, hatred, happiness, and anger. From some of these minor emotive portrayals we may gain a sense of how the Chinese feel as well as how they think.

Thus, the analysis of the content of popular media in China can be revealing and illustrative, if the findings are interpreted with caution. Even if the analysis does not adequately show the contours of the new Chinese culture, it can nevertheless provide an indication of the direction in which the Chinese are being prompted to think and feel, a direction which, given enough time and practice, they may eventually adopt.

PROCESS OF DIRECTED CULTURAL CHANGE

The popular media can also be fruitfully examined because they illustrate the process by which the Party leadership is prompting the Chinese to unlearn the old and learn the new, thus directing the course of cultural change. We shall discuss their role in the perspective of the process of directed culture learning.

Two related elements unique to human cognitive processes play essential roles in culture learning. One element is the use of symbols. Symbolic processes enable us to extend our mental world beyond the immediate environment and thus reach a high level of abstraction in our thinking. The other element is our tendency to rely on secondary sources for a basis of validity and not to seek direct verification of the content in our cognitive field. These secondary sources are often what we call "authority figures," persons whom we have come to trust and follow. They derive their authority in part from their knowledge and in part from the normative support they command in their social and cultural environment, in the sense that other authoritative figures in similar positions think and act in like manner.

It is through symbolic processes, reinforced with the support of authority figures, that individuals growing up in a culture learn values and beliefs which may have no immediate relevance to their limited role behavior and which they probably would otherwise be unable to generalize from their day-to-day behavioral patterns. Loyalty to the emperor, as a traditional Chinese value, is an example. The average peasant had no direct interaction with the emperor. In fact, he had no means by which to verify empirically the existence of the emperor. Yet he had come to accept the emperor not only as the embodiment of absolute authority, but also as the "Son of Heaven," who deserved total obedience and sacrifice from his subjects. The peasant was able to form this ideational concept partly because of his ability to abstract, which enabled him to project from the powerful landlords in his village to this unreachable "Son of Heaven," but also partly because he accepted the words of the village elders at face value without asking for empirical verification. In a similar manner, the Chinese for centuries endorsed without question the idea of ancestor worship, which uplifted the status of deceased parents and grandparents close to that of guardian angels.

The act of learning values and beliefs of this kind, however, does not rely on the words of authority figures alone. In any culture, one usually finds legends and stories, in the form of drama, narrative, or lyric, that symbolically portray behavioral patterns in support of the relevant values and beliefs. The depicted events that elicit those behavioral patterns are usually beyond what an average person would normally encounter. For instance, a peasant would almost never find himself in a situation where he could demonstrate his loyalty to the emperor through personal sacrifice. But in a play or a folk tale, he could experience indirectly, through the behavior and symbolic affirmation of the main characters, what absolute loyalty means and how important it is. Through dramatization, he could identify with the characters, rejoicing in their triumphs and suffering in their trials, and eventually accept their values as his own. In other words, a value such as absolute loyalty to the emperor was something the village elders could strongly affirm, but not something they could vividly demonstrate to the peasants. It is the function of folk tales, drama, and popular fiction to illustrate for the peasants the meanings, relevance, and importance of those values and beliefs that lie beyond their daily experience, in an emotional, dramatic context with which they can readily identify. Thus, folk media aided the symbolic process of culture learning.

In this process, folk media can extend beyond what is directly experienceable and serve the vital function of communicating to a society's large population certain unifying themes that bind them together into one cultural group. It seems that the Party authorities in China fully recognize the importance of this function when they go beyond the technically advanced, Western-originated mass media of newspapers, radio, and television and use Chinese opera, fiction, songs, and serial pictures (similar to comic books) as major communication channels for propagating the new Chinese culture. It is a case of using traditionally accepted forms of communication to (1) illustrate the exceptional circumstances that crystallize pertinent new values, and (2) provide an emotive basis of identification to aid their acceptance. This is how the popular media in China serve the function of cultural transmission, in Harold Lasswell's terms.[8]

Such considerations prompt us to analyze the popular media in China as a process of directed cultural change. Stated another way, some of the new values and beliefs the Party wants to establish may be difficult for the majority of the Chinese people to assimilate. Because they are somewhat abstract, these ideas normally do not enter the people's daily lives. The abstract nature of some of the new values means that the social context of the average person's daily interactions, in and of itself, may not provide an ideal setting for learning the new culture. A social-cultural vacuum would thus be created and the pace of change slowed. The popular media—including revolutionary drama, fiction, serial pictures, and children's songs—can aid the symbolic process of culture learning to fill that vacuum. By providing concrete meanings that the majority of Chinese can understand, by laying an emotive basis of identification and acceptance, these popular media can serve the integrative function of propagating new unifying themes and, at the same time, can keep up the momentum of cultural change.

POPULAR MEDIA EXAMINED

Of the various popular media currently used in China, we have selected five because of their pervasiveness and the availability of materials. Two of the media are directed primarily at children: serial pictures and revolutionary children's songs. Both forms have been popular among Chinese children for generations. I remember the days in Hankow before World War II when many of my after-school hours were occupied by reading serial picture books. The most popular theme during those days was *kung fu*. But other themes—palace conspiracy, historical events, and even romantic love—were also present. Children's folk songs have been part of Chinese culture for ages. Passed from generation to generation in the process of child-rearing, many children's folk songs dealt with parental love and family life, although the themes varied somewhat regionally. In the rural areas, Chinese teenagers used to sing folk songs that were timid expressions of romantic love. "The Shepherd's Song of Love," for instance, was so popular that it was incorporated into the traditional Chinese opera. In China today, the old format of serial picture books and children's folk songs has been used extensively to transmit new messages to the present generation of children when they are still at an impressionable age. The style and content of serial picture books are analyzed by John Hwang in Chapter 3, and the content and themes of revolutionary children's songs are discussed by Leonard Chu in Chapter 2.

Although serial pictures and folk songs are intended for children, the Chinese opera is an important medium primarily for adults. Unlike Western opera, the Chinese traditional opera is a folk art as well as an elite art; it has been extremely popular among the rural population in its various regional versions, even though in the past most of the accomplished artists performed only in big cities. The much-disputed transition of the Chinese opera from its traditional format to its current revolutionary style and the process of creating the revolutionary opera are traced by Godwin Chu and Philip Cheng in Chapter 4. In Chapter 5, Cheng has further undertaken a comparative analysis of the traditional and revolutionary operas in terms of the predominant values they espouse. Using both quantitative content analysis and factor analysis, techniques that have been only occasionally applied to China studies, he is able to draw an intriguing picture of continuity and change between the old and the new.[9]

Unlike popular songs and opera, which can be sung and understood by the Chinese people at large, short stories as a medium are for those with a certain level of education. Unlike the opera, however, which accentuates the dramatic and the extraordinary, often expressed in a capsule format, short stories strive to portray more complex situations of reality. Even though this "reality" may only be that seen through the eyes of the Party theoreticians, thus leaving few surprises for the readers, the attention to the details of interaction, the dialogues, and the stress on vividness and a lifelike quality can reveal nuances of modes of thinking, acting, and valuing. A thorough analysis of Chinese short stories of the 1970s, compared with those of the 1950s and 1960s, is undertaken by Ai-li Chin and Nien-ling Liu in Chapter 6.

The last medium discussed in this volume is different from the others in several ways. This is the unique, omnipresent *tatzepao*, the big-character posters. It is true that posters, like folk songs, opera, and short stories, have been part of Chinese culture for a long time. Siao Yu, a playmate of Mao Tse-tung, recalled that during his childhood posters were used by the villagers as a way of exposing injustice and airing grievances.[10] The posters were also used in those days for public announcement of important events. But the prominence and extensive use of this medium, penetrating as it were the life of practically every adult in the country, have been the result of deliberate advocacy by the Chinese Communist Party. In that sense, it is a new element in the Chinese culture.

Another difference may be noted about *tatzepao*. While serial picture books, opera, and short stories are largely "spectator" media, in the sense that the audience is basically the recipient of the messages, China's *tatzepao* is more of a "participant" medium. One not only reads the posters but is also urged to participate in producing posters for others to read and criticize. It is also an "expressive" medium, for it gives ordinary people a channel for bringing petty grievances and minor problems to the attention of the authorities.[11] If the old Chinese culture was one of reticence and noninvolvement—typified by the saying, "Let's each sweep the snow in front of his door, but never mind the frost on other people's roofs"—then the *tatzepao* has initiated a major change, for today one has to get involved, to speak out. Although much of what one says usually follows the Party policy, the very fact of expressing oneself, of getting involved, represents a new cultural pattern not found in old China. In Chapter 7, David Poon discusses the historical background of the *tatzepao*, its growing significance in China today, and some of the limitations of its efficacy as a means of ideological communication.

Other popular media besides those examined here are being actively employed by the Party for transmitting the new culture. Examples are storytelling, puppet shows, vernacular plays, variety shows, and poster art. They all convey revolutionary messages through a popular form of communication and can be rewardingly analyzed. The various studies we have included here are but a beginning of what should be a much broader effort to understand the new Chinese culture, for much of it, just like the mountain in a traditional Chinese painting, still lingers beyond our observation and requires further probing.

NOTES

1. A. L. Kroeber and Clyde Kluckhohn, *Culture, A Critical Review of Concepts and Definitions* (New York: Random House, 1963), p. 357.

2. Edward Sapir, "Communications," In *Encyclopedia of the Social Sciences*, 1st ed., vol. 4 (New York: Macmillan, 1935), p. 78.

3. For a discussion of cultural uniformity versus diversity, see Anthony F. C. Wallace, *Culture and Personality* (New York: Random House, 1961). The idea of core values is implicit in the definition by Kroeber and Kluckhohn. See also Francis L. K. Hsu, ed., *Aspects of Culture and Personality* (New York: Abelard-Schuman, 1954); and Alex Inkeles, "Some

Sociological Observations on Culture and Personality Studies," in *Personality: In Nature, Society, and Culture*, ed. Clyde Kluckhohn, Henry A. Murray, and David M. Schneider (New York: Alfred A. Knopf, 1965), pp. 577–592.

4. Francis L. K. Hsu, *American and Chinese: Reflections on Two Cultures and Their People*, 2nd ed. (New York: Doubleday & Company, 1970).

5. See for instance David Aberle, "The Psychosocial Analysis of a Hopi Life-History," in *Comparative Psychology Monographs* 21:1 (Berkeley: University of California Press, 1951); William E. Henry, "The Thematic Apperception Technique in the Study of Culture-Personality Relations," *Genetic Psychology Monographs* 35 (1947); William Henry, "Projective Tests in Cross-Cultural Research," in *Studying Personality Cross-Culturally*, ed. Bert Kaplan (Evanston, Ill.: Row, Peterson and Co., 1961), pp. 587–596; Eleanor E. Maccoby and Nathan Maccoby, "The Interview: A Tool of Social Science," in *Handbook of Social Psychology*, vol. 1, ed. Gardner Lindzey (Reading, Mass.: Addison-Wesley Publishing Co., 1954), pp. 449–487; Clyde Kluckhohn, "The Personal Documents in Anthropological Science," in L. Gottschalk et al., "The Use of Personal Documents in History, Anthropology and Sociology," *Social Science Research Council Bulletin* 53: 79–173; Weston LaBarre, "Folklore and Psychology," *Journal of American Folklore* 61 (1948): 382–390.

6. For a detailed analysis of psychological research in the People's Republic of China, see Robert and Ai-li Chin, *Psychological Research in Communist China: 1949–1966* (Cambridge, Mass.: The M.I.T. Press, 1969). The Communist Chinese epistemology is further discussed in the paper by Ai-li Chin and Nien-ling Liu in this volume.

7. Among the few studies available are: Alan P. L. Liu, *The Use of Traditional Media for Modernization in Communist China* (Cambridge, Mass.: The M.I.T. Press, 1965), and Frederick T. C. Yu, *Mass Persuasion in Communist China* (New York: Praeger Publishers, 1964). The chapter on *tatzepao* in Yu's book is the first known analysis of this unique Chinese medium.

8. Harold D. Lasswell identifies three major functions of communication: (1) the surveillance of the environment, (2) the correlation of the parts of society in responding to the environment, and (3) the transmission of social heritage from one generation to the next. See Lasswell, "The Structure and Function of Communication of Society," in *The Communication of Ideas*, ed. Lyman Bryson (New York: Institute for Religious and Social Studies, 1948).

9. The purge of Chiang Ching has so far had little effect on the status of the revolutionary opera, which she used to claim as her creation. For fur-

ther discussion of this point, see the paper by Godwin Chu and Philip Cheng in this volume.

10. Siao Yu, *Remembering My Boyhood* (Taipei, Taiwan: Yih Wen Chih Monthly Publications, 1969), pp. 77–80.

11. These functions of *tatzepao* have been discussed in Godwin C. Chu, Philip Cheng, and Leonard Chu, *The Roles of Tatzepao in the Cultural Revolution: A Structural-Functional Analysis.* (Carbondale, Ill.: Southern Illinois University, 1972).

CHAPTER 2　Sabers and Swords
for the Chinese Children:
Revolutionary Children's
Folk Songs
Leonard L. Chu

Revolutionary children's folk songs are fine weapons.
Like sabers and swords, they kill all ferocious foes.
Mold myriad sabers and swords
To kill them all—all the world's old foxes.
　　　　　　　　　—Revolutionary children's folk song[1]

Folk songs, created and circulated among the common people, are one of society's spontaneous forms of communication. In Chinese, folk songs are called *min ko,* or "people's
songs," to mean that they are the songs of the people, not the
songs of the aristocrats or the literati. Because of their spontaneity as well as their simplicity and beauty, they are cher-
ished and enjoyed by the common people and literary writers
alike. Children's folk songs, *erh ko,* differ from *min ko* only
in that they are recited and circulated among children.
Throughout China's long history, *min ko* and *erh ko* have
largely retained their original characteristics. This, however,
is changing. Under direction of the Chinese Communist Party, this grassroots form of communication has been politi-
cized. The songs are still called *min ko* or *erh ko,* and their
forms have remained largely the same, but they have acquired new content and new functions. This chapter analyzes

some of the changes that have taken place by examining the revolutionary children's songs *(ke ming erh ko)* now being promoted in China.

THE PRE-1949 YEARS

Folk singing had long played important roles in China's social communication network. Together with theatrical performance and storytelling, folk singing was an integral part in traditional China's complex value and information system.[2] Children's folk songs played similar roles. Their functions as carriers of cultural heritage and reflectors of public opinions and social conditions received particular attention. Since *erh ko* were often satirical of national or local political figures as well as of adults and children in the region, scholars and moralists watched them closely for clues of deviations from ethical norms. So did rulers and bureaucrats for clues of public dissatisfaction or disobedience.[3] It was common for old historical novels to include one or two episodes in which children's folk songs were used to spread rumors to help create a favorable climate for the insurgents. To what extent this actually happened is difficult to document because of lack of written records. These episodes, however, do demonstrate the importance of children's folk songs in Chinese society.

During the Republican years, children's folk songs continued to receive attention. In the early twenties, a group of professors at the National Peking University organized a folklore society to collect and study China's folk songs. To publish their collection, a *Folk Songs Weekly* was issued.[4] In South China, folk songs also attracted a group of professors at the Sun Yat-sen University in Canton.[5] In the thirties, the Republican government began to look into China's folk songs. During this period, both the Ministry of Education and the Ministry of Interior were engaged in the collection and study of folk songs for the purpose of "remolding the nation's character."[6] As a result, many collections were published. It was Japan's all-out war against China that aborted such efforts.

The Chinese Communist Party was founded in 1921, coinciding with the national interest in folk songs. Engaged in heated struggles against the Kuomintang to win the support of the masses, the Communists tried to utilize every possible source of manpower. Early Communist history indicates that children were organized to perform a variety of duties, including acting as messengers and spying on suspicious intruders in Communist-occupied areas. Rich in metaphor and prophecy and oftentimes satirical of social injustice, children's folk songs were utilized by the Communists to socialize the children and the people as well as to help highlight dissatisfaction and whip up enthusiasm among the masses. Children's folk songs conducive to the Communist causes were included in school textbooks and carefully sorted out for popularization. In addition, new ones were created and propagated.[7]

The pre-1949 years in general were characterized by a national interest in folk songs. The war against Japan and the Nationalist-Communist civil war were the major deterrents to the collection and study of children's folk songs. Though the Communists did try to utilize children's folk songs in an organized effort to achieve their objectives of mass mobilization, their activities were limited to the areas under their control. Coordinated efforts on the national level to put children's folk songs under direct political control did not come about until after the founding of the People's Republic of China in 1949.

THE PRE-CULTURAL REVOLUTION YEARS

After the People's Government was proclaimed in late 1949, the Chinese Communist Party soon began to organize all communication media, traditional and modern, for the purpose of creating a breed of socialist Chinese. Attention was focused on resocializing the adult population as well as on bringing up the children in a new cultural milieu. To do so, a movement to create and spread a new kind of children's literature was launched. Chinese writers were urged to learn from the models set by their counterparts in the Soviet Union and aim at producing works that could cultivate a socialist breed of healthy, courageous, and honest children who would love the country, the people, manual labor, science, and public property.[8]

During this period, efforts were made to collect folk songs from around the country and publish them for dissemination. In the eight years between 1951 and 1958, about four hundred fifty titles were produced. These folk songs and children's folk songs were reminiscences of the early hardships of the Chinese Communists during various stages as well as commemorations of the achievements made during the first decade of China under Communism.[9] Steps were also taken to weed out undesirable children's folk songs and to create new ones for propagating the Communist ideology and glorifying such achievements as the Great Leap Forward and the people's communes in the late fifties.[10]

During the first half of the sixties, China's split with the Soviet Union gradually intensified. The field of children's folk songs still followed basically the same policies established in the fifties, although any suggestions of learning from the Russians were dropped.[11]

Two criteria were set for weeding out bad children's folk songs: first, whether the content of a song had any educational value, and second, whether it was artistically created, rich in imagination, and sophisticated in the choice of words.

Specifically, three kinds of traditional children's folk songs were criticized and deleted. The first kind perpetuated superstition, feudalism, or fatalism. Children's folk songs suggesting the pursuit of wealth or worship of deities were also considered bad and excluded from dissemination.

The second group made fun of other people's physical deformities or those meant to scare children with frightful monsters or hideous characters. For instance,

Red eyes, green nose.
Four hairy legs.
Clanging while walking.
Hungering to eat the kids.

This song was considered to do too much harm to children. It was criticized and excluded.

The third kind described the hardship of the laboring masses and women but did not identify them with the old society. The rationale was that these things no longer existed in China under Communism. Mothers and children were urged not to recite them lest there be confusion between the past and the present. These songs, however, were still cited in publications as references to the old society.[12]

Following these criteria, the traditional children's folk songs retained were those of educational value. They taught children to love hygiene, cherish friendship, and respect manual labor. Others taught the children simple arithmetic or helped enrich the children's imagination. It was said that only very few "bad" children's folk songs were retained out of carelessness.[13]

While undesirable children's folk songs were being screened and deleted, new ones were created and disseminated. The following two, reported in the early sixties, are typical examples. One, called "Praise the Communes," reads: "Little, little birds, singing on the trees, praising the oxen and goats growing so strong; praising the grain piled up so high; praising the ponds teeming with fish and shrimp; praising the communes so good."[14] The other, called "Support the Young Black Brothers," reads: "Little white pigeons, you are really beautiful! Fly to Africa quickly, to tell the young black brothers that we support them forever."[15]

To sum up, socialist and nonsocialist children's folk songs coexisted during the first seventeen years before the Cultural Revolution. This policy was soon to be criticized as "revisionist" and revolutionary children's folk songs would prevail.

REVOLUTIONARY CHILDREN'S FOLK SONGS

Revolutionary children's folk songs were one of the so-called "socialist newborn things" which have emerged from the Cultural Revolution.[16] Together with other forms of literature and art, they are considered "powerful weapons for teaching Marxism, Leninism, and Mao Tse-tung thought." Or, in Communist terminology, the battlefront of children's folk songs has been completely occupied by the proletarian class.[17]

Unlike their counterparts in pre-Cultural Revolution years, revolutionary children's folk songs are referred to as powerful weapons for class struggle. They are not only used to criticize bad children's folk songs but are also tied into every political movement—the criticism of Lin Piao and Confucius, the criticism of the legalist school's bourgeois thinking, the counterrevolutionary line advocated by Teng Hsiao-ping and, most recently, the condemnation of the "Gang of Four" and the praising of China's new Party chairman, Hua Kuo-feng.[18]

For other purposes, revolutionary children's folk songs are used to teach children good sanitary habits, to pay tribute to Mao Tse-tung, to hail the Party, to urge people to learn from the model Tachai Brigade, and to promote other socialist newborn things.

The efforts to create revolutionary children's folk songs are almost unprecedented. For instance, Hsiao Wei is a student with the title of "Red Little Soldier" at an elementary school in Peking. He was reported to be composing almost

one revolutionary children's folk song a day for the purpose of propagating Marxism-Leninism and Mao Tse-tung
thought: glorifying Chairman Mao, the Party, and the Cultural Revolution, and criticizing capitalism, revisionism, and
Teng Hsiao-ping.

Hsiao Wei wrote that he alone composed more than ten
revolutionary children's folk songs when Mao called upon
the country to criticize the classic novel *Shui Hu* (Water
Margins) and capitulationism. His primary school produced
more than twenty thousand revolutionary children's folk
songs in only a few years.

In April, 1976, when the Communist Party Central Committee announced its two decisions to relieve Teng Hsiao-
ping of his duties and to appoint Hua Kuo-feng as the
premier, Hsiao Wei immediately wrote nine revolutionary
children's folk songs to show how much he loved Chairman
Mao and how much he hated Teng Hsiao-ping.[19] One of his
creations reads like this:

> Party Central's decisions warm the people's hearts,
> Pointing the direction for us to march forward.
> With Teng Hsiao-ping's duties stripped,
> The whole nation, from below and above, is elated.
> In celebration, gongs and drums are beaten,
> Spurring more energy in counterattacking the wicked wind.
> Resolutely criticize Teng Hsiao-ping, for
> Chairman Mao is the one who is backing us!

While the case of Hsiao Wei may be unique, composing
revolutionary children's folk songs has in fact become a national activity. In Tientsin, one primary school composed
more than ten thousand revolutionary children's folk songs in
the campaign to criticize the "Right deviationist wind to
reverse correct verdicts."[20] In Yuncheng County of Shansi
Province, twelve schools produced more than fifty thousand
revolutionary children's folk songs in six months to criticize

and condemn Teng Hsiao-ping.[21] Even the less productive schools reportedly turned out revolutionary children's folk songs in the hundreds and thousands.[22]

AUTHORSHIP AND DISSEMINATION OF REVOLUTIONARY CHILDREN'S FOLK SONGS

It is not easy to determine the age of authors of revolutionary children's folk songs. Those published in books and in the press show that both children and adults, especially workers, peasants, and soldiers, are among the composers. The age of children authors ranges from about six to mid-teens. Most of them were elementary school students, with a smaller percentage enrolled in middle schools. Of the more than eight hundred revolutionary children's folk songs (dated 1973-1976) analyzed for this study, more than 87 percent are attributed to single authorship. Coauthorship by two or three accounts for about 7 percent. Next comes "collective authorship," about 5 percent, attributed to either a "revolutionary children's folk song group" of a school or a production unit's spare-time writing group. Only very few, less than 1 percent, are attributed to anonymous authors.

To propagate revolutionary children's folk songs, a variety of media are utilized and organized:

1. Revolutionary children's folk songs are being taught at schools and nurseries. The children are taught not only to recite them but also to create new ones. Some songs are included in school textbooks. Others use the *pin yin* system of Romanization to enable younger children to read.[23]

2. Revolutionary children's folk songs are disseminated through the mass media. Newspapers and magazines—for instance, the *Serial Pictures* monthly and *Poems* monthly—as well as radio all carry revolutionary children's folk songs.

3. Recitation and competition meetings are organized for children to participate in reciting and publishing their own

creations. Such contests may be held as often as once a week or twice a month.[24] The *Kwang Ming Daily* reported that a fifth-grade class held a recitation contest of revolutionary children's folk songs especially for the condemnation of Teng Hsiao-ping and the Tienanmen Square Incident of April 5, 1976.[25]

On November 25 and 26, 1976, Peking held a massive poetry recital to celebrate Hua Kuo-feng's succession to Mao as chairman of the Communist Party and the crushing of the "Gang of Four." At this gathering, political lyrics, epics, and children's folk songs as well as "verses accompanied by gongs and drums" were recited. Theatrical troupes and a variety of other cultural and art groups were also present.[26]

4. Books and pamphlets are among the major media used to propagate revolutionary children's folk songs. These publications use attractive illustrations. Those aimed at younger children are usually printed in color and each song is accompanied by a picture. Some books are written in Chinese characters together with their *pin yin*. These books are published by either Peking or Shanghai's People's Press and are distributed by Hsin Hua (New China) Bookstores throughout the country.

To facilitate circulation, the cheapest of these publications sell for only about 5 US cents. Most sell for about 10 US cents, with the most expensive ones priced at about 15 US cents.

Large quantities are being printed. The press run for one collection was 800,000 copies. Even the smallest press run had 150,000 copies.

Another way of disseminating revolutionary children's folk songs is by printing them on "calendar cards" (Figures 2–1—2–5). On one side, a revolutionary children's folk song is printed. On the other side is a calendar for the whole year. Beautiful illustrations in color are included in the designs. These cards sell for about 1.5 US cents apiece.

5. Since children's folk songs all have simple rhymes, they

Children's Folk Songs Calendar Cards

Children's folk songs by: Liu Meng
Designs by: Mao Sui-hsien

红小兵，学工忙，
开机床，隆隆响。
做颗革命螺丝钉，
"铁人"叔叔是榜样。

FIGURE 2–1.

Red little soldier is busy learning to operate the machine.
Switched on, the lathe sounds "boom boom."
I want to be a revolutionary screw.
Uncle "Ironman" is my model.

红旗飘，呼啦啦，
学军课上练打靶。
敌人胆敢来侵犯，
一枪一个消灭它。

FIGURE 2–2.
Red flags are flapping.
In military drills, we aim at the target.
If the enemies should dare to invade,
They will be eliminated, one after the other.

红小兵，喜洋洋，
肩并肩，学习忙。
从小爱读革命书，
红心永向红太阳。

FIGURE 2–3.
Red little soldiers are so happy.
Side by side, they are busy studying.
They love to read revolutionary books since young.
Red hearts are always facing the red sun.

学农课堂在田头，
叔叔教咱开铁牛。
广阔天地学本领，
争当人民老黄牛。

FIGURE 2-4.
I am learning agriculture on the farm.
The uncle teaches me how to drive the iron buffalo (tractor).
Learning skills in this vast land,
Everyone is eager to be the people's cow.

红小兵，志气高，
基本路线记得牢。
个个争当小闯将，
批林批孔立功劳。

FIGURE 2-5.
Red little soldiers are ambitious.
They learn the basic lines by heart.
Everyone is eager to become a brave little general.
To establish meritorious deeds in criticizing Lin Piao and
    Confucius.
[Note that the child is writing a *tatzepao*.]

can be easily memorized and sung. Thus, they are made into
record albums and put on sale.[27]

CONTENT OF REVOLUTIONARY CHILDREN'S
FOLK SONGS

More than 90 percent of the revolutionary children's folk
songs we examined are ideologically oriented. Most deal with
current events, such as the glorification of Mao or Hua and
the Party, or the condemnation of Teng Hsiao-ping and now
the "Gang of Four." (See Figure 2–6.) Others recall historical events, such as the war against Japan, the Long March,
and life under greedy capitalists or landlords.

FIGURE 2–6. "Every Revolutionary Children's Folk Song Expresses Our Heroic Spirits" by Lo Chia-pen. The banner headline
says "Heartily Hail the Victorious Convention of the Fourth People's Congress." Note the sun and sunflowers in a picture on the
wall (upper left corner). The two Chinese characters above the sun
and sunflowers are *erh ko*, children's folk songs. This illustration is
reproduced from *Serial Pictures* monthly (February, 1975), p. 21.

The 10 percent of the revolutionary children's folk songs are about exercising, sports, and hygiene. Even these are not totally devoid of political tones. "Rope Skipping," for instance, is one such folk song:

Skip a single rope. Skip a double rope.
Let's all skip a fancy rope.
First we line up as the geese do.
Then skip as fast as the wind.
Scarves are red as fire and the faces, too.
Never stop moving on the road of revolution.[28]

Political and ideological tones are even more evident in "Grenade Throwing":

That little grenade
Scares the enemies to death.
Today we practice grenade throwing.
Tomorrow we annihilate the enemies.
Class hatred and national hatred
Are burning hot in the chest.
Turn hatred into strength,
Attack all imperialists, revisionists, and
counterrevolutionaries.[29]

Given this heavy ideological orientation, the content of revolutionary children's folk songs covers almost all aspects of life in present-day China. The songs deal with going to a night school for the study of Mao Tse-tung thought, attending a special criticism session, or participating in a "remember-bitterness-think-of-sweetness" meeting. Or they deal with life in a commune, an oil field, or a neighborhood factory, and so on.

CHARACTERS

In terms of characters, children's folk songs cover people from all walks of life. These characters include: children, who usually appear as *hung hsiao pin* (red little soldiers);

family members, who appear on political occasions rather than in family settings per se; national figures, including both those who, like Mao Tse-tung, Hua Kuo-feng, or Ironman Wang Ching-hsi, are praised, and those who, like Teng Hsiao-ping and Lin Piao, are denounced; workers, peasants, and soldiers, who are described as working hard and as models for children; youth settling down in the countryside; cadres and Party secretaries, worker propagandists, militia; barefoot doctors; foreigners, including the condemned "imperialist superpowers" and Japanese, and the praised "foreign friends" and "foreign guests"; and capitalists, landlords, "class enemies," who are criticized or condemned.

Animals and birds appear in only a few of the children's folk songs. One song describes birds singing happily while another depicts how two grandparents, wanting to protect the commune's property from being damaged, rescued a lamb in a storm.

We will take a look at the different types of characters who are treated in the folk songs.

HEROES

The greatest hero to appear frequently in children's folk songs is Chairman Mao Tse-tung. Almost without exception, he is glorified in absolute terms and compared to the sun. Take the "Red Little Soldiers Follow Chairman Mao" for instance.

Red Sun,
Chairman Mao,
Every sunflower faces you.

Your books,
We study.
Your instructions we memorize by heart.

Red little soldiers
Follow you
In revolution forever![30]

Other heroes who appear frequently are workers, peasants, and soldiers; young intellectuals settling down in rural villages; barefoot doctors; the model Tachai Brigade or the Taching oil field. In general, however, they are referred to collectively. Besides Mao, and recently, Hua Kuo-feng, other individual heroes are limited to such national figures as Lei Feng, the Ironman Wang Ching-hsi, and Huang Shuai,[31] the few nationally recognized in the official media. In all other cases, heroes appear nameless. They are described as "uncle worker," "uncle policeman," "red salesclerk," "auntie barefoot doctor," and so on.

Two examples will be used to illustrate how heroes are presented. First, a "collective hero" in a children's folk song entitled "Bright Shining Sky over the Motherland":

Newborn things emerge in the thousands.
White smoke is puffing out from the chimneys.

Little brother asks his sister,
Who says, smilingly:

"It was created by uncle workers,
Who cleared the smog to prevent pollution.

Efforts are so well coordinated and utilized
That bright sky is shining over the motherland."[32]

The following, "I Want to Learn From Lei Feng's Model" is about an individual hero:

Little Grassy was singing happily.
She hopped all her way joyfully.
She walked into a book store to buy a poster.
A portrait of Lei Feng was selected.
Asked why she picked out that one,
Smiling and raising her head, she said:
"Lei Feng devoted his life to the people
And dedicated his red heart to the Party.
The uncle was a sunflower.
I want to learn from Lei Feng's model!"[33]

VILLAINS

Villains are those characters condemned or criticized in the children's folk songs. Among those children's folk songs with villains, about two dozen deal with foreign villains. Domestic villains are the landlords, the usurers, the capitalists, the Nationalists, the "bad" children's folk songs, the "bad" books, and so on. Lin Piao, Confucius, Teng Hsiao-ping (before his most recent reinstatement), and the "Gang of Four" are the only Chinese condemned by name in folk songs. Others appear nameless.

Compared with those that glorify heroes or model deeds, children's folk songs condemning villains are much fewer, accounting for about one eighth of the total collected for analysis. We will take a look at several examples.

The first song comdemns those "bad elements" in society who are propagating bad books and bad children's folk songs. It is entitled "We Should Be Brave Little Revolutionary Generals."

Little Chin, Little Chuan, and Little Kan
Were discussing in their classroom about the current situation:
"Look at these bad stories.
Who is telling them?
Look at that bad children's folk song.
Who is teaching it?
Red little soldiers, beware.
Watch closely the new direction the class struggle
    turns into."

Check the east.
Check the west.
Once the masses were mobilized,
The bad egg had no place to hide—
That smiling wolf under watch
Had always been trying to poison us secretly.
Red spear in hand,

Our combatting spirits were high and strong.
Repudiated, the bad egg lowered his head.
He handed out a whole box of bad books.

Little Chin, Little Chuan, and Little Kan
Spoke out at the criticism session:
"We red little soldiers
Have bright eyes and bright minds.
Always remembering class struggle by heart,
We should be brave little revolutionary generals!"[34]

Lin Piao and Confucius are described with such epithets as "wolves," "crooks," "big bad egg," or "bandits." Take for instance the following song, entitled "We Are Determined to Exercise Dictatorship":

Who are bad?
The jackals and wolves are.
Yet Lin Piao was even worse.

Bandit Lin Piao was
Pregnant with ghosty plots.
He said we were "dictators."

What he was getting at
Is crystally clear.
He wanted to usurp the Party's power
And restore all ghosts and monsters to power.

Red little soldiers
All said no, and
Aimed their artillery fire at Lin Piao.
Over all five black classes,
We are determined to exercise dictatorship.[35]

Since the downfall of Chiang Ching, the "Gang of Four" has been added to the list of villains. Children's folk songs denouncing the "Gang of Four" seem to have replaced those denouncing Teng Hsiao-ping. It has become the turn of the "Gang of Four" to be attacked as "insidious wolves,"

"bloodsuckers," "capitalist roaders," or "traitors." Take for
instance the following, entitled "Resolutely Crush the 'Gang
of Four' ":

> Full of courage and full of spirit,
> Red little soldiers march to the battleground.
> Each children's folk song is a sword.
> And each sword is aimed at the "Gang of Four."
>
> The "Gang of Four" is a pack of insidious wolves.
> They were engaged in restoration and splitting the Party.
> They flattered foreigners and wanted to be their slaves.
> They were so treacherous that they wanted to usurp the Party
>   and seize its power.
> Swords are unsheathed and rifles loaded.
> Red little soldiers march toward the battleground.
> We fight under Chairman Hua's command.
> We will resolutely crush the "Gang of Four"![36]

Landlords, capitalists, and others form another group of
villains in the children's folk songs. They are considered to
belong to the old society but are brought up again in
"remember-bitterness-think-of-sweetness" sessions. "I Knock
Him Down to the Ground" is one such children's folk song.

> The boss was really wicked and cruel.
> He forced me to work from morning till dark.
> I was tired and sweating.
> And hunger weakened my legs.
> Falling by the machine,
> I shed a puddle of blood.
> The fierce and cruel boss
> Whipped at me:
> "You are pretending illness.
> Get up and work!"[37]

FOREIGNERS

There are thirty-two children's folk songs (about 4 percent)
that have foreigners in them. (Americans are mentioned only

in passing. There are only two such children's folk songs.) Eight of them depict a warm and friendly relationship between the Chinese and people in other parts of the world. These folk songs are all about welcoming "foreign friends" visiting China or about uniting with foreign peoples in the struggle against the two "imperialist powers."

"Hearts of the World's People Are Linked Together" reads like this:

Listen! Listen!
The planes are arriving.

Foreign guests! Foreign guests!
From five continents and four seas, they are coming
    to Peking.

Welcome! Welcome!
Hearts of the world's people are linked together.

Unite! Fight!
Revolutionary friendship is forever green.[38]

The Soviet Union is the number one foreign villain in the children's folk songs. It is referred to as the "new czar," an aggressor anxious to invade China, who, however, is always prepared to defend herself against such invasion.

The old czar and
The new czar
Are all wicked wolves.

Wicked wolves
Are full of bad plots,
And always wanting to bite China like a piece of meat.

Plotting rebellions and
Engaged in expansionism,
The superspy is doomed to meet death.

New China
Can never be imposed upon.
This piece of fat meat is hard and strong.

Stop dreaming.
Stop fancying.
A May fly can never move a tree.

Wicked wolves,
If you dare take any mad actions,
Seven hundred million pairs of fists are there for you to bite![39]

Another foreign villain is Japan, who, however, appears in a historical context only. In a collection entitled "Songs of Children's Anti-Japan Corps," eighteen children's folk songs describe how children helped the Communist troops fight the Japanese "wolves" and "bandits" by acting as spies or by participating in battles.[40]

M. Antonioni, the Italian film director who produced a documentary called *China* in the early 1970s, is the only individual foreigner singled out for attention. One children's folk song characterizes him as a "big bad egg."

Antonioni
Was a big bad egg.
Lying on the ground and pointing his legs into the sky,
He shot his film, purposely mixing black and white.
How cunning he was!

Antonioni,
You will never deceive anyone.
New China is growing in prosperity.
Friends from the five continents are praising her.
To hell, all imperialists, revisionists, and antirevolutionaries.[41]

CHILDREN

In all the children's folk songs, as they would be, children—boys and girls—play the leading role. They are all presented as heroes actively engaged in carrying out the Party's various directives. They are depicted as lending a helping hand on a farm or in a factory. They are described as eager to learn from model workers, peasants, and soldiers. Children at play appear in a very limited number of the folk songs, about forty. Others describe children as hygiene-loving. Two different examples will be given here for illustration. The first one, entitled "Red Little Soldiers Receive Military Training in the Drill Ground," is about children playing as soldiers.

Red flags, red scarves, and red spears.
Red little soldiers are receiving their military training
  in the drill ground.
All lined up neatly,
They look like a strong wall.
They run as fast as a gust of wind, and
They climb up the poles just like that.
After grenade throwing, they practice bayonets.
The heads of their spears are shining brightly.[42]

The second one, entitled "Seesaw," is about children playing at seesaw. It is one of the few with a light, nonideological tone.

The seesaw
Can be high and low on either side.
Let's sit still and hold the handles tight.
One side is low and
The other is high.
High and low; we laugh "ho, ho."
Unite tightly,
Coordinate well.
The more we play, the more interested we are.[43]

THEMES AND SCENES

Themes of revolutionary children's folk songs are various. An overwhelming majority of the songs present more than one theme. Clearcut classification is difficult because most themes are closely tied together into one general topic, namely, revolution and ideological struggle.

We have found that children's folk songs touch upon

almost every aspect of life in today's China. They deal with everything from watching a model revolutionary opera to fighting with the Russians at Chen-pao Island (in northeast China), from showing determination to liberate Taiwan to exalting China's satellites, and from hailing peasants who till the land to celebrating the completion of a new railway in southeast China. These themes can be captured in one phrase—glorifying the achievements made in China and attributing them to the leadership of the Party and its chairman, Mao Tse-tung.

Other than these themes, there are those describing how the people, and the children as well, are enthusiastically supporting the Party by studying Mao Tse-tung thought or by actively participating in various political movements. There are themes that describe children eagerly modelling themselves after "brothers and sisters who settle down in rural areas," or workers, peasants, and soldiers.

Family settings do appear in children's folk songs, but they are presented in a political context, not as family gatherings per se. There are songs about a father going to the "May Seventh School," about parents sending their children off to settle in villages, about a child escorting his grandma to a night school of Mao Tse-tung thought, or about family members together condemning Teng Hsiao-ping. None of these is about parents and children enjoying family life.

Children playing, one of the major themes in the songs, is presented in a political light, too. The children are depicted in military drill or condemning all sorts of "enemies."

Other themes that appear less frequently are aimed at reminding the children of the "bad old society" before 1949. Their purpose is to contrast the present with the past so as to make the children cherish the present.

Songs teaching children to love hygiene, to form sanitary habits, and to exercise do exist. They are, however, greatly outnumbered by other kinds of folk songs praising the official policy.

APPROACH AND STYLE OF REVOLUTIONARY
CHILDREN'S FOLK SONGS

The approach and style of revolutionary children's folk songs produced after the Cultural Revolution are identical with those in other fields of literature and art. Basically, they are proletarian as defined by the Party and epitomized in the model revolutionary operas promoted by Chiang Ching. Although Chiang Ching is now disgraced and has lost her power, the style of literary creation that has flourished in China for the past decade has remained. So far there are no signs that it will be changed in the near future.

The purpose of the "proletarian style and approach to literature and art" is to create a uniform image of the Party-sanctioned proletarian heroes. Thus, folk songs glorify a "grandpa poor peasant," "an uncle miner," "uncle Lei Feng," "an auntie barefoot doctor," or "a big sister going to settle down in rural villagers," and so on. All these are intended to implant in the children the correct images of workers, peasants, and soldiers so that the children themselves will follow these models when they grow up.[44]

Another feature of revolutionary children's folk songs is their activism and militancy. They deal not only with what belongs to the children's world, such as playing or saying innocent things, but also with what is generally considered within the realm of adult political life. Thus, you find children responding to every move the Party makes and joining, as their parents do, in current political campaigns. Not only that, revolutionary children's folk songs are at the same time full of highly abstract ideological terms, such as "restoration of rites," "using the three directives as the key link," the "Right deviationist wind to reverse correct verdicts," just to name a few.

In terms of militancy, revolutionary children's folk songs liberally apply such phrases as "opening fire at," "smash them," "repudiate until they stink," "pierce through their black hearts." (See Figure 2–7.) Simplicity and childlikeness, features characteristic of traditional children's folk songs, are not prominent. It seems that the Chinese Communist leaders want to bring up a new generation of militant Chinese rather than docile ones. It is not accidental that one Chinese writer should have said that old children's folk songs are "little sheep" while new children's folk songs are "brave little warriors."[45]

While Chinese children's folk songs have changed a lot in content, their form has retained many of the traditional

FIGURE 2–7. "A Children's Folk Song Is a Piece of Artillery" by Li Chieh et al., Third Grade, Ling Hai W. Rd. School, Shanghai. The banner says, "Anti-Lin Piao and Anti-Confucius Children's Folk Song Recital." This picture is reproduced from *Serial Pictures* monthly (June, 1975), cover.

features. Generally, short sentences are used and most songs are not long. The most frequently used form is one or two three-character phrases followed by one or two seven-character phrases. This form is not new. It is a combination of the old traditional three-character verses and the seven-character poems. In fact, it is the same as the form of children's folk songs popular in Taiwan. Even the rhymes are of the same pattern. That is, the first, the second, and the fourth verses, but not the third, rhyme together. Overall, it is another case of the Chinese Communists using old cultural patterns to serve new political purposes.

Rhymes and rhythms in revolutionary children's folk songs continue to be simple. Except for a very few long ones, they can be easily memorized. In fact, many of them have been set in music.

Realism and directness also characterize today's children's folk songs. Even the metaphors used are easy to detect. For instance, in one song hailing the Taching oil field, oil pipes are likened to a huge river in China.[46] In another one describing a beautiful rural scene, the "mountains are smiling and dancing."[47] Nevertheless, the almost omnipresent metaphor is the sun for Chairman Mao and sunflowers for the Chinese people and children.

Lack of a distinctive demarcation between children's folk songs and poems, either created by adults or children, is another feature. In style, it is difficult to tell a children's folk song from a poem written by adults. The two literary forms use the same style and the same format in today's China. They often deal with the same topics for the same purposes.[48]

FUNCTIONS OF REVOLUTIONARY CHILDREN'S FOLK SONGS

Revolutionary children's folk songs perform at least three major functions: socialization, communication, and social control.

SOCIALIZATION

Children are like sheets of white paper; you can paint them almost any color. The Chinese Communist leaders have realized this fact for a long time. To create a new breed of socialist Chinese, they know they have to start with the children as early as possible to make the task easier. Folk songs are what the children learn and memorize even before they are old enough to go to school. The Party regards folk songs as so essential that it has decided not to leave them to the parents, who may consciously or unconsciously recite songs that contain values contradicting those advocated in Communism. One way of achieving this is constantly to criticize "bad" songs and at the same time supply new desirable ones.[49]

COMMUNICATION

Revolutionary children's folk songs also serve an information dissemination function. Children may listen to the radio and then immediately compose new songs based on what they have just heard. When the Fourth People's Congress was held in Peking in early 1975, Chinese children composed folk songs about the convention. When the Communist Central Committee announced its decision on April 7, 1976 to strip Teng Hsiao-ping of all his duties and appointed Hua Kuo-feng as the premier, the children were composing new songs to show their support. Again, when the "Gang of Four" was crushed and Hua Kuo-feng was appointed chairman of the Communist Party, the various celebrations and demonstrations of support also included the composition of children's folk songs.[50]

Other children's folk songs are aimed at publicizing China's latest developments, such as the recently completed Chengtu-Kunmin Railway, the Nanking Bridge over the Yangtze River, the Red Flag Canal in Shensi Province, the visiting of foreign friends, and the latest educational reforms.

By incorporating all these items of information in children's folk songs, the Party can be sure that not only the people but the children as well are kept informed of the latest policies and the direction which they should follow.

SOCIAL CONTROL

Content of revolutionary children's folk songs indicates that they closely follow the Party lines, be it the criticism of Lin Piao, the condemnation of the "Gang of Four," or the hailing of the Tachai Brigade. This contributes to an atmosphere of consensus in which few would venture to deviate from the officially approved directives. Whether Chinese children chanting the songs really can comprehend the meanings matters little; the important thing is that the adults who hear the chanting know very well what the implications are. Furthermore, quite a few children's folk songs unequivocally relate to children's surveillance roles as contributing to the capture of "bad elements" in the country and to the location of "bad" books. As mentioned earlier, organizing children for social control or surveillance has long been a Chinese Communist practice that can be traced back to their Yenan years.

CONTRAST WITH THE PAST

Children's folk songs are indeed being revolutionized in China. Their content is almost beyond recognition by people who are familiar with traditional children's folk songs. This, of course, is because time has changed. But it is also because the Chinese Communist authorities are purposely politicizing this medium to create a new culture. Such an attempt has never before been carried out on such a massive scale, in China or elsewhere.

Traditional children's folk songs can be divided into two major categories. One category is what the parents or grandparents taught their children. These songs may have been passed on from generation to generation or they may have been the parents' own creations. The children gradually learned them by heart. The other category is what children sang while playing. These songs may have been created by adults or by children themselves.[51]

In contrast with the past, children's folk songs in today's China are distinguished from traditional ones in at least four major areas:

1. *Process of creation:* People-created (past) versus authority-created (now). Traditional children's folk songs were created either by the parents or grandparents or by children themselves, or they were inherited from former generations. They more or less spontaneously originated from the masses since there were no political sanctions against nonproduction or political approval for production. Their creation was largely an exercise of individual decision. It was for enjoyment rather than for any political purposes ordered from above. In contrast, revolutionary children's folk songs, though still created by children or adults from among the masses, are either initiated or directed from above. Except for a very few, most of them have a clear and distinctive purpose. It is the Communist Party or, more accurately, those in power within the Party, that decides what is to be composed and when. This is exactly why children's folk songs denouncing Teng Hsiao- ping have quickly disappeared and new ones condemning the "Gang of Four" have flourished recently.

2. *Content:* Primary relationship or love (past) versus "socialist" relationship or revolutionary ideologies (now). Since traditional children's folk songs were created on the people's own initiative, it is only natural that such songs touched mostly upon experiences in people's immediate environment, namely, the family or the neighborhood. Thus, they were characterized by parental love and close family relationship. These themes, however, are almost totally absent in children's folk songs in China today. Instead, the new songs invariably refer to the revolution or the Party. Al-

though the concept of family does appear in them, it is always introduced in the context of the Communist revolution or Maoist ideology. Thus, they are not about family members enjoying life together per se but about family members praising the Party's achievements or recounting their experiences in the various political movements. Their purpose is apparently to do away with traditional family relationship and replace it with a "socialist" relationship bonded by Maoist ideologies.

3. *Social indicators:* Public opinions (past) versus official policy (now). Revolutionary children's folk songs also differ from traditional ones in being generally glorifying in tone, while the latter were oftentimes critical or satirical. Those revolutionary children's folk songs that are critical are directed at the past or foreign villains or the so-called "class enemies" in society. They are never critical of the Party or the government. On the contrary, they always praise the current official policy, whether or not the policy contradicts or lends support to previous ones. In other words, they are not necessarily social indicators of today's China, although they may point out her desirable goals and values. On the other hand, traditional children's folk songs may be taken as indicators of public opinions, because many were indeed critical of political wrongdoings or social injustice.

4. *Process of dissemination:* Slow and spontaneous (past) versus fast and organized (now). Closely related to the distinctions just mentioned is the process of dissemination. Traditional children's folk songs, having originated from among the ordinary people, took much longer to emerge and circulate since there were no organized efforts behind them. Both the creation and the circulation had to depend on word of mouth. It is almost impossible to identify the authors or to locate the places where they originated.[52] Also, it is very difficult to collect traditional children's folk songs since they were usually not recorded and printed. This is not the case

with revolutionary children's folk songs, whose authors and originating localities can be readily identified. (Note that less than 1 percent of the revolutionary children's folk songs are by anonymous authors.) Moreover, they are not only mass produced but also mass circulated via all kinds of media.

There is yet another difference besides all these distinctions. In pre-Cultural Revolution years, both traditional and revolutionary children's folk songs coexisted, and the latter were not promoted on such a massive scale as they are now. Further, in pre-Cultural Revolution years, the task of creating new songs and weeding out undesirable old ones was largely assigned to professional literary workers. Since the Cultural Revolution, however, the Chinese children themselves have been involved in the task of creating and weeding. They are playing two roles simultaneously: that of socializers and that of socialized.

One last point needs to be mentioned. That is, do nonrevolutionary—that is, traditional—children's folk songs still exist and circulate in today's China? References to "bad" children's folk songs in revolutionary children's folk songs and in other publications indicate that they do exist and are perhaps liked by some people. Since Chinese children are constantly reminded to keep an eye on those "bad" children's folk songs, it is very likely that traditional songs circulate slowly and within a relatively small radius. Those that do survive are most likely the true indicators of today's China.

Folk songs and folk arts are liked because they are simple and uncontaminated by worldly concerns. Children's folk songs are liked by both adults and children for the same reasons. Today, as a result of the Party's determination to carry out its unprecedented social experiment, Chinese children's folk songs have become a political instrument. What impact this policy will have on the children of China deserves continued research attention.

NOTES

1. Hsiao Wei, "I Join the Battle by Writing Children's Folk Songs," *Poems* [Shi Kan] (June, 1976), p. 84.

2. Alan P. L. Liu, *The Use of Traditional Media for Modernization in Communist China* (Cambridge, Mass.: The M.I.T. Press, 1965), pp. 1–19.

3. Chang Yu-fa, *Communication and Its Cultural and Political Impacts During the Pre-Chin Period* (Taipei: Chia Hsin Foundation, 1966), pp. 17–22; Hu Hwai-sheng, *A Study of Chinese Folk Songs* (Hong Kong: Pai Lin Bookstore, photo edition of a 1925 book), pp. 10–13.

4. *Folk Songs Weekly*, vols. 1, 2, 3, were published between December 17, 1922, and June 28, 1925, and between April 4, 1936, and June 26, 1937, by the Peking University's Society of Folk Song Research. The three volumes were reprinted in 1970 by Taipei's Orient Cultural Services; Li Chin-hui, Wu Chi-jui, Li Shih, eds., *Children's Folk Songs from Twenty Provinces in China*, 2 vols. (Peking: National Peking University, 1925, reprinted 1970 by Orient Cultural Services, Taipei).

5. Liu Wan-chang, *Children's Folk Songs in Canton* (Canton: Sun Yat-sen University, 1928).

6. Wang Hsiao-yu, *Songs and Ballads from Shensi* (Taipei: Tien I Press, 1974; reprint of a 1935 edition), pp. 1–3.

7. Examples are plentiful in children's folk songs and stories published in China both before and after 1949.

8. Chen Po-tsui, "Learn from the Advanced Children's Literature in the Soviet Union," in *Essays on Children's Literature* by Chen Po-tsui (Wuhan: The Yangtze River Literary and Art Press, 1959), pp. 221–300.

9. Association of Chinese Folk Art and Literature, ed., *Materials of Chinese Songs and Ballads*, 3 vols. (Peking: Writers' Press, 1959), pp. 388-1–388-16.

10. Li Yao-chung, "Promote with Great Efforts the Creation and Collection of Folk Songs," *Poems* (January, 1976), p. 35; Liu Chao, "Talks on Children's Folk Songs," in *A Collection of Essays on Children's Literature* (Wuhan: Yangtze River Literary and Art Press, 1956), pp. 79–90.

11. Liu, *Traditional Media*, pp. 79–80.

12. Liu Chao, "Talks."

13. Ibid.

14. Liu, *Traditional Media*, p. 80.

15. Ibid.

16. These "newborn things" include "revolutionary committees," "theory contingents," "barefoot doctors," "model revolutionary operas," "workers, peasants, and soldiers attending universities," "youth settling down in the rural areas," and so on.

17. Hsiao Chiu, "Work Hard to Promote Children's Literature," In

48 POPULAR MEDIA IN CHINA

Essays on Literature and Art (Peking: People's Literature Press, 1974), pp. 162–163.

18. The "Gang of Four" included Chiang Ching, Chang Chun-chiao, Yao Wen-yuan, and Wang Hung-wen. They were arrested in early October, 1976, less than one month after the death of Mao Tse-tung. In "I Fight under Chairman Hua's Command," *Poems*, no. 12 (December, 1976), pp. 48–50, six children's folk songs were published. They were all about the glorification of Hu Kuo-feng and the condemnation of the "Gang of Four."

19. Hsiao Wei, "I Join the Battle."

20. The campaign was closely related to the criticism of Teng Hsiao-ping. New China News Agency, "Red Little Soldiers in Tientsin Are Brave Little Generals in Criticizing Teng," *People's Daily*, June 1, 1976, p. 1.

21. "Red Little Soldiers Fight Together to Deepen the Criticism of Teng Hsiao-ping," *Kwang Ming Daily*, June 1, 1976, p. 2.

22. "Utilize the Fighting Function of Revolutionary Children's Folk Songs," *People's Daily*, June 1, 1976, p. 4; "Red Little Soldiers Resolutely Criticize Teng Hsiao-ping," *People's Daily*, June 1, 1976, p. 1.

23. "Experiences in Using Characters and Pin Yin in Compiling Language Textbooks for Elementary Schools," *Kwang Ming Daily*, December 19, 1976, p. 4; "First Graders Can Join the Battle Too," *Kwang Ming Daily*, May 21, 1976, p. 4.

24. Yin Chih-kwang, "Peking's Poetry Recitation Activities Organized by the Mass," *Poems* (January, 1976), p. 96; "Utilize the Fighting Function of Revolutionary Children's Folk Songs"; "Red Little Soldiers Fight Together."

25. "Red Little Soldiers Fight Together."

26. "Songs Dedicated to Chairman Hua; Daggers Aimed at the 'Gang of Four,'" *Poems* (December, 1976), p. 20.

27. The author located two such records in Hong Kong. One is called "I Am a Sunflower," the other, "Embroidering a Red Star." Both were issued by Peking's China Record Company.

28. "Rope Skipping," *Athletic Flowers Are Blooming toward the Sun* (Peking: People's Sport Press, 1974).

29. "Grenade Throwing," *Athletic Flowers Are Blooming*.

30. "Red Little Soldiers Follow Chairman Mao," *Revolutionary Saplings Are Growing* (Shanghai: People's Press, 1974).

31. Lei Feng was a model soldier, regarded as "Chairman Mao's good soldier." Wang Ching-hsi was a model worker at the famous Taching oil field. Huang Shuai was a middle school student. She used to be hailed as a national model for her courage in daring to criticize her teacher. Since

Chiang Ching's downfall, however, she has been critizied as a negative model in the Chinese media.

32. Chia Tien-hao, "Bright Sun in the Motherland's Sky," *One Generation Is Better than the Other* (Shanghai: People's Press, 1975), p. 104.

33. Lu Tien, "I Want to Learn from Lei Feng's Model," *Revolutionary Saplings Are Growing.*

34. "We Should Be Brave Little Revolutionary Generals," *Songs of Worker's Village* (Shanghai: People's Press, 1974).

35. Wang Chao-yang, "We Are Determined to Exercise Dictatorship," in *We Are Brave Little Generals* (Peking: People's Literature Press, 1974), p. 56.

36. Wang Ya-tung and Huang Tong-fu, "Resolutely Crush the 'Gang of Four,' " *Poems* (December, 1976), pp. 48–49. It should be noted that the "Gang of Four" was not named individually but referred to as a group.

37. "I Knock Him Down to the Ground," in *The Train Is Heading toward Shaoshan* (Shanghai: People's Press, 1973), pp. 105–106.

38. Chang Tong-fan, "Hearts of the World's People Are Linked Together," *One Generation Is Better than the Other*, p. 152.

39. Liu Yu-hsien, "Seven Hundred Million Pairs of Fists Are There for You to Bite," *We Are Brave Little Generals*, pp. 73–74.

40. *Songs of Children's Anti-Japan Corps* (Shanghai: People's Press, 1975).

41. Ho-chien Road School, Shanghai, Children's Folk Song Group, "Antonioni Was A Big Bad Egg," *One Generation Is Better than the Other*, pp. 28–29; *Remin Ribao* [People's Daily] commentator, "A Vicious Motive, Despicable Tricks" (Peking: Foreign Language Press, 1974).

42. Huang Yi-po, "Red Little Soldiers Receive Military Training in the Drill Ground," *One Generation Is Better than the Other*, p. 134.

43. Hu Peng-nan, "Seesaw," *Let's All Exercise* (Shanghai: People's Press, 1974).

44. Yin Shih-lin, "Rains and Dews Nourish the Rice Saplings: On Reading Revolutionary Children's Folk Songs," *Poems* (June, 1976), pp. 80–82.

45. Ibid.

46. Shen-yang Cable Factory's Primary School, "Two Children's Folk Songs," *People's Daily*, June 18, 1976, p. 2.

47. Ibid.

48. To identify the revolutionary children's folk songs for this study, the author relied on a Chinese book catalogue published in March, 1976 by a Communist bookstore in Hong Kong. Only those designated "revolutionary children's folk songs" or "children's folk songs" were analyzed.

Others designated "children's songs" or "children's poems" were excluded from this analysis.

49. Mao Yuan-hsin, Mao Tse-tung's nephew and, before the arrest of the "Gang of Four," political commissar of the Shen-yang Military District, reportedly was taught to recite children's folk songs such as "Little Soldiers of the Eighth Rout Army Want to Go to Yenan" as a means to strengthen his faith while he was a child. Cheng Ju-shih, "The Rising Generation," *Ming Pao Daily*, September 21, 1976, p. 11.

50. *People's Daily*, November 4, 1976, p. 3.

51. Chu Chih-ching, *Essays on Chinese Ballads and Songs* (Peking: Writers' Press, 1957), pp. 137–142.

52. Chu Chieh-fan, *Treatises on Chinese Songs and Ballads* (Taipei: Chung Hua Bookstore, 1974), pp. 315–382. Chu gave many examples of how certain children's folk songs were circulated and originated. Chu has been collecting and studying Chinese folk songs for forty years.

CHAPTER 3   *Lien Huan Hua:*
Revolutionary Serial Pictures
John C. Hwang

Even though many comic books in the West are serious in nature, often reflecting social ills and conditions of the times,[1] and have become a social force in the molding of public opinions,[2] the term "comic strips" or "funnies" as widely used tends to conjure up the impression of a popular medium intended for light entertainment or amusement.

It would be misleading, however, to describe a seemingly identical popular medium in the People's Republic of China, generally known as *lien huan hua* (serial pictures), as "comic books," for the Chinese Communists are deadly serious about using the medium as a means of social change and indoctrination, and the comic element is clearly not a professed function. In practice, the term "serial pictures," encompassing a much wider variety of picture-story books than merely drawn strips, is more indicative of the nature and scope of this Chinese medium.

HISTORICAL PERSPECTIVES
Like many other popular literary and art forms, the origin of serial pictures in China is difficult to trace. There are, how-

ever, two recognized forerunners of the popular medium—
the traditional drawings in books or novels, and New Year's
pictures.

As Chiang has noted, many story books of the Sung (A.D.
960–1279) and the Yuan (A.D. 1279–1368) Dynasties often
had illustrations at the top of each page.[3] During the Ming
(A.D. 1368–1644) and the Ching (A.D. 1644–1911) Dynasties, popular romantic novels often included portraits of the
main characters at the beginning of the novels and sometimes
at the start of each chapter.

Another precursor of serial pictures is the traditional New
Year's pictures, which are often mounted on screens in serial
form, with sixteen, twenty-four or thirty-two pictures to a set.
A similar art form is serial wallpaintings, such as the 112
paintings portraying the life of Confucius in the Confucius
Temple at Chu-fu, Shantung Province. Traditional New
Year's pictures were usually color prints of stories of legendary heroes and episodes of operas. Tales such as *Twenty-
Four Legends of Filial Piety*, *Legend of the Cowherd and the
Weaving Girl*, and *Romance of the Three Kingdoms* are
favorite subjects of New Year's pictures. This kind of folk art
was extremely popular among the peasants who traditionally
purchased it during the Lunar New Year holidays.

During the late Ching Dynasty, contemporary themes
began to creep into serial pictures. For instance, there was a
serial on the devastating effects of opium on the families of
opium smokers; another portrayed episodes of the Boxer Re-
bellion. The inroads of Western cultural influence also found
their way into many serial pictures of this period. For instance, one series was found depicting the ladies of Shanghai
using sewing machines and another dealing with a young
sportsman falling off a bicycle. All these were printed on
large sheets, each carrying the whole story.[4]

It was not until the May Fourth Movement of 1919, however, that serial pictures began to flourish in China, particu-

larly among residents of the "concession" cities under the control of Western powers. Many foreign comics were translated into Chinese and circulated among families with foreign contacts. Comics featuring such Western characters as Mickey Mouse, the Phantom, and Mandrake were among the popular ones. Before long, original Chinese comics modelled after the imported ones were rolling off the press of specialized publishing houses and their circulation spread from the coast to the interior of China.[5]

The popularity of comic books during this period also aroused controversy in literary circles. Some condemned it as a corrupting force; others, most notably Lu Hsun, who was hailed by Mao Tse-tung as the most important pioneer revolutionary writer, defended it as a medium of educational significance. Lu urged Chinese artists to take this art form seriously and personally promoted it fervently, because, as he argued, "the masses want it; the masses appreciate it."[6]

During the Japanese invasion, both the Kuomintang (the Nationalists) and the Communists used serial pictures as a means of inspiring patriotism among the Chinese people and of mustering their support against the invaders. In the area under Communist control, serial pictures were used for the purpose of education and indoctrination; in the Kuomintang-controlled area, however, in addition to didactic and patriotic comics, many foreign, especially American, comics continued to be translated and circulated.

When the Communist Party took over the Chinese mainland, serial pictures became an important tool of ideological indoctrination for the general masses. Traditional themes and subject matter were altered to reflect the new revolutionary policies set by the Party. For instance, in the eyes of the Party, the old themes and formats of New Year's pictures were superstitious and feudalistic, unsuitable for the education of the masses. This attitude is voiced in a special article in the *People's Daily:*

Since the Liberation, it is estimated that more than 2 million copies of New Year's pictures are sold each year. Unfortunately, for hundreds of years, these pictures had been dominated by themes and subjects of gods and ghosts, kings and ministers, and scholars and beauties, and had been used by the ruling class as tools to fool the people with feudal and superstitious ideas. Since the birth of new China, constant reforms and improvements have been made on these pictures so that they will have a revolutionary content. . . . Of more than two hundred different kinds of New Year's pictures published, 95 percent have taken up new and contemporary themes—praising the Party, Chairman Mao, socialism, heroes of the new era, workers, peasants, and soldiers.[7]

The volume of serial picture books increased tremendously during the first few years of the People's Republic. Some 21 million copies were printed in 1952; 52 million copies were issued in 1955; and by 1956, well over 100 million serial picture books had been printed! By the same token, 670 different titles were issued in 1952; five years later, the number jumped to 2,300. A peak was reached in 1958 during the Great Leap Forward; in the first six months alone, more than 1,600 titles were circulated, and of those, 700 were new titles.[8] It is estimated that between 1949 and 1963, at least 12,700 different titles of serial pictures were published and more than 560 million copies were circulated.[9]

Until the Cultural Revolution, serial picture books continued to take on a relatively large variety of themes and subject matters. Even though most of the serial picture books dealt with stories of revolutionary struggles and the reconstruction of the new socialist republic and heroic models, some titles were devoted to stories of historical figures and popular legends such as *Romance of the Three Kingdoms*, *Lady White Snake*, and *The Western Chambers*.

Apparently the effort to limit the stories treated by serial picture books to those of revolutionary themes and subjects was not a total success. The impact of the traditional themes and subject matter became a deep concern among many sectors of the country. A letter to the editor of Peking's *Worker's Daily* in 1965 illustrates the point:

Comrade Editor:
   One day as I came home to rest, I found my children together with several small friends of the same alleyway deeply engrossed in drawing pictures. What they drew was not bad. But a close look showed that their drawings were all unhealthy in content, involving emperors, generals, prime ministers, scholars, beauties, and the like. I asked myself what had put such things into the minds of these small friends. Involved here was quite a big problem. Later, I had a talk with my oldest child. I asked, "Who told you to draw such things?"
   "I drew them just for fun!"
   "Did you work all this out from imagination?"
   "No, I read serial pictures and copied them."
   Afterward, I took a look at the serial picture books they had borrowed. Some of them even dealt with stories from such old novels as *Cases of Shih Kung, Cases of Peng Kung,* and *Living Buddha Chi Kung.* . . . At present, available for hire in book-stores are many good serial pictures reflecting life in the struggle of socialist construction and revolution. . . . However, available at the same time are some hackneyed serial picture books with pictures of emperors, generals, prime ministers, scholars, or beauties. . . . Therefore, I suggest that the leadership depart-ments concerned should check and purge according to plan all the serial picture books to be published, issued, or offered for hire. The unwholesome serial picture books should not be al-lowed to poison the minds of our youths and children.[10]
                  Pan Yu-chun,
                  Chinshan hsien, Shanghai Municipality

   The Cultural Revolution answered the call of that reader. Many serial picture books were either banned or revised to be rid of "revisionist, black" literary lines. As it has upon other literary and art forms, the Cultural Revolution has left clear imprints on the creative process of serial pictures. The selec-tion and treatment of themes and subject matters now follow rigid guidelines, the political awareness of the artists in the profession has been heightened, and the creation of "successful images of proletarian heroes" has become the raison d'être of serial pictures.

Since the Cultural Revolution, there has been a decline in the number of new titles published. For instance, in the first half of 1958, 700 new serial picture books were issued; less than 150 new titles, however, including children's picture books, were published in 1972.[11]

TYPES OF SERIAL PICTURES

Serial picture books in the People's Republic of China come in many forms. Some are series of movie stills with accompanying captions. The serial picture book *Tunnel Warfare*, for example, was compiled with a collection of stills extracted from a movie of the same title. Occasionally, animated stills of marionette film are also used to create serial picture books. One such example is *The Cock Crows at Midnight*, a story about the oppressed peasants who rose under the organization of a Communist in a successful struggle against the local landlord.

Stage photos or hand-drawn pictures adopted from famous stage plays and revolutionary Peking operas are another popular form of serial pictures. The most popular ones include, among others, *Taking the Tiger Mountain by Strategy*, *The White-Hair Girl*, *Lei Feng*, *The Red Women's Detachment*, *Mine Warfare*, and *The Red Lantern*.

Sketches based on reports in the *People's Daily* are another popular form of serial pictures. A great many serial pictures of this kind use episodes of the Vietnam War as their subject matter. For instance, *Attacking a Train by Strategy* is based on a report carried in the *People's Daily* that portrayed the successful raid of a South Vietnamese train by the Vietcong.

Prints from woodcuts, paper cuts, traditional black-and-white sketches, and sketches in color ink or gouache are other art forms used for serial pictures.

Even though no clear distinction is made between serial pictures for children or adults, a large number of serial pictures are obviously designed for younger children. These usually come in shorter texts and use simpler characters; when a more difficult character is used, romanized pronunciation would be added next to the character.

The subject matters treated in serial pictures fall into four categories.

1. Serial pictures which mold the heroic image of the proletariat. Since in the People's Republic of China the major mandate of serial pictures is to "create successful images of proletarian heroes," a large number of picture-story books are created for this purpose. Pictorial books of this category—many of them fictitious—tend to focus exclusively on the main character; the so-called "middle character" or secondary characters are not allowed to play any significant role in the story. Examples in this category include, among others, *Liu Hu-lan, Lei Feng, Taking the Tiger Mountain by Strategy, Tan Tseng* and *The White-Hair Girl* (see Figure 3-1).

2. Serial pictures dealing with Chinese Communist revolutionary history and contemporary reconstruction campaigns. In this kind of pictorial book, the hero figures are more diffused and success of any kind is invariably attributed to the teaching and guidance of Chairman Mao and the cooperation of the masses. *Tunnel Warfare, Sparks of Youth*, and *Red Flag Canal* are serial pictures of this category (see Figure 3-2).

3. Stories based on traditional folklore. A large number of serial pictures of this category have been banned since the Cultural Revolution because they are considered to be a glorification of the past. A few traditional stories that can be interpreted in a revolutionary perspective have been played up. One example is the uprising by Chen Sheng, a peasant who revolted against the Second Emperor of the Chin Dynasty (221–206 B.C.; see Figure 3-3). Another is the denuncia-

FIGURE 3-1. A scene from *Liu Hu-lan*, a serial about the Chinese heroine who died a martyr in her attempt to save the people of her village from the persecution of the landlords.

FIGURE 3-2. *Tunnel Warfare*, a serial depicting the use of tunnels by the Chinese peasants and the Red Army in Hopei Province to defeat the Japanese during the Sino-Japanese War.

FIGURE 3-3. A scene from *Chen Sheng and Wu Kuang*, the legendary heroes who led the peasants in an uprising against the Second Emperor of the Chin Dynasty (221–206 B.C.).

tion of Confucius by Liu-hsia Chi, a rebel at that time (see Figure 3-4).

4. Serial pictures dealing with the history of international Communist movements and struggles. Examples include, among others, *Lenin in October*, *My Universities* (based on Maxim Gorki's story), *Vietnamese Hero Yuan Wen Chui* and *Hsieh Shih Chiao—A Heroine* (see Figure 3-5).

THE FUNCTIONS OF SERIAL PICTURES

The roles and functions of all literary and art forms in China, serial pictures included, are spelled out in one of Mao's most important works—*Talks at the Yenan Forum on Literature and Art*. This speech not only laid the philosophical foundation for China's revolutionary literature and art but also set

FIGURE 3–4. Pictures show the towering rebel leader Liu-hsia Chi condemning Confucius.

FIGURE 3–5. *Hsieh Shih Chiao—A Heroine*, a serial based on a report in the *People's Daily* depicting the brave deeds of a Vietcong heroine.

in motion the direction and the thrust of literary and artistic creation. It stipulates that literature and art in China is to serve workers, peasants, and soldiers.

As a unique art form that combines both narrative and picture in one medium, serial pictures can serve as "a powerful instrument for propagating the Party's policies, for cultivating the thought of the people, and for enhancing the people's understanding of history, science, and class struggle," according to the *People's Daily*.[12]

Undoubtedly, a pivotal function of serial pictures in China is "to create successful images of proletarian heroes." As internal power struggles and political campaigns unfold, however, one finds that the medium is charged with additional tasks related to the struggles. An article in the *People's Daily* in 1974 by a veteran artist of serial pictures illustrates this point and reveals the following objectives of serial pictures in contemporary China:[13]

1. To create successful images of proletarian heroes and reflect the life and struggles of workers, peasants, and soldiers.

2. To ensure the prevailing victory of the proletariat.

3. To protect the Communist system from the inroads of capitalism.

4. To recount revolutionary history.

5. To extol the thoughts of Chairman Mao.

6. To praise the educated young people who choose to go to the countryside and factories and labor with the masses.

7. To criticize feudalistic, bourgeois, and revisionistic ideologies; to educate the masses with revolutionary traditions and to criticize Confucius class ideologies spread by Liu Shao Chi and Lin Piao.

8. To awaken and raise class consciousness and to inspire revolutionary enthusiasm among the masses.

9. To criticize "revisionist, black" literature and to

praise the new literary developments fostered by the Cultural Revolution.

These objectives are reflected in the Chinese serial pictures currently available in Hong Kong.

MESSAGES OF SERIAL PICTURES

PROCESS OF MESSAGE CONSTRUCTION

There are essentially two ways of creating serial pictures. The first is less complex and involves the compilation of stage or motion picture stills or the drawing of serial pictures and the adaptation of dialogues from the movies or stage plays to reflect original themes. Serial pictures produced this way are part of a carefully conceived campaign and are designed for the masses who may not otherwise be reached by such media as radio, television, newspapers, motion pictures, and performing troupes. In the form of serial pictures, the mechanical barriers of motion pictures and theater production no longer present an outreach problem. In the pictorial format, the serial books can reach those who are isolated in remote areas and those who find novels hard to read.

Another way of creating serial pictures is more elaborate. It is not necessarily directed from above. At the initiation stage, the idea can be conceived and presented by any of the following teams—professional serial picture artists, lay artists, or just ordinary people in various factories, communes, production brigades, and units of the People's Liberation Army in different locales. No matter who initiates the idea, several distinct traits are present in the process of message creation.

1. The messages are conceived to reflect the thoughts of Mao and contemporary Party policies. This is clearly enunciated in the *People's Daily:*

> The process of the creation of the image of proletarian heroes in serial pictures is also the process of fierce struggle for two

classes and ideologies. During the creative process, only through the insistence of the supremacy of the proletariat, the broadening of active ideological struggle, the criticism of the teachings of Confucius and Mencius and the poisonous revisionistic black literature, and through the resistance of the inroads of capitalistic ideology, can we insure that the creative process would follow the correct direction set by Chairman Mao, portray the image of Communist heroes of high class consciousness and acute awareness of class and party line struggles. . . . [14]

2. Serial pictures are collective products of teams of artists and writers. In fact, a Three-in-One Union creative guideline has become the norm of the trade—that is, serial pictures are created under the "concrete leadership" of the Party and the cooperation of the professionals and amateurs.[15] Under this policy, the rank and file of serial picture artists has been expanded to include not only the professionals but a sizable number of workers, peasants, soldiers, students, and teachers as well.[16] Most recent releases, in fact, tend to bear the collective authorships of various creative teams of different Army units, communes, and local and regional government propaganda departments.

3. An extensive feedback mechanism is built into the creative process. The first feedback input tends to come from members of the professional team itself, which can immediately detect any deviation from Party policies and make corrections. When the first draft of the product is completed, it is presented to various groups of people for criticism before the final revision. For instance, a professional creative team, in attempting to portray a Communist martyr, painted his face with deep grief when he was about to be separated from his relatives and executed by the enemy. The mother of the martyr, upon seeing the drawing, criticized the picture for failing to convey the bravery and determination of a Communist martyr. This comment alerted the creative team and the first draft was revised accordingly.[17]

Delayed, large-scale feedback is sought from readers in

various parts of the country. It is not uncommon to see the following statement included at the end of serial picture books:

> To The Reader:
> Chairman Mao teaches us: "Be serious in perfecting the work of publication." We earnestly hope that the great masses of workers, peasants, soldiers, and young readers, after reading this as well as other pictorial books published by this publisher, will send us their precious opinions to help us better our literary and art work under the guidance of Chairman Mao's revolutionary literary line.

Another unique feature of the collective creative process is that professional artists are asked to spend a period of time each year living and working among the masses. This is to guard against the development of an elite mentality and to enable the artists to portray faithfully "the life and struggle of the masses."

VERBAL MESSAGES

Except for those dealing with the Vietnam War, serial pictures published after the Cultural Revolution almost without exception devote the first page to a quote from Mao's works. Undoubtedly, this practice is intended to legitimize Mao as the only supreme leader of China.

After the quote from Mao, a synopsis of the story is presented. Since the medium is primarily intended for children and adults who are either illiterate or newly literate, verbal messages are very simple and straightforward. Romanized pronunciations of difficult characters are included to assist the reader.

There seems to be a general tendency to do away with verbal messages contained in "balloons," and captions have emerged as a standard vehicle. The use of captions instead of "balloons" may be due to two reasons: First, more narrative information can be included in captions. Second, as Kunzle has pointed out, the inclusion of balloons in comic strips makes drawings look "busy" and less aesthetic.[18]

Serial pictures published after the Cultural Revolution frequently plant Mao's quotes or teachings at strategic points in the story. Specifically, the quotes often appear at the moment when the hero or the heroine is about to make a critical decision or to undertake a colossal task. In all cases, Mao's teachings become the inspiration which guides the hero/heroine to steer the course of events to a correct conclusion. For instance, in *The Triumphant Song of Unity and Victory*—a story about the successful effort of a PLA unit in Tsintao to plug a leak in a major dam—when the leak widened and threatened to wipe out the local communities, the soldiers began to chant a quote from Mao—"First, we are not afraid of hardship, second, we are not afraid of death." The quote gave strength to the soldiers, who eventually plugged the leak and saved the communites from the disaster.

By the same token, the denouement of each serial picture book inevitably entails a quote, a teaching of or a pledge to Chairman Mao. For instance, in *Fighting North and South*, the concluding captions (scenes 169 and 170) read:

> Amid great rejoicing the division commander mounted a captured tank to congratulate the assembled crowd on the great victory due, he pointed out, to following Chairman Mao's military line. On the broad plain, army men and people cheered and shouted in response: "Long live Chairman Mao! A long, long life to Chairman Mao!"

In the same vein, the denouement of another serial, *The Red Lantern*, ends with this caption (scene 172):

> The sun shines on the Red Flag. Swords and guns dance in the song. Tieh Mei raises the Red Lantern; the warriors are determined to raise the banners of Chairman Mao's thoughts in their march. The Red Lantern emits the rays of victory. "Only through the sacrifice of the brave can we usher in a new era." [a quote from Chairman Mao]

Contemporary political struggles and campaigns are often reflected in the verbal messages contained in captions. For example, in *Ten Thousand Willow Branches in the Spring Breeze*—a story about the heroic deeds of a military medical team which removed a gigantic uterus tumor from the body of a poor worker's wife—out of 122 scenes, Liu Shao-chi's revisionism is criticized and attacked in 11 scenes. Many legends and slogans in the pictures also reflected the anti-Liu campaigns. In scene 27, for instance, the drawing carries the slogan "Thoroughly criticize Liu Shao-chi's antirevolutionary revisionistic line of medicine."

NONVERBAL MESSAGES

Kunzle argues that even though comic strips are essentially a hybrid, partly verbal and partly pictorial, the pictorial element must be considered their primary feature, because it carries the bulk of the message.[19] It is possible that serial picture artists in China share the same idea, for the pictorial (nonverbal) part of the medium has received close study by many artists. As a result, a number of conventions have developed as guidelines of pictorial message construction:[20]

1. The drawing of scenes and minor characters is to serve the main proletarian hero or heroine; there is no place in the revolutionary art form to practice "art for art's sake."

2. The main character always occupies the center of the picture; this convention is intended to portray the "prevailing force of the right against the wrong" (see Figure 3–6).

3. In addition, in order to make the hero/heroine stand out from the background, close-ups of the hero/heroine are used as frequently as possible. In *Taking the Tiger Mountain by Strategy*, for instance, out of 190 scenes, more than 50 are close-ups or full-length portraits of the hero, Yang Tzu-yung, in dominant view (see Figure 3–7).

FIGURE 3–6. A scene from revolutionary opera, *The Red Lantern*, in which hero Li Yu-ho defies his Japanese captors.

4. Contrasts between light and shade, between solid object and space, and between different angles are used to reflect the relationship between the hero/heroine and the enemy.

As an article in *Chinese Literature* points out, the artists use "negative characters as foils for the heroes, using perspective to put the enemy under the foot of the hero or by giving him half a body or half a head. The positive characters stand towering high while the negative characters are shadowed aside." (See Figure 3–8.) This method "negates the naturalism of the old bourgeois picture-story books in which positive and negative characters were placed on equal footing."[21]

Furthermore, "enemies of the masses" are always drawn with a stereotypical, sinister look and are portrayed from a higher angle "to make them appear more despicable and sinister"[22] (see Confucius in Figure 3–4).

FIGURE 3–7. Scenes from revolutionary opera, *Taking the Tiger Mountain by Strategy*, showing hero Yang Tzu-yung.

FIGURE 3–8. Scenes from the *White-Hair Girl*, revolutionary ballet. Hsi-erh, the girl, finally confronts her oppressor-landlord.

IMPACT OF SERIAL PICTURES

It appears that the Chinese Communist leaders are fully aware of the fact that for propaganda to have impact, it must first overcome the problem of reaching an audience. Apparently, the Party has been successful in building an effective network all over the country for the distribution of serial pictures. According to Nebiolo, serial picture books are available at bookstores, schools, commune libraries, factory cafeterias, department stores, military barracks, village markets, post offices, bus terminals, and fruit stands.[23]

While it is difficult to assess accurately the impact of serial pictures in a social system like Communist China because we know little about the composition and the reactions of the audience, the following observations can be made:

1. Serial pictures serve as an important "verbal conductor" in the propagation of Communist doctrines and policies.

2. The constant extolling of Chairman Mao as superhero helps to legitimize him as the orthodox supreme leader of China.

3. The molding of model heroic images sets examples for the country to follow.

4. In serial pictures, many historical events are reinterpreted from the socialist perspective; this would help to reshape history in socialist terms.

5. Serial pictures help to focus and intensify contemporary political campaigns launched under the direction and guidance of the Party.

CONCLUSION

According to the revolutionary literary philosophy of Mao, serial pictures in China closely reflect the Communist social order. Unlike most Western comic books, in which didactic messages are often latent, the intended political messages in serial pictures in China are manifest. Besides reflecting and propagandizing the Communist doctrines, serial pictures in China serve as an important tool for contemporary political campaigns and Party power struggles. Since the Cultural Revolution, heroes/heroines in serial pictures are extracted from the masses—the workers, peasants, and soldiers. Many serial pictures which dealt with traditional themes and subject matters are either banned or revised.

Partly because of the need to cater to a relatively unsophisticated readership and partly because of the paucity of subject matters and thematic variations beyond the officially sanctioned ones, the characterization of heroes/heroines and villains tends to be "black and white." Middle characters are kept from playing any significant part in the development of the story. As a consequence, there is a relatively limited spectrum of subjects that creative artists can work with.

The creation of serial pictures is essentially a collective process. The picture books are normally created by a team of artists under the guidelines of the Party and subject to the criticism and feedback of the masses. Revisions are often made after criticism is voiced. This intensive feedback and criticism process serves to reduce the chances of deviation from the Party line by an individual writer or artist working alone.

NOTES

1. Kenneth Eble, "Our Serious Comic," in *The Funnies: An American Idiom*, ed. David Manning White and Robert Abel (New York: The Free Press of Glencoe, 1963), pp. 99–108.

2. David Kunzle, *The Early Comic Strip* (Berkeley: University of California Press, 1973), p. 1.

3. Wei-pu Chiang, "Chinese Picture Story Books," *Chinese Literature* 3 (March, 1959): 144–147.

4. Gino Nebiolo, *The People's Comic Book*, trans. E. Wilkinson (Garden City, N.Y.: Doubleday & Company, Inc., 1973).

5. Ibid.

6. Chi Cheng, "New Serial Pictures," *Chinese Literature* 2 (1974): 111–117.

7. Ma Ke, "Cheers to the New Achievement of the Serial Picture," *People's Daily*, December 29, 1963.

8. Chiang, "Chinese Picture Story Books."

9. Ma, "New Achievement of the Serial Picture."

10. Pan Yu-chun, letter to the editor, *Workers' Daily*, May 18, 1965.

11. Yu-ning Li, "A Selected Bibliography of Humanities and Social Science Publications in China since 1969," *Chinese Studies in History* (Fall-Winter, 1973–74): 27–47.

12. Ma, "New Achievement of the Serial Picture."

13. Sung Yin, "A Talk on Moulding the Characters of Serial Pictures," *People's Daily*, July 6, 1974.

14. Ibid.

15. Ibid.

16. Chi, "New Serial Pictures."

17. Sung, "Moulding the Characters of Serial Pictures."

18. Kunzle, *Early Comic Strip*, p. 3.

19. Ibid.

20. Sung, "Moulding the Characters of Serial Pictures."

21. "Drawing Heroes," *Chinese Literature* 12 (1970): 105–109.

22. Chi, "New Serial Pictures."

23. Nebiolo, *The People's Comic Book.*

CHAPTER 4   Revolutionary Opera:
            An Instrument
            for Cultural Change

Godwin C. Chu
Philip H. Cheng

Our purpose is to ensure that literature and art fit well into the whole revolutionary machine as a component part, that they operate as powerful weapons for uniting and educating the people and for attacking and destroying the enemy, and that they help the people fight the enemy with one heart and one mind.
—Mao Tse-tung, *Talks at the Yenan
Forum on Literature and Art*

INTRODUCTION

China today is undergoing one of history's most daring attempts at cultural change. The objective, according to Chairman Mao Tse-tung, is to produce a new breed of Chinese who are not bound by the old traditions, beliefs, and culture of China. A number of communication media, mostly unfamiliar to the Western world, have been employed to achieve this objective. One medium that has been used with some degree of success is the Chinese opera. It is the purpose of this study to examine both the transformation of traditional Chinese opera into its current revolutionary format and the function of opera as an instrument of cultural change.

SOURCES OF DATA

Studying a social institution at a distance presents formidable obstacles, for the institution is not accessible to direct observation and the researcher usually has to rely on whatever written materials might be available to him.[1] In this particular case, the authors were able to examine not only official statements attributed to important leaders of the People's Republic but also accounts by Chinese opera writers and players about their own experience. These personal accounts, we believe, add meaning to the official announcements because they often provide a glimpse of the social processes involved in the institution of Chinese opera.

In our search for relevant materials, we have relied heavily on two professional journals: *Xiju Bao* (The Theater Journal), and *Qu Yi* (Operatic Art), both published in China and both suspended during the Cultural Revolution. Other materials include the writings of Chairman Mao, the pronouncements of Chiang Ching, wife of Mao, the *People's Daily* and other publications from China, and the various contemporary operatic plays published by the Chinese Communist Party. Occasionally we have made reference to publications in English by Westerners who have visited China. We have made no attempt here to analyze the content of themes and values in the Chinese opera, a research which is undertaken in Chapter 5 by Philip H. Cheng.

The term "Chinese opera" has been used to include both Peking opera, which is the most important representative of Chinese opera, and local operas. The latter are similar to Peking opera in their themes, costumes, and style of acting, although the music is somewhat different. While Peking opera has nationwide popularity, local operas have their audience in their respective regions.

BRIEF HISTORY OF CHINESE OPERA

Chinese opera has its ancient origin in the Tang Dynasty.[2] The first operatic school of China was established at the Pear Garden by Emperor Ming (A.D. 712–755) of that dynasty for the training of young players in singing and dance. Emperor Ming himself often directed the dances for his beautiful concubine, Yang Kuei Fei. Under his patronage, dance and drama flourished.

The Pear Garden performing art developed into a new form, the "variety show," officially known as *tsa chu*, in the Sung Dynasty (A.D. 960–1126). In this period, dances were acted out with a story. Another important development took place with *Yuan chu* (Yuan melody), a new form of drama which emerged during the Yuan Dynasty (A.D. 1280–1368). It combined speech, song, and dance in a four-act story.

After a period of refinement in the Ming Dynasty (A.D. 1368–1643), the formal version of Peking opera emerged during the Ching Dynasty (1644–1911). Emperor Chien Lung (1736–1796) was considered the ruler who started the Chinese national theater, *Ching hsi*, or "Drama of the Capital." On the Emperor's birthday, opera troupes came from various provinces to the capital to perform. When some of the troupes decided to stay permanently in the capital, the curtain for a new era of Chinese opera went up.

The essential features of Peking opera are described in the following sections.

SYMBOLISM

Stage props and costumes are mostly symbolic. Generally, the stage is bare, with perhaps only one table and two chairs, covered with colorful embroidery. The table stands sometimes for a dining table, sometimes for a mountain.

The most popular item, considered to be the symbol of Peking opera, is the horse whip. Actors merely wave a horse whip to symbolize riding on a horse.

Because of the nature of symbolism, Peking opera is almost totally unrestrained by material artifacts. The stage can be used to represent a room, a court, a battleground, or the universe.

TOTAL THEATER

Peking opera is a total theater which embodies many of the major facets of Chinese culture—philosophy, history, literature, language, dance, music, and acrobatics.

Chinese plays are concerned with the full range of human drama but lean toward a preoccupation with loyalty, filial piety, wars, and romance. Most stories are several hundred years old, deriving largely from historical events and popular folklore. Authorship is usually unknown.

ROLE TYPES

Classically speaking, there are four major theatrical role types of acting in Peking opera; each of these is subdivided into a number of narrower specialties.

1. *Sheng:* Male roles of scholars, emperors, statesmen, gentlemen, or warriors. The actors are bearded but wear no painted make-up.

2. *Tan:* Female roles of queens, ladies, beautiful girls, heroines, or the like. In the past they were impersonated by male players, including Dr. Mei Lan-fang, an internationally known actor.

3. *Ching:* Male roles with painted faces to represent the figures of warriors, bandits, evil politicians, righteous judges, gods, ghosts, and other supernatural entities.

4. *Chou:* The clown, who alone may use colloquial speech. Performers of other role types must use classic language.

FROM TRADITIONAL TO REVOLUTIONARY OPERA

The transition of Peking opera from the traditional to the revolutionary involves a long ideological debate among the

Chinese Communist leaders and is part of a political struggle between two lines—radical and revisionist.

As early as the 1930s, while the Chinese Communists were still in the caves of Yenan, Mao Tse-tung had advocated a political orientation for art and literature, including the opera. In 1942, Mao outlined the political application of drama in his much-quoted *Talks at the Yenan Forum on Art and Literature.* These talks, which have since become a basic text for writers and artists in China, stated that art and literature should serve the proletariat—workers, peasants, and soldiers, exposing evils while extolling good.[3]

From that time on, the question of "for whom" has been debated, off and on, among Communist theoreticians, artists, and political leaders. Nevertheless, Mao's instruction on art and literature began to gain momentum in "the fighting years," during which time a great number of war plays emerged along with the traditional Peking opera. These plays contributed greatly to the Communist campaigns at the front in mobilizing farmers' support to fight the Nationalist troops and the Japanese invaders.

The Communist Party's movement for revolutionalizing Peking opera suffered its first setback shortly after the war against the Japanese, as the general masses began to tire of the war plays. They preferred the colorful style and familiar content of their traditional Peking opera.

A heated debate developed soon after the establishment of the People's Republic. Some Party leaders, in view of the popularity of traditional Peking opera among the people, called for a return to the classic drama. They considered the classic Peking opera a cultural heritage. On the other hand, the more radical elements of the Party condemned the traditional opera as part of the feudal past containing elements harmful to the new society. Mao, in his position as the Party leader, took swift action and cut off the prolonged debate by announcing a new slogan: "Weed through the old to let the new emerge."

Following the new policy, there came a long period, from

the late 1940s to the early 1960s, during which a great number of traditional Peking opera plays were staged. The Communist leaders, in an attempt to use the traditional Peking opera for their political purposes, carried out the new policy through selecting and modifying the old plays or writing new ones.

Among the classic plays selected by the Communist Party for perfomances, the most popular ones were *Snow in Midsummer*, a traditional play from the Yuan Dynasty (1280–1368), and *Driven to Join the Liang Mountain Rebels*, also an old play. These plays were chosen for their merits of exposing the injustice and evils of feudal society or for showing the fighting spirit of farmers throughout history in struggling against the ruling classes. Communist writers in that period also demonstrated their talents in modifying classic plays, including *Lady White Snake* and *The Removal of Three Dangers*.

Yet the most significant feature of this period was the new plays contributed by writers and artists. Among the most important playwrights were Tien Han, Hung Shen, Ouyang Yuchien, and Wu Han, who authored the controversial *Dismissal of Hai Jui*, the play which, in a way, touched off the Cultural Revolution.[4]

It should be noted that the traditional Peking opera enjoyed an astonishing development in every aspect during this period, particularly in acting, music, and playwriting. Many outstanding young actors and actresses made their appearances during the flurry of new plays.

The development could be the result of a series of moderate policies on culture and education by Liu Shao-chi, who was later ousted as chairman of the National Congress, and Teng Hsiao-ping, the secretary general of the Chinese Communist Party who stepped down with Liu during the Cultural Revolution. The Ten Points on Literature and Art, a policy never officially announced but circulated in August, 1961 under the name of Chou Yang, then vice minister of the Central Propaganda Department, has revealed a great deal about the official stand during that period.

According to *Wen-hsueh Chan-pao*, a Red Guard tabloid published during the Cultural Revolution, the Ten Points advocated that it was necessary not only to create more and better new works of art but also to allow the people to enjoy the excellent literary and art works handed down from the past. It added:

> . . .We should express in our literature and art not only strong political content but also such content which is not political but gives people wisdom of life and enjoyment of aesthetics. . . . If literature and art is to serve politics, we should let one hundred flowers bloom, not just let one flower bloom; it should be a road which is the broadest, not the narrowest.[5]

The policy envisioned a broad scope in which literature and art could serve the needs of the people, not merely as an instrument for political struggle. Although it recognized that literary and art works should have a correct political content, the policy also stressed the importance of art form:

> The forms and styles of literature and art should be as varied as possible. Each form or style has a merit and characteristics of its own, and, at the same time, its limitations.[6]

Concerning cultural background, the policy noted that the development of socialist literature and art requires selective inheritance of Chinese cultural legacies as well as selective absorption of the culture of foreign countries. In short, the Ten Points on Literature and Art seemed to be an outgrowth of Mao Tse-tung's guideline of "letting a hundred flowers bloom" and "weeding through the old to let the new emerge." It allowed the traditional drama to flourish while developing the new plays.

The first indication that the Ten Points policy was beginning to undermine Communist ideology came in the aftermath of the controversial classic Peking opera, *The Dismissal of Hai Jui*, which was a turning point between the traditional Chinese opera and revolutionary drama.

The Dismissal of Hai Jui was a historical opera written by Wu Han, then deputy mayor of Peking, and published in *Peking Literature* in January, 1961. (Wu, a professor of history at Tsing Hua University and a well-known historian, later became the first victim of the Cultural Revolution).

Wu's play closely followed another historical play, *Hai Jui Admonishes the Emperor*, presented by actor Chou Hsin-fang as a gift to commemorate the tenth anniversary of the People's Republic in 1959. A famous traditional Peking opera actor and director, Chou was then chairman of the Shanghai branch of the Union of Chinese State Artists and president of the Shanghai Institute of Peking Opera. (Chou also came under severe attack during the Cultural Revolution.)

Hai Jui, the leading character of the two plays, was an official of the Ming Dynasty who undertook a "legitimate face-to-face struggle" against the emperor for reform programs in social welfare. In the plays he was portrayed as a scholar of great wisdom and integrity who had the courage to remind the emperor of his many mistakes. The emperor responded by removing Hai Jui from the office. The plays received enthusiastic response from the audience.

It soon became clear, as revealed later during the Cultural Revolution, that *The Dismissal of Hai Jui* and *Hai Jui Admonishes the Emperor* were disguised dramatic allegories to criticize Mao Tse-tung for dismissing his Minister of Defense Peng Teh-hui in 1959 and replacing him with Lin Piao.[7] The emperor in the plays supposedly stood for Chairman Mao. This implication was clearly recognized in an article in the *Wen Hui Pao* of Shanghai:

> . . . Chou Hsin-fang collaborated with a few ghosts and monsters in a conspiracy to carefully produce the big poisonous weed *Hai Jui Admonishes the Emperor* and to launch a frantic attack on the Party and socialism. In this play, he sang aloud a rebellious

song, threw malicious curses at the new society, and attacked our respected and beloved Party Central and Chairman Mao.[8]

The plays of Hai Jui appeared to have sounded the alarm for the Communist leaders, especially the radical group, that something was wrong with traditional operatic theater. More important than the political undertone of the Hai Jui plays was the realization that traditional opera as a whole was serving to perpetuate old ideas and old customs by vividly enacting the past before mass audiences.

It was Chiang Ching, Mao's wife, who first took public action. She sent a statement to reproach to Hsia Yen, an active member of the All-China Federation, calling attention to the "reactionary political tendencies of the Hai Jui plays." Then the Party organized a "Forum of Theatrical Workers Participating in the Festival of Peking Opera on Contemporary Themes," held in Peking in July, 1964, at which Chiang Ching formally launched the campaign for completely revolutionalizing Peking opera. She said:

It is inconceivable that, in our socialist country led by the Communist Party, the dominant position on the stage is not occupied by the workers, peasants, and soldiers, who are the real creators of history and the true masters of our country. We should create literature and art which protects our socialist economic base.[9]

Criticizing the traditional Peking opera, Chiang Ching said:

At the same time, it has always depicted ancient times and people belonging to those times. Therefore, it is comparatively easy for Peking opera to portray negative characters and this is what some people like about it so much. On the other hand, it is very difficult to create positive characters, and yet we must build up characters of advanced revolutionary heroes.[10]

This criticism was seconded, though in a somewhat moderate tone, by Peng Chen, then mayor of Peking, in a speech at the same festival:

During the past, many of our Peking operas only portrayed emperors and courtiers, talented young scholars and beautiful ladies, or masters and madames, etc., to eulogize the manipulative ruling class and ridicule the working class. . . . For a long time, Peking opera served only the interest of feudalism and capitalism. . . . From now on, we must reform Peking opera and make it a performing art that serves the interest of workers, peasants, and soldiers, and the interest of socialism.[11]

Other than its generally negative social influence, the traditional Peking opera was found objectionable because it posed a dilemma to Communist atheism by constantly bringing ghosts and gods to the stage. This dilemma was discussed at length in an article entitled "Atheistic Education and Ghost Opera," which appeared in the theatrical journal *Xiju Bao*.[12] Ghosts and gods often appear in traditional Peking opera, the article noted; to play these roles in front of the audience would imply the existence of ghosts and gods. Even worse is the fact that ghosts and gods in Peking opera often play the roles of righters of injustice or revengers of evil acts. Themes of this kind would not only create favorable impressions of ghosts and gods but would also divert the attention of the oppressed people away from their present plight and lead them to place their hope in an afterlife. Instead of actively engaging in class struggle, the people would tend to indulge in fantasy. Traditional Peking opera was thus considered an instrument for perpetuating superstition and whitewashing the inequities of feudalism. The solution was that Peking opera should stop aiding superstition and, furthermore, should become an active instrument of the Party in the fight between atheism and religion.

The ban of traditional opera was only partial at first, as indicated in a speech by Tao Chu, then First Party Secretary of Southern China, in 1965:

Of course, we do not intend to ban all traditional opera from now on. After a while, when revolutionary opera has been well accepted on the stage, you can still stage some traditional opera shows. But you have to be selective, and present only those that have educational meaning.[13]

This policy was followed only for a short time. By 1966, during the height of the Cultural Revolution, performance of all traditional opera was banned. Only five revolutionary operas, personally approved by Chiang Ching, were permitted.[14] Since then, three new revolutionary operas have been introduced.[15] After the purge of Chiang Ching and her followers—this was the liquidation of the "Gang of Four" in October, 1976—the status of the revolutionary opera appeared for a while to be in doubt. About a month later, in a semiofficial policy statement attributed to the Criticism Group of the People's Publishing Press and published on the front page of the *People's Daily*, the Party reaffirmed the authentic position of the revolutionary opera.[16]

Calling Chiang Ching a "political pickpocket who established her false reputation by cheating the world," the article said that the initiation, preparation, and development of the revolutionary operas were undertaken by the mass of people, including artistic performers, writers, workers, peasants, and soldiers, under the direct supervision of Chairman Mao. For Chiang Ching to claim the credit and leadership for the revolutionary operas was a "shameless lie."[17]

As a symbolically significant demonstration of the Party's approval, two of the revolutionary operas—*The Red Lantern* and *Shachiapang*—were staged in Peking during the 1977 New Year to celebrate the victory over the "Gang of Four" and the inauguration of Hua Kuo-feng as the new Party chairman.[18]

DIFFERENCES BETWEEN TRADITIONAL AND REVOLUTIONARY OPERAS

The differences between the traditional and revolutionary operas can be summarized as follows:

1. *Themes:* The traditional Peking opera depicts historical characters (real or imagined), mostly emperors, queens,
princes, generals, ministers, scholars, beauties, and sometimes gods, ghosts and monsters, while the revolutionary
opera deals only with the workers, peasants, and soldiers
—the proletariat class of the contemporary time.

2. *Costumes:* The figures in traditional opera are mostly
clad in the colorful embroidered costumes of ancient times
while the characters in the revolutionary opera appear
mostly in military uniforms, everyday clothes, or Mao
jackets.

3. *Stage properties:* In traditional opera, only a few symbolic items, such as flags standing for wind, water, or
waves, are allowed on the stage. Realistic scenery and
other properties are seldom used. Occasionally, skilled
fighters use real knives and swords. In revolutionary opera,
realistic scenery and artifacts—spears, machine guns, and
rifles—are used in the performances.

4. *Role types:* In traditional opera, different theatrical
role types, such as Sheng, Tan, Ching, Chou, are distinctly
classified in performances. In revolutionary opera, there
are no clearcut theatrical role types, although the general
types—both male and female—are cast either as heroes or
villains.

5. *Singing:* Singing style of traditional opera is generally
kept unchanged in revolutionary opera, except for more
emphasis on the quick tempo portions to achieve a mood of
vigor and force.

6. *Music:* The music and instruments of traditional
opera are generally retained in revolutionary opera, with
some Western instruments such as piano and violin also
used.

Although the revolutionary opera has abandoned some of
the old cultural values prominent in the traditional opera—
for instance, filial piety, chastity, and scholarly dignity—it
has implicitly retained other virtues by giving them a dif-

ferent interpretation. For instance, the traditional opera praised loyalty to the emperor and obedience to authority figures. The revolutionary opera glorifies loyalty to the Party and obedience to the teachings of Chairman Mao. The traditional opera portrayed sacrifice for the emperor or master. The revolutionary opera dramatizes sacrifice for the proletariat cause. The traditional opera stressed humanity, family love, and brotherhood. The revolutionary opera emphasizes comradeship. Personal valor and ingenuity have found their places in both traditional and revolutionary opera, although in different settings. While the significant characters in the traditional opera included the emperor, officials, generals, as well as scholars, beauties, and courtesans, their counterparts in the revolutionary opera are relatively few: the Party, the peasants, the workers, the soldiers, the revolutionary leaders, and (frequently referred to) Chairman Mao. There are villains in both. It would seem that a considerable degree of similarity in approach exists between the traditional and revolutionary operas although their specific contents are quite different.

This rather puzzling feature—that is, the marked difference in specific content but basic similarity in general approach between the old and the new—can be illustrated by one of the five revolutionary operas, *Taking the Bandits' Stronghold*.[19] The original version of the play, which first appeared on stage at the Shanghai Peking Opera Theater in 1958, portrayed a detachment commander of the People's Liberation Army, Yang Tze-yung, who was presented as a hero much in the traditional swordsman style of the old Chinese opera. Except for its contemporary setting and costumes, the play sounded like the traditional opera *Lien Huan Tao*. Personal courage and resourcefulness stood out in the play, but ideological affirmation was not clearly in evidence. A revised version was presented under the direction of Chiang Ching during the Cultural Revolution; the singing and acting remained unchanged, and the plot, though basically the same, was cast in the broad perspective of revolution. Commander Yang was still shown as a soldier of great wisdom and courage; these were no longer individual qualities, however, but rather reflections of his "boundless loyalty to the Party, the people and the revolutionary cause, his bitter hatred of the reactionary ruling class, and above all, his learning of the great wisdom of Chairman Mao Tse-tung." In the play, whenever Yang faces a critical problem, he pauses and rehearses the teachings of Mao, draws his inspiration there, and acts decisively and triumphantly.

The similarity between the old and the new is even greater in the music, the style of singing, and the modes of acting. Basically the same music has been retained, with only minor modifications. This is important because certain basic melodies in the traditional opera have almost become part of Chinese life. Changing the music would destroy the basis of popular acceptance of Chinese opera as a folk art. The traditional singing styles have largely been retained, although archaic, literary phrases are replaced by simple, expressive terms. Certain traditional theatrical pronunciations were found difficult to understand when placed in the context of modern dialogue and Communist terminology. These have been replaced by commonly spoken pronunciations of the Peking dialect. The style of acting has largely remained unchanged, although certain movements and postures from the traditional opera, which looked out of place with actors in military uniforms, have been modified. These minor innovations were apparently well received by the audience. The masses of workers, peasants, and soldiers were said to be in favor of this kind of reform,[20] and judging by the continual popularity of the Chinese opera, it would seem that the audience has accepted these changes.

REVOLUTIONARY OPERA AS AN INSTITUTION

The revolutionary opera is a new social institution in which several major components—the Party, the playwrights, the performers, and the audience—play their respective, essential roles. The processes of their interactions and feedback, as well as resistance to change, will be discussed.

The roles of the Party are to set the policy, to select the plays considered suitable for the propagation of socialist ideology, to reeducate the playwrights and performers, and to evaluate the effectiveness of the various operatic plays on the basis of feedback from the audience as well as the performers and playwrights. These roles were clearly outlined in an editorial in the *People's Daily*.[21]

Under the Party's new policy of serving the proletarian class, the players are required not only to perform for workers, peasants, and soldiers, but actually to live among them and work with them as part of their own reeducation. At the village level, the guiding principle is: "When the peasants are busy, work with them. When they have spare time, perform for them." Thus, actors and actresses were reported to be helping the peasants in their harvest, carrying water, chopping vegetables, doing household chores, mending pig sties.[22] Despite the Party's directives, however, there appeared to be considerable reluctance among the players about going to the villages. The Faku Opera Troupe of Liao Ning Province provided an example. The troupe was formed in 1955, and by 1963 it had begun to perform for the villagers. According to one report, many actors were complaining about the poor living conditions and food.[23] There was a feeling that by spending their time mostly in the villages, they would become uncultured. A common complaint among the players was: "You lose 500 years of personal cultivation if you stay in the village for one month." Some ran away and went back to the city; others remained with the troupe but their "hearts [were] in the city." They did not get along well with the villagers. There appeared to be a tendency among the city-bred actors and actresses to look down on the peasants and regard manual work with contempt, and the villagers seemed to be aware of it. Living in the village, however, necessitated

some behavioral adaptations and brought about minor attitude change. According to a report cited earlier, "Some girls
were previously so picky about food and clothes. Now they
have adapted themselves to a simple lifestyle."[24] One actress
at first could not stand the sweat and odor of the peasants but
became accustomed to it after a while.

One reason for sending the players to the villages and military units was the fact that most of them had been accustomed to the traditional theatrical parts and did not know
how to play the roles of peasants and revolutionary soldiers.
The comments of Liu Yuan-jo, a well-known actress in
Shanghai, were indicative of the general situation. She said
she had been playing the traditional love themes so long that
her personality had been affected. She simply could not act
the revolutionary parts with genuine feelings and admitted
that she was using all kinds of excuses for not playing in revolutionary opera. It took her a long time to overcome her old
background. The audience too seemed to prefer the traditional opera, when they still had a choice. Once actress Liu's
troupe went to a commune and presented *The Golden Fan
Lost*, a traditional love story. People in the commune liked it
so much that "all they talked about every day was the play
—the emperor did this or the emperor did that. People just
did not want to go and work in the field." On a different oc-
casion her troupe was playing in another rural area and this
time they performed a revolutionary opera. She asked a
young girl how she liked it. To her surprise, the girl said she
liked the traditional opera better. "What I like best is the
talented scholar and his beautiful lady, wearing gorgeous silk
costumes of the old time. Now you all wear cotton dresses,
and you just don't look good." Actress Liu noted that this girl
was a member of the Youth Pioneers, and "yet she has been
so badly contaminated by the poison of the traditional opera,
which is serving only the interest of capitalism and feudalism."[25]

It was such attitudes that the Party was attempting to
change through revolutionary opera as part of the nation-

wide socialist reeducation campaign. The effectiveness of revolutionary opera in this regard will be discussed later.

Another objective of bringing the playwrights, performers, and the audience together through close interaction was to obtain feedback, so that the playwrights could revise the plays and the performers would be able to portray the lives of peasants and soldiers with feeling. This was what Chiang Ching called the Three-in-One Union of the leadership, the playwrights, and the masses for creative art. Citing the play *Great Wall along the Southern Sea* as an example, she described the process as follows:

> First the leadership set the theme. Then the playwrights went three times to acquire experience of military life, even taking part in a military operation to round up enemy spies. When the play was written, many leading members of the Kwangchow Military Command took part in discussing it, and after it had been rehearsed, opinions were widely canvassed and revisions made.[26]

Under this system, it is clear that playwriting is no longer a matter of individual creativity but an outcome of collective efforts. The leadership—the Party—chooses the themes, the playwrights write, the players perform, and the personnel or military units concerned give advice on both techniques and content. This system seems to allow little room for anti-Party elements to make use of the stage. It was meant to be an effective device by which Chairman Mao Tse-tung's thought could occupy all the positions in literature and art.[27]

Then there is the audience, whose role is to participate by attendance, to learn the content of the new Chinese opera, and to apply the new norms and values to their behavior. Feedback from the audience regarding the revolutionary opera is communicated through the organizational channels to the actors, the writers, and the Party. Revisions are made on the basis of audience feedback as well as official evaluation by the Party to achieve greater effect.

So thorough was this system of feedback that one revolutionary opera about the Liberation Army, *Shachiapang*, was revised fourteen times.[28] During that period, the playwrights and actors enlisted as soldiers in a military unit to live the life of soldiers.[29]

A vivid example of the process of feedback was *Red Youth*, a revolutionary opera that eulogized a shepherd boy, Chang Kao-chien, who died in a class struggle. The intended audience was children.

At first the play presented a chronological account, and the young audience called it "superficial." Many anecdotes were then added. For instance, in the play Chang got poor grades because he had to spend time tending the sheep. This was intended as a small crisis, but many children did not like it. So Chang received good grades. One of Chang's playmates, Little Lu, was shown to be habitually wiping his running nose. This was intended to add humor. The reaction was: "Little Lu is careless about his hygiene." So no more running nose. Some of Chang's playmates were shown to be absorbed in playing cards. This was later dropped. The most dramatic example of audience pressure concerned the ending. In the earlier version, shepherd Chang died as a result of the class struggle, just as it actually happened, but many children were upset. "How nice if Chang were still alive!" In the final version, Chang triumphed over his class enemy.[30]

One major mechanism for communicating the feedback to the Party was the opera forum discussion, attended by performers, playwrights, Party officials, and often some members of the audience, mostly soldiers and peasants. During the discussion, the participants would bring up their difficulties and shared each other's experiences in solving these difficulties. Admissions of errors were frequently made. Advice was sought from those members of the audience who happened to be attending the forum. The discussion would usually conclude with a reaffirmation to serve the interest of the proletarian class. Contents of these discussions were published in the two professional journals, *Qu Yi* and *Xiju Bao*.

Another important medium of communication has been the Revolutionary Opera Festival Demonstration, first held in Peking in the summer of 1964 and since then in various provincial capitals. At the Peking demonstration, attended by Party officials, performers, and playwrights, a number of revolutionary operas were staged to illustrate how to solve technical and content problems during the transition from traditional opera to revolutionary opera, and to elicit comments and suggestions. Important Party officials would deliver speeches to outline the policy of the Party regarding the roles of revolutionary opera. There were generally a few sessions at which exchange of experiences among playwrights and performers was encouraged.

The general patterns of social processes in revolutionary opera are summarized in Figure 4-1. At the top is the Party, which sets policy objectives and gives basic instructions for the playwrights and performers. Operating within these instructions, the playwrights and performers work together to produce a revolutionary opera. Close interactions with the audience are maintained during the production and performance stages. Feedback from the audience is discussed and incorporated into the opera. After most of the difficulties are solved with some success, an initial model revolutionary opera is staged by the Party at a Revolutionary Opera Demonstration Festival for other performers and playwrights. Further discussion by performers and playwrights may be pursued and additional feedback from the audience may be sought in order to improve the initial model. The product will be a revised model opera, which will be disseminated at provincial opera demonstration festivals to performing troupes throughout the country.

SOCIAL FUNCTIONS OF REVOLUTIONARY OPERA

For generations, Chinese opera has been functioning as a socializing agent. Traditionally, above every stage hung a huge

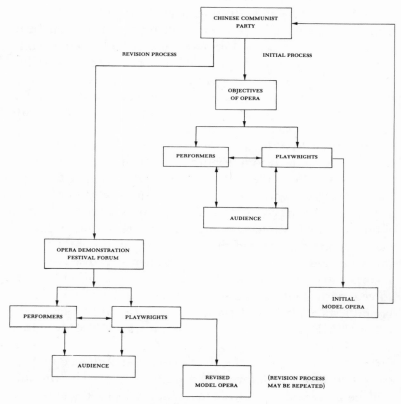

FIGURE 4-1. Communication processes in revolutionary opera production.

plaque bearing four characters: *Kao Tai Chiao Hua*, meaning "High Stage Educates and Influences." Another plaque
often appeared on the stage: *Yu Ming Tung Lo*, meaning
"Entertainment for the People." This concept of influence
through entertainment was clearly recognized in an article
written by a Chinese Communist commentator, Tai Pu-fan,
back in 1961:

> In fact, the opera of our country has always been presenting to
> the audience what they like to hear and love to see. We give
> them entertainment, through which they are being influenced so
> that customs and mores can be modified. We both entertain and
> educate. In fact, we build education within entertainment,
> which is a prominent tradition of Chinese opera.[31]

Tai mentioned many traditional Chinese opera shows and
characters, which he said were "household words to us."
Even a "three-foot tall boy will get excited about them and
discuss them, judging which is a good character and which is
a rotten egg. These characters have been deeply engraved in
our hearts, influencing the people of our country from
generation to generation." The performance of one single actor on stage was judged by Tai to surpass "a hundred lec-
tures" for its educational function because "philosophy and
theory are abstract but art and performance are concrete."

Unlike the European opera, which is essentially an elite-
spectator art, Chinese opera is a popular-participant art, for
many of the arias are sung by the Chinese like folk songs. A
common scene in a Chinese village during the past would be
a group of peasants gathered together during the evening,
singing and acting some part of the Chinese opera.

Because of its popularity and wide acceptance as a source
of entertainment and social standards, and above all because
it can involve the audience as active participants, Chinese
opera has been chosen by the Communist Party as an instrument to bring about changes in behavioral norms and cultural values and to mobilize support for the regime's policies.

The stated goals of the revolutionary opera are these: destroying the old and establishing the new; fostering proletarian ideology and eradicating bourgeois ideology; combatting egoism and repudiating revisionism; heightening political consciousness; reshaping the Chinese culture. The overall objective is cultural transformation.[32]

Admittedly, the functions of the revolutionary opera are difficult to demonstrate because of the extensiveness of the campaign and the fragmentary nature of available data. Nevertheless, some limited inferences can be made on the basis of the materials we have on hand.

First, as a cognitive function, the very shift from traditional opera to revolutionary opera should indicate to the people the Party's preference regarding behavioral norms, cultural values, and appropriate ideological commitment. This shift would serve clear notice that the old should be abandoned and the new adopted. Noteworthy is the fact that the new behavioral norms and values are presented not in abstract slogans, but through concrete, colorful, and dramatic models which the peasants and workers can readily understand and follow.

Second, the revolutionary opera has the instructive function of explaining to the people the new policies and directives of the Party in order to elicit their support. For instance, in Shansi Province, while the Party was publicizing the New Marriage Law, the Provincial Opera Group of Shansi staged a special opera to illustrate what the new law meant.[33] In Yunnan, during a movement of Winter Production, the Party had outlined eight objectives for the peasants. These were organized into an opera and sung in local folk music. The most dramatic example came from a troupe of twenty-one actors and actresses who went from village to village in an area inhabited by Tibetan tribesmen on the Burmese border. Singing in opera style but in Tibetan dialect, this troupe presented the various policies of the Party in the form of short skits and dances. Often the performers would take a recent local event and turn it into a skit. Thus, members of the audience were able to identify themselves with the story and see, in the play, characters they could recognize. The audience's reactions were highly favorable. According to the troupe's report, nearly every performance had to be repeated several times to satisfy the demands of the villagers. As some of the villagers stated it, "These policies have been explained to us before by Party members, but we did not understand them too well. Now that we have seen your performances, the ideas have firmly sunken into us."[34]

The effects of these performances were demonstrated in several concrete cases. One ironsmith who had long refused to join the commune changed his mind after seeing an operetta. In another village, some of the young tribesmen had been reluctant to help build a nearby highway, but they reported to work after they had seen one of the performances. After seeing one operetta that emphasized the need for food conservation, people in one village decided to go without their customary annual feast after harvest.

This same report mentioned several rather convincing cases where the opera troupe succeeded in changing health-related superstitions of the tribesmen. In those tribes, few people had ever gone to see a doctor. When a person became sick, his family would recite Buddhist scripts and plead to Buddha for mercy. To dispel this superstition, the troupe prepared a special operetta called "To Catch a Ghost," in which a magician staged a number of stunning displays of magic to win the faith of the villagers, then showed the audience that all the "feats of magic" of the Buddha they had just witnessed and believed were only tricks. As a result, the villagers realized that there were no ghosts or Buddhas, and said, "From now on, if we get sick, we'll see a doctor."[35]

Another function, one which the revolutionary opera shares with its traditional predecessor, is to provide an emotive outlet for the common people. Traditional operas such as *The Fisherman's Revenge* have long served as a social mechanism for the relief of frustration and anger of common men. In a similar vein, the evils of exploiters, capitalists, corrupt officials, landlords, and foreign invaders are portrayed extensively in the the revolutionary opera to arouse an emotional basis for antagonism against the past and commitment to the present.

Evidence available in the Communist publications suggests a relatively high degree of acceptance of revolutionary opera by the people as a form of entertainment and source of information. One reason for its popularity is the degree of emotive empathy which seems to have been achieved between the performers and the audience. This point was repeatedly stressed by many actors and actresses while discussing their experience. As one actor put it, "You must touch the heart of the audience." Another reason is the relevance of the subject matter to the audience: "We must go deep into real life to look for materials."[36] What is noteworthy is the fact that these factors alone have not brought about the same degree of popularity for other types of performance. For instance, the peasants did not seem to like movies, because they could not follow the shift of scenes.[37] In many cases the mobile movie team had to explain to the peasants what the movie meant.[38] Vernacular stage shows, which have no singing part, did not seem to be as popular as Peking opera.[39] Thus, a main reason for the continued popularity of revolutionary opera would appear to be the familiar old music and style of acting that it has inherited from traditional opera with only minor modifications.

Despite its popularity, we do not know to what extent revolutionary opera has succeeded as an instrument of socialization in changing the basic values and beliefs of the Chinese people. There is evidence to show that when the hero or heroine of a play is engaged in a struggle against the landlords, or fighting the enemy, the audience demonstrates a high degree of emotional identification with the hero or heroine. Take the revolutionary opera *Liu Hu-lan*, the life of a courageous peasant woman who died in a battle. In the early version of the opera, the scene of her supreme sacrifice was treated in a rather unconvincing manner. The audience expressed great disappointment. That scene was revised many times until the audience was satisfied and offered comments like: "This girl has guts, she is not afraid of anything," or "What a fight, she sure scares the class enemy with her big knife." Thus some degree of politically oriented consciousness in favor of class struggle seemed to have been fostered by revolutionary opera.[40]

Before traditional Peking opera was completely banned, however, even important leaders of the Party had to admit that if given a choice, most peasants would prefer the traditional opera. This can be seen in the audience responses to two plays in 1958, when traditional opera was still permitted. One was a modern revolutionary opera, *Taking the Bandits' Stronghold*, about the heroic deeds of the Liberation Army. The other was a traditional local opera, *Liang Shan-po and Chu Ying-tai*, a tear-jerking love story which had been part of Chinese folklore, in which the dominant themes were obedience to parents, love and devotion, chastity and faithfulness, and self-sacrifice for the sake of romantic love.[41] *Taking the Bandits' Stronghold* could hardly be described as a success and had to be dropped after a brief run,[42] but the love story of *Liang Shan-po and Chu Ying-tai* engulfed the entire country for months. Everywhere, people were singing *Liang Shan-po and Chu Ying-tai*. Audience preference of this nature could hardly indicate a fundamental change in the values and beliefs of the Chinese. In fact, Peng Chen, then mayor of Peking, observed in 1964 regarding the traditional opera:

Frankly speaking, there are people who live a life of contradiction today. Their bodies have moved into a socialist society, but their heads still remain in the feudalistic or capitalistic society. Their bodies and heads reside in two different worlds, which necessarily stretch their necks so long. . . . They live in a socialist society, but they think like a feudalist or a capitalist.[43]

At this point, one may wonder whether the "feudalistic or capitalistic" thinking was confined to those Chinese intellectuals who received their education in pre-Communist days, or whether the old values and beliefs might have permeated a large section of the population. We would be the first to recognize the possibility of differences in the embodiment of old Chinese culture between the intellectuals and the peasantry. Allowing this possibility of diversity within a culture, we would still assume some degree of uniformity of core values—however limited—that were shared by the intellectuals as well as the peasantry.[44] One example of this uniformity was furnished by actress Liu of metropolitan Shanghai and the Youth Pioneer peasant girl in one of the villages where Liu performed. Despite the vast differences in their backgrounds, both were fascinated by something in the traditional opera. The controversy about ghosts and gods in traditional opera provides another example. There is no question about the importance of ghosts, gods, and Buddha in the belief system of the Chinese peasants. It is interesting to note that many intellectuals came to defend the ghosts and gods as salutary features of the traditional opera when the Party attempted to brandish them off the stage on atheistic grounds.[45]

Following the purge of the "Gang of Four," a rather interesting revelation was made about the artistic taste of Chiang Ching. According to an article published in the *People's Daily* in November, 1976, during a visit by Chiang Ching to the model Tachai Brigade in September, 1975, the brigade propaganda team put on for her a program of revolutionary shows. The wife of Chairman Mao sat for not quite half an hour, became impatient, and left. Two days later she arranged a program of four traditional operas by a group of performers she had brought with her to Tachai from Peking. She was enthralled, and applauded continually.[46]

If we use these episodes as a basis of inference, we are inclined to be skeptical about the immediate effects of the revolutionary opera in changing the old cultural values and beliefs of the Chinese people. Indeed, one would hardly expect any great change to take place within a space of ten years in a culture that has been able to resist change for centuries. Such a change would seem to be unlikely in view of the fact that for nearly fifteen years after the establishment of the Peking government, the people of China were allowed partial reinforcement of their old values and beliefs through the content of the traditional opera. It seems clear that traditional opera functioned as a major link with the cultural heritage of the past until it was totally banned during the Cultural Revolution. In this sense it might be more appropriate to speak of the socializing effects of revolutionary opera not in terms of the present or even the near future, but in terms of the next generation—that is, if the ban on traditional opera remains in force. If the Party's embargo against the past should remain unrelenting—an assumption which may be challenged—then one would wonder how long the old Chinese culture could survive while links with the past are severed one after another. [47]

NOTES

1. One excellent example is Ruth Benedict, *The Chrysanthemum and the Sword* (Boston: Houghton Mifflin Company, 1946). Also Godwin C. Chu, Philip H. Cheng, and Leonard Chu, *The Roles of Tatzepao in the Cultural Revolution: A Structural-Functional Analysis* (Carbondale, Ill.: Southern Illinois University, 1972).

2. It is described in "The History of Rite and Music," *The Tang Book.* Also Josephine Huang Hung, *Classic Chinese Plays* (Taipei: Mei Ya Publications, Inc., 1971), p. 4; L. C. Arlington, *The Chinese Drama* (New York: Benjamin Blom, 1966).

3. Mao Tse-tung, *On Literature and Art* (Peking: Foreign Language Press, 1967), p. 3.

4. A brief account of how the *Hai Jui* play written by Wu Han touched

off the Cultural Revolution is given by Harrison E. Salisbury, *To Peking—And Beyond* (New York: Quadrangle/the New York Times Book Co., 1973), p. 45.

5. *Wen-hsueh Chan-pao* [Literary War Bulletin], combined issue nos. 17–18, June 30, 1967.

6. Ibid.

7. Lois W. Snow, *China on Stage* (New York: Random House, 1972).

8. Kao T. Shun, "Tear Off the Mask of Anti-Communist Veteran Chou Hsin-fang," *Wen Hui Pao* (Shanghai), July 11, 1966.

9. Chiang Ching, *On the Revolution of Peking Opera* (Peking: Foreign Language Press), p. 1.

10. Ibid, p. 5.

11. Peng Chen, "Speech at Festival of Peking Opera on Contemporary Themes," in *Qu Yi* 63 (July, 1964): 8.

12. Ya Han-chang and Tang Hai, "The Question of Atheistic Education and the Ghost Opera," *Xiju Bao* 185 (May, 1964): 39–43.

13. Tao Chu, "The Revolutionary Opera Will Completely Occupy the Stage," *Xiju Bao* 200 (August, 1965): 2–7.

14. The five revolutionary operas are: *Taking the Tiger Mountain by Strategy, The Red Lantern, Shachiapang, The Raid on the White Tiger Regiment,* and *On the Docks.* For their stories, see Chapter 5 in this volume.

15. The three major revolutionary operas introduced since the Cultural Revolution are:

The Dragon River: In the spring of 1963, a coastal district in southeast China is suffering a serious drought. The revolutionary committee of the Dragon River District Brigade decides to build a new dam which could help fight the drought. Under the leadership of Miss Chiang Shu-ying, secretary of the committee, the commune members have to fight the drought on the one hand and face the challenge of a sabotage by class enemies on the other. Using Mao Tse-tung thought as their weapon, the secretary and her followers carry out their mission and crush the sabotage.

Azalea Mountain: In 1928, on Azalea Mountain in central China, the civil war between the Chinese Communists and Nationalists reaches a climax. Ko Hsiang, a female Communist Party representative of the peasants' self-defense corps, is rescued from execution by Lei Kang, leader of the self-defense corps. Under the leadership of Ko, the farmers soon build up their base as a stronghold. A few months later, the antirevolutionary elements launched another surprise attack. Granny Tu, known as the mother of the revolutionaries, is arrested. Lei Kang, while trying to rescue Granny Tu from jail, is detained by the antirevolutionary forces. On a dark night, Ko leads the corps in a surprise raid on the enemies and rescues both Granny Tu and Lei. Immediately after the successful raid, Ko and Lei join the forces led by Mao Tse-tung in the mountain area in Kiangsi.

War in the Plain: During the Sino-Japanese War, Chao Yung-kang, a platoon commander of the Communist Eighth Route Army, organizes the villagers in the plain near Tahang Mountain to attack a Japanese garrison along the railway. Chao repeatedly outwits the Japanese commander in a number of maneuvers, including a personal visit to the Japanese headquarters. He blows up the Japanese ammunition depot and destroys the Japanese forces.

16. Criticism Group of People's Publishing Press, "Chiang Ching is a Political Pickpocket Who Established Her Reputation by Cheating the World," *People's Daily*, November 22, 1976.

17. Ibid.

18. "1977 New Year Programs to Celebrate Inauguration of Comrade Hua Kuo-feng as Chairman of the Chinese Communist Party and Chairman of the Central Military Committee, and the Victory over the 'Gang of Four'," *People's Daily*, January 2, 1977.

19. Union Research Institute, *Taking the Bandits' Stronghold*, *Union Research* 46:5 (January 17, 1966): 66, translated from *China News Service* 4632 (December 12, 1965). The title of this opera was later changed to *Taking the Tiger Mountain by Strategy*.

20. Union Research Institute, *Taking the Bandits' Stronghold*, pp. 67–68.

21. Editorial, *People's Daily*, August 1, 1964.

22. Chu Ping, "The Cultural Hussars Active in the Mountainous Villages," *Qu Yi* 70 (April, 1965): 63.

23. The Faku Opera Troupe of Lian Ning Province, "Facing the Village, to Serve the People and to Be the Red Cultural Hussars," in *The Good Troupes Marching on the Revolutionary Road* (Peking: The Chinese Theater Publication Association, 1966), p. 92.

24. Chu Ping, "Cultural Hussars."

25. Liu Yuan-jo, "To Serve the Workers, Peasants, and Soldiers, and to Be the Art Fighters of the Proletariat Class," *Qu Yi* 70 (April, 1965): 6–8.

26. Chiang Ching, *Revolution of Peking Opera*, p. 4.

27. The Revolutionary Committee of the China Peking Opera Theater, "Let Heroic Images of the Proletariat Shine on the Peking Opera Stage," in Chiang Ching, *Revolution of Peking Opera*, p. 35.

28. Acrobatic Team of Peking's Chinese Opera Troupe, "Strive to Create a Model of a Revolutionary Hero," *Wen Hui Pao* (Shanghai), June 2, 1965.

29. Military Acting Team of the Peking Opera Troupe, "To Exert Ef-

forts to Model the Images of Our Revolutionary Heroes," in *Collection of Commentaries on Peking Opera Shachiapang*, ed. Chinese Dramatists' Association (Peking: The Chinese Theater Publication Association, 1965), p. 170.

30. Yao Ying-hua, "How Did We Model the Image of Hero Chang Kao Chien?" in *Red Youths* (Shanghai: Shanghai Cultural Publishing Co., 1965), p. 75.

31. Tai Pu-fan, "Influence and Education through Entertainment People Like to Hear and See," *Xiju Bao* 145/146 (November and December, 1961): 10.

32. "Pursue to the End the Socialist Revolution on the Front of Art and Literature," editorial, *People's Daily*, August 1, 1964; "Vigorously Develop the New Socialist Opera," editorial, *People's Daily*, February 5, 1964. "The Most Fundamental Lessons for Revolutionary Operatic Words," *Qu Yi* 70 (1965).

33. Shansi Cultural Bureau, "Facing the Villages, Red in the Villages," in *Good Troupes Marching*, p. 136.

34. The Propaganda Department, the Workers' Committee of Ti King County of Chinese Communist Party's Yunnan Branch, and the *Yunnan Daily*, "The Red Cultural Hussars in the High Land," in *Good Troupes Marching*, pp. 12–23.

35. Ibid.

36. "Again Discuss Why 'Fire in the Swamps' is Successful," editorial, *Peking Daily*, May 11, 1964.

37. *Yunnan Daily*, "Red Cultural Hussars," p. 18.

38. Alan Liu, "Movies and Modernization in Communist China," *Journalism Quarterly* 43 (Summer, 1966): 319–324.

39. One report noted that the peasants were not accustomed to vernacular stage shows. See Li Ma, "Swatow Vernacular Stage Show Troupe Seeking Roots in Villages," *Xiju Bao* 173 (May, 1963): 8.

40. Yang Lan-chun, "On the Performance of Contemporary Opera for Peasants," *Xiju Bao* 173 (May, 1963): 7–9.

41. Union Research Institute, "Extol Symphony Shachiapang and Decry Violin Concerto 'Liang and Chu'," *Union Research* 48:1 (July 4, 1967): 1.

42. Union Research Institute, *Taking the Bandits' Stronghold*, p. 63.

43. Peng Chen, "Speech at Festival of Peking Opera on Contemporary Themes," *Qu Yi* 63 (July, 1964): 12.

44. For a discussion of cultural uniformity versus diversity, see Anthony F. C. Wallace, *Culture and Personality* (New York: Random House, 1961).

45. Ya Han-chang and Tang Hai, "Atheistic Education."

46. Tachai Brigade Propaganda Team, "Expose the Face of Chiang

Ching as One Who Worships Foreigners and Wants to Restore Traditions," *People's Daily*, November 19, 1976. The four traditional operas ordered by Chiang Ching were:

The General Ordered His Son's Execution: Commanding General Yang of the Sung Dynasty orders that his son be executed because he has failed in his mission to take an enemy fortress. The execution is stopped by his son's girl friend, Mu Kuei-yin, who later succeeds in destroying the enemy forces.

The Emperor's Robe Was Executed: Emperor Jen of the Sung Dynasty unknowingly commits the sin of offending his mother. Judge Pao discovers the truth and confronts the emperor with his error. The penalty for such a breach of filial piety would be death. As a symbolic punishment, the emperor's robe is executed in place of himself.

The Strategy of the Unguarded Fortress: Chukuo Liang, the best-known Chinese military strategist during the dynasties of the Three Kingdoms, suddenly finds himself surrounded by a large enemy force while his troops are away. He deceives the enemy by abandoning all guards and leaving the fortress gates wide open. The enemy commander, suspecting a trap, hastily retreats.

At the Broken Bridge: The title refers to the beginning scene in the romantic love between Hsu Hsien, a handsome scholar, and Pai Shu-cheng, a beautiful lady who is actually a white serpent. It is at the Broken Bridge near the West Lake in Hangchow that they first meet.

The predominant values in these traditional operas are: *The General Ordered His Son's Execution* (loyalty to the emperor, obedience to father, romantic love); *The Emperor's Robe Was Executed* (loyalty to the emperor, supremacy of the emperor, filial piety, integrity, law, and justice); *The Strategy of the Unguarded Fortress* (intelligence, bravery, and ability); *At the Broken Bridge* (romantic love). The last-mentioned opera also reflects the Chinese belief in superstition.

47. On June 12, 1978, the official New China News Agency *(Hsinhua)* announced the rehabilitation of forty-five traditional operas "following Chairman Mao's thoughts on revolutionary art and literature." These operas, described by *Hsinhua* as highly popular among the Chinese, either portray the struggle of the oppressed class or extol the patriotism, diligence, courage, and intelligence of the people. Many are historical plays about warriors and generals. *Fisherman's Revenge*, analyzed by Philip Cheng in this volume, is one of the forty-five, which also include *At the Broken Bridge* and *The Strategy of the Unguarded Fortress*, said to be among Chiang Ching's favorites. See "Traditional Peking Opera Shines Again," *Ta Kung Pao* (Hong Kong), June 13, 1978.

CHAPTER 5   A Comparative Value Analysis:
Traditional versus
Revolutionary Opera

Philip H. Cheng

This study compares the values that are reflected in traditional Chinese opera of the past and the revolutionary opera
of today. Using quantitative content analysis and factor
analysis, the writer examined ten Peking opera plays, five
traditional and five revolutionary.

As a popular art, Peking opera has been widely accepted
for centuries as a source of entertainment and education
because it can involve both the performers and the audience
as active participants. Because of this characteristic, Peking
opera has been chosen by the Chinese Communist Party as an
instrument to bring about changes in behavioral norms and
social values and to mobilize support for the Party's policies.

METHODOLOGY

The theoretical and methodological orientations guiding this
research are taken from three areas: cultural values, content
analysis, and factor analysis.

The value system recommended by Milton Rokeach provided a theoretical basis for analyzing the themes of the ten
Chinese opera plays.[1] Working mostly in psychological
research, Rokeach has suggested two kinds of cultural values,

terminal and instrumental. Terminal values are basic ends and goals that we seek in our life. Instrumental values are personal qualities and attributes that are considered important and desirable as means toward achieving the basic goals. Rokeach's value system consists of eighteen terminal values and eighteen instrumental values that can be used to provide a hierarchical rank-ordering along a continuum of importance. These values can serve as operational categories for analyzing the content of popular literature and mass media as indicators of dominant cultural values.

Since Rokeach's system is likely to reflect generally Western perceptions, however, some modifications are desirable to adapt it to Chinese culture. For the purpose of subsequent cross-cultural comparison, the writer kept all thirty-six terminal and instrumental values recommended by Rokeach, even though some of them may not be prominent in the Chinese value system. In addition, on the basis of an initial reading of the revolutionary operas and a trial analysis of two traditional plays, four new categories were included. They are "new hope" (prospect of new life), as a terminal value, and "patriotic," "loyal," and "grateful," as instrumental values. These values figure prominently in either traditional Chinese society or in the new Communist Chinese system. Altogether this study uses nineteen terminal values and twenty-one instrumental values after the modification (see Table 1) as major categories for the content analysis.

Five traditional Chinese opera plays were chosen on the basis of popularity and variety of themes: *The Tragedy of a Brave King and His Favorite Queen*, *Lady White Snake*, *The Fisherman's Revenge*, *The Pass at Yu Meng*, and *The Feast at the Yellow Crane Tower*. The five revolutionary opera plays analyzed were: *Taking the Tiger Mountain by Strategy*, *The Red Lantern*, *Shachiapang*, *The Raid on White Tiger Regiment*, and *On the Docks*.

The following are brief summaries of the ten Chinese operas in the analysis.

TABLE 1. The Terminal and Instrumental Values

Terminal Values	Instrumental Values
A Comfortable Life (a prosperous life)	Ambitious (hard-working, aspiring)
An Exciting Life (a stimulating, active life)	Broadminded (open-minded)
A Sense of Accomplishment (lasting contribution)	Capable (competent, effective)
A World at Peace (free of war and conflict)	Cheerful (lighthearted, joyful)
A World of Beauty (beauty of nature and arts)	Clean (neat, tidy)
Equality (brotherhood, equal opportunity for all)	Courageous (standing up for your beliefs)
Family Security (taking care of loved ones)	Forgiving (willing to pardon others)
Freedom (independence, free choice)	Helpful (working for others' welfare)
Happiness (contentedness)	Honest (sincere, truthful)
Inner Harmony (freedom from inner conflict)	Imaginative (daring, creative)
Mature Love (sexual, spiritual intimacy)	Independent (self-reliant, self-sufficient)
National Security (protection from attack)	Intellectual (intelligent, reflective)
Pleasure (an enjoyable, leisurely life)	Logical (consistent, rational)
Salvation (saved, eternal life)	Loving (affectionate, tender)
Self-respect (self-esteem)	Obedient (dutiful, respectful)
Social Recognition (respect, admiration)	Polite (courteous, well-mannered)
True Friendship (close companionship)	Responsible (dependable, reliable)
Wisdom (a mature understanding of life)	Self-controlled (restrained, self-disciplined)
New Hope (prospect of a new life)	Patriotic (loving to nation)
	Loyal (dedication to nation, leaders)
	Grateful (thankful to others)

FIVE TRADITIONAL OPERAS

The Tragedy of a Brave King and His Favorite Queen. Hsiang Yu, known as Pa Wang (peerless emperor), and Liu Pang, the founder of the Han Dynasty (202 B.C.–A.D. 220), are competing for supremacy in China after the downfall of the Chin Dynasty. Lady Yu Chi, Hsiang's favorite, is a beautiful and brave female warrior who serves as a fighting mate, sweetheart, and boon companion of the king. Hsiang is eventually defeated by Liu because of his failure to enlist and keep the support from other outstanding scholars and military strategists. On the eve of the death of the peerless emperor, Lady Yu Chi offers him wine and dance as a farewell greeting before she kills herself.

Lady White Snake. This is a supernatural play based on a very popular folktale in China. A white snake, by virtue of supernatural power, has been transformed into an immortal in the form of a pretty young girl. She meets by chance a young and poverty-stricken scholar, Hsu Hsien, and falls in love with him. They lead a happy and prosperous life after their marriage. Their life becomes disastrous, however, when the young husband is told by a monk that his pretty wife is a snake. Under the instigation of the monk, the husband forgets all her love and kindness. He joins the monk's scheme, which turns the wife back to a snake and puts her in permanent imprisonment under a pagoda on the West Lake in eastern China.

The Fisherman's Revenge. Hsiao En, a national hero of the Sung Dynasty (A.D. 960–1126), returns to an obscure life as a fisherman with his daughter after retiring from a long military service. A few years later, he becomes the victim of oppression by a landlord and a group of corrupt government officials. In despair, the old hero takes the law into his own hands and kills the landlord. He then begins his fugitive life with his daughter.

The Pass at Yu Meng. The play tells how the Silk Road

linking the East and the West is opened by a young hero named Pan Chao in the first century A.D. The young scholar defeats a strong barbarian tribe and puts a total of thirty-six small kingdoms under the rule of the Chinese emperor, thus expanding the Chinese territory to the far north and strengthening national defense against the northern barbarians. As a result, he has been regarded as one of the most outstanding national heroes in Chinese history.

The Feast at the Yellow Crane Tower. During the Three Kingdoms Period (A.D. 221–265), Shu in the west and Wu in the east are struggling for the possession of Ching Chou, a large territory in central China. Liu Pei, the King of Shu, is invited to a feast by General Chou Yu, commander-in-chief of Wu, at the Yellow Crane Tower. Chou plans an ambush in order to force Liu to sign documents which would promise the return of Ching Chou to Wu. Under the careful strategy of Chu Ko Liang, the prime minister, Liu escapes Chou's scheme successfully without surrendering the territory to Wu. This victory paves the way for Liu's forty-year rule over the western part of China.

FIVE REVOLUTIONARY OPERAS

Taking the Tiger Mountain by Strategy. The story takes place in northern China in the winter of 1946. A Chinese Communist Liberation Army detachment of thirty-six men, led by regimental chief of staff Shao Chien-po and platoon leader Yang Tze-jung, penetrate a stronghold of the Chinese Nationalist troops. The Communist heroes eventually defeat the Nationalists and seize the military base by successful strategy.

The Red Lantern. The story takes place in northern China under the Japanese occupation during the Sino-Japanese war from 1937 to 1945. Li Yu-ho, a Chinese Communist underground fighter, is assigned to deliver a secret code with instructions to a guerrilla's base in a mountain. Betrayed by a traitor, Li is arrested by the Japanese troops before he is able to carry out the mission. Anxious to obtain the secret code, the Japanese troops also detain Li's mother and daughter to force him to surrender the code. The seventeen-year-old daughter, Tieh-mei, performs the mission successfully after her father and grandmother are tortured to death by the Japanese invaders. Because of the heroic deed of the young girl, the Japanese troops are finally defeated by the Chinese Communist troops.

Shachiapang. Shachiapang is a small town in Kiangsu, eastern China. The story occurs under the Japanese occupation during World War II. Sister Ah-ching, an underground Chinese Communist agent, is assigned to run a tea shop as a business to cover a group of wounded Communist soldiers planning to cross the enemy lines to the rear. Under the assistance of the local community, Sister Ah-ching defeats a series of raids by the Japanese and Nationalist troops. She then fulfills her mission and leads the wounded Communist soldiers to safety.

The Raid on the White Tiger Regiment. This is an international play. The setting is Anpingli, Korea. The hero is Yang Wei-tsai, leader of the reconnaissance platoon of the Chinese People's Volunteers Regiment. The Chinese Communist soldiers, portrayed as supermen, launch a surprise attack by flying over deep gorges and mined areas against the Korean White Tiger Regiment, which is under the strong support of the American troops. The successful raid smashes the joint efforts by the American-Korean forces.

On the Docks. This is the only play among the five model revolutionary plays that involves no fighting, shooting, and killing. The play, internationally oriented, depicts a struggle in the industrial background—on the docks. The story takes place in Shanghai in 1963 when a group of dock workers, under the leadership of Miss Fang Hai-chen, secretary of the Chinese Communist Party branch of the dock workers' brigade, defeats a reactionary scheme. The dock workers crush the sabotage, which tried to delay the shipment of 8,000 sacks of seed rice to Africa as part of the international duty by the Chinese people. The villain is discovered and killed and the seeds are delivered on time for the plant season.

METHODS OF ANALYSIS

Three judges were assigned to analyze the ten plays on the basis of the value system given in Table 1. The judges, all versed in Chinese language and Chinese opera, also had training in content analysis. They read all dialogues and singing parts in every play and recorded which values, if any, were contained within each sentence.

Before reading the plays, the judges were given training on two traditional plays which were not included in the ten for this study. They were required to read and record the values according to Rokeach's system. They were also asked to list additional values which were frequent but not included in Rokeach's system. They ended their training sessions with a final list of nineteen terminal values and twenty-one instrumental values.

Interjudge reliability coefficients were obtained. The correlations (Pearson product-moment coefficient) are between the frequencies obtained by all judges, tested one against the others, for the forty values. The reliabilities on the terminal and instrumental values were obtained separately. Since the reliability coefficients ranged from .75 to .84, it was felt that the judges performed reliably and their data could be used in this study.

The data were factor analyzed by two Q-solutions, one on the nineteen terminal values and the other on the twenty-one instrumental values. The two analyses are run on the themes as they appear in the plays.

The Q-factoring was used mainly to identify various groupings of plays that were similarly oriented to the terminal or instrumental values. These play types were also analyzed to determine which values characterize the opera plays in a particular type. The prominence of these values is expressed in terms of standard z-scores that are high and positive.[2]

It is assumed that the Chinese operas can be categorized into different groups because of their orientations. Among the traditional operas, for example, some of the themes and plots deal with family love and personal feelings. Based on the values identified in the dialogues and singing parts, the factor solutions determine accordingly which type an opera will fall into.

We recognize that there are hundreds of traditional Chinese opera plays, most of them hundreds of years old, and that five plays may seem insufficient to represent an overall picture. The reason for selecting only five was to match in number (for the purposes of factor analysis) the five model revolutionary plays officially adopted by the Chinese Communist Party in 1972 when the research project began.

The results of the content analysis, then, provided a basis for two Q-factor analysis solutions. Information related to the number of factors, as well as the relationship between the factors and the plays, is contained in Appendix A.

FINDINGS

FOUR-FACTOR Q-SOLUTION FOR NINETEEN TERMINAL VALUES

In the factor analysis, a simple structure matrix of the nineteen terminal values (Appendix A) yielded a four-factor Q-solution that accounted for 73.06 percent of the total variance. By factor, the variance accounted for was: Type I—27.33 percent; Type II—22.70 percent; Type III—16.52 percent; and Type IV—6.51 percent.

Type I includes four revolutionary opera plays: *The Red Lantern, Shachiapang, The Raid on the White Tiger Regiment,* and *Taking the Tiger Mountain by Strategy.* This type of opera highly accentuates salvation values (z-score = 3.051) and true friendship (z-score = 2.128). Rokeach defines salvation as "saved, eternal life," and true friendship as "close companionship." In this study, salvation also refers to liberation, that is, being saved in a practical sense.

The four plays in this category are generally military in nature. *The Red Lantern* is an anti-Japanese story, and *Shachiapang* is similar in background. *The Raid on the White Tiger Regiment* is an anti-American and anti-Korean war drama, highly international in orientation. *Taking the Tiger Mountain by Strategy* is the only play in this type about the civil war between the Nationalists and the Communists.

It is interesting that salvation and true friendship appear so closely related in this type. This fact might be interpreted to mean that, in Communist philosophy, comradeship is the cornerstone of salvation. That is, salvation—a saved and meaningful life—becomes a major cause of friendship—a comradeship.

The meaning of salvation (liberation) through comradeship is prominent in many parts of the four revolutionary operas. For instance, Tieh-mei, the little girl who carried out the heroic mission against the Japanese invaders, describes her devotion to salvation through close comradeship with her own father:

> Granny has told me the story of the red lantern,
> The words are few, but meaning is deep.
> Why are my father and uncle not afraid of danger?
> Because they want to save China,
> Save the poor, defeat the Japanese invaders.
> I realize I should act as they do,
> And be a person like them.
> I am seventeen, no longer a child,
> I should share my father's worries.
> If he's carrying a 1000-pound load,
> I should carry 800.[3]

Type II contains only one traditional Chinese opera, *The Pass at Yu Meng*. This type emphasizes national security (z-score = 4.098). No other values have high z-scores in this type. National security is defined by Rokeach as "protection from attack," which is the theme of this traditional play.

The Pass at Yu Meng, an historical account, has been very popular in China. It tells how young Pan Chao distinguished himself by expanding the Chinese influence as well as the territory to the northwest, and thus built a strong national defense against the northern tribes in an international struggle. The sentiments of national security are evident in almost every major melody and dialogue throughout the opera. One of the young hero's lyrics reads:

> Let me throw away my pen,
> It is the very time to join the military service.
> Beyond the Pass at Yu Meng, there is 3,000 miles of land,
> It is the best place for young men,
> To build up their bright future and the national defense.

It may be noted that the theme in this opera is concentrated in two subjects—the heroic deed of the young scholar and the urgent need for national security. There is no mention of either the emperor or the royal court.

Type III consists of three traditional Chinese operas: *The Tragedy of a Brave King and His Favorite Queen*, *Lady White Snake*, and *The Fisherman's Revenge*. This type is oriented toward family security, as all three plays are characterized by family love—between husband and wife, between king and queen, and between father and daughter. Family security, as a terminal value, is the only one of the nineteen terminal values to have a high, significant, positive z-score (3.609) in this type. Self-respect has a relatively low but significant z-score of 0.930. All other values were nonsignificant.

Family security is defined by Rokeach as "taking care of loved ones," and self-respect as "self-esteem." The plots of these plays illustrate vividly a kind of human passion which is universal both in traditional Chinese society and Western society as a whole. It is clearly indicated in a melodic part of *Lady White Snake*:

So you want us to go back to Omei,
And leave my beloved husband behind.
Even if you are a living Buddha,
You won't be able to make us do that.
Please, O Abbot, please give back my husband,
So that we may have an early reunion.
Alas! When love is concerned, I just can't control myself.

Type IV comprises two operas, one traditional and one revolutionary, both emphasizing a sense of accomplishment. The plays are *The Feast at the Yellow Crane Tower*, and *On the Docks*. The terminal value, "sense of accomplishment," has the highest z-score (3.277) in this type. Two other values, national security and social recognition, also have significant z-scores, 1.756 and 1.280, respectively. Sense of accomplishment is defined by Rokeach as "lasting contribution," social recognition as "respect, admiration." This is the only type that contains both a traditional play and revolutionary play within the same category of terminal values. Both are non-military.

To sum up, in the four plays in Type I, revolutionary causes are emphasized, generally for the salvation of the poor, the oppressed, and the underprivileged. In Type II, heroic deeds are portrayed and national defense is emphasized in a traditional opera.

A sharp difference between salvation and family security can be noted between Type I (revolutionary cause) and Type III (family love).

Both Type II and Type III contain only traditional operas. These plays all involve military action or violence. In Type II, the hero is depicted as a model for national survival in a struggle against the northern barbarians. In Type III, the heroes and heroines are described as fighters for love, family, or romance. The former deals with the security of the nation while the latter deals with personal emotion.

National security as a value is present in both Types II and IV. The finding that national security is regarded as an important value in those plays (in Type IV) in which a sense of accomplishment is strongly emphasized seems to suggest that the Chinese, in the past as well as today, perceive accomplishment in a national or collective framework. On the other hand, while a hero is fighting for national defense or survival, as was Pan Chao in *The Pass at Yu Meng*, he is not necessarily concerned with a sense of accomplishment as a personal goal. This can be seen in our finding that "sense of accomplishment" scored low in the Type II opera *(The Pass at Yu Meng)*. Taken together, these findings suggest that collective goals take precedence over individual goals among the Chinese, in the past as well as the present.

TWO-FACTOR Q-SOLUTION FOR TWENTY-ONE INSTRUMENTAL VALUES

With the application of a simple structure matrix (Appendix A), two types of opera are identified for the twenty-one instrumental values. This matrix is the result of a repeated effort to carry out the analysis from different factor levels. All these attempts resulted in a similar two-factor solution.

The two-factor solution accounted for 61.33 percent of the total variance as follows: Type I—42.84 percent; Type II—18.49 percent.

Type I can be considered a "loyal" type, featuring such values as being "loyal," "courageous," and "capable." The z-scores of these values are significant: 2.266, 2.200, and 1.999, respectively.

"Loyal" is defined as "devotion to nation, leaders"; "courageous" as "standing up for your beliefs"; and "capable" as "competent, effective."

This type contains all the five revolutionary operas and two of the five traditional operas. The revolutionary ones are *The Red Lantern, Shachiapang, The Raid on the White Tiger Regiment, Taking the Tiger Mountain by Strategy*, and *On the Docks*. The traditional plays are *The Pass at Yu Meng* and *The Feast at the Yellow Crane Tower*.

It appears consistent that these three instrumental values —loyalty, courage, and capability—hold the highest z-scores. Literally speaking, they represent three qualities which are closely related in individual behavior. A hero, either of the revolutionary or traditional type, must be, first of all, capable and courageous so that his high quality of loyalty can be fully manifested in his brave deeds. While all three are qualities a hero must have to distinguish himself, it is interesting to note that loyalty is given overwhelming importance in both revolutionary and traditional opera.

In terms of loyalty as an instrumental value—whether to the emperor, the nation, the people, the Party, or the leader— these Chinese operas, regardless of their political orientations, present a high degree of similarity. This finding provides insight into the social functions of Chinese opera. It seems that both in the past and today, the performing art has been applied for political socialization by the governing institutions. There are differences, however, in the degree of application. Among traditional Chinese opera plays, only some —in this analysis, two out of five—manifested this characteristic. Today, under the government of the People's Republic, the utilization of this art form for political purposes has been enlarged in our sample to 100 percent, five out of five plays.

Type II is characterized in the instrumental value analysis as a "loving" type, consisting of three traditional plays—*The Tragedy of a Brave King and His Favorite Queen*, *Lady White Snake*, and *The Fisherman's Revenge*. The three values with significant and positive z-scores are: "loving," 3.516; "courageous," 1.272; and "capable," 1.123, indicating that these values are prominent themes.

"Loving" is defined as "affectionate, tender." "Capable" and "courageous" have just been described in the previous section. It may be noted that the two instrumental values, "capable" and "courageous," are related to "loving" just as they are to another value, "loyal," discussed in Type I. It appears that these values can cluster together because the

power of love, as generally understood, is able to make people sacrifice willingly for others, thus enhancing the qualities
of capability and courage. In *The Tragedy of a Brave King
and His Favorite Queen*, the heroine, Lady Yu Chi, takes her
own life without any hesitation because of her love for the
king. The heroine of *Lady White Snake* goes even further in
devoting herself to love by challenging the whole world.
Even in *The Fisherman's Revenge*, which accentuates the
grievance of the poor people, the theme of affectionate love
stands out in the father-daughter relationship.

Another significant finding is that the three traditional
operas in this type are the same ones that fall in the family
security type of the nineteen terminal values. This offers
more conclusive evidence that family security and loving are
closely related in terms of traditional Chinese value orientations. This finding also draws a clear line between the traditional and revolutionary operas. Loving and family security
seem to be the basic criteria for the traditional Chinese
opera, but not for the revolutionary opera.

As we have noted, the two most outstanding differences in
instrumental values between Type I and Type II concern
"loyal" and "loving." Operas in Type I stress the importance
and significance of the national cause and emphasize the
heroic deeds by the younger generations, to royal courts,
emperors, and the nation of the past and to the Party, the
leaders, and the people of the present. The Type II plays, on
the contrary, emphasize the qualities of love and affection.
These, of course, involve mostly personal feelings, individual
emotion, or natural impulse acting upon the heart.

"Intellectual" and "patriotic," two instrumental values
found to be related to loyalty in Type I, may be briefly
discussed. In the revolutionary operas, such as *Schachiapang*
and *Taking the Tiger Mountain by Strategy*, the heroes and
heroines are portrayed as so intelligent that they could carry
out their difficult missions successfully in any kind of situation. In such "loyal" operas, including the traditional as well

as revolutionary, the heroes or heroines are depicted as supermen or superwomen who are always able to succeed against
impossible odds. Also, since these operas all deal with national affairs or revolutionary causes, patriotism is usually
cited as a value to justify the themes. On the other hand, in
the "loving" operas, the themes and plots are mostly presented in an emotional tone. They appeal to human feelings,
neither rational nor intellectual. In this context, patriotism
does not need to be emphasized as a value.

We found, however, that the operas in the "loving" type
stress two other instrumental values, those of being "helpful"
and "logical." When the heroes and heroines are suffering
from pain or sorrows, they are actually portrayed as doing
something rational to help their beloved ones. That is, even
though such devotion or self-sacrifice may seem lacking in
justification to the audience, to the person directly involved
such actions would be consistent with love and thus, rational
and logical.

CONCLUSION
"LOVING" AND FAMILY SECURITY

We may recall that three traditional plays, *The Tragedy of a
Brave King and His Favorite Queen*, *Lady White Snake*, and
The Fisherman's Revenge, are grouped together both in the
instrumental value analysis and the terminal value analysis.
They are oriented toward "loving" and family security. The
relationship can be presented in a model as this:

"Loving" (instrumental value) → family security (terminal
value)

It can be interpreted that in the traditional Chinese culture, love is the basis of family security and family security
comes from love. Love, sometimes presented in the form of
romance, is part of human nature. In revolutionary opera,
however, love and family security have been generally ex-

cluded. Even when some family affairs are mentioned, the norms are modified and carefully redefined in a new way, in which the family stands as a unit of comrades united under the same revolutionary cause, such as the family structure in *The Red Lantern.* It is not presented as a unit of close and warm kinship relations.

Thus love, one of the most popular themes in traditional Chinese opera, has disappeared completely in the revolutionary plays because it is considered bourgeois. The Communist leaders believe that love, if the term is proper, should be expressed as a kind of passion, enthusiasm, or dedication to the cause of the proletariat class, the people, the Communist Party, and most of all, Chairman Mao. Under this conviction, family, family love, and romance—the most frequent themes in traditional Chinese opera—are given no prominence in revolutionary plays.

THE "LOYAL" TYPE

In our analysis of instrumental values, seven operas, both traditional and revolutionary, are identified in the "loyal" type. They are: *The Pass at Yu Meng, The Feast at the Yellow Crane Tower, The Red Lantern, Shachiapang, The Raid on the White Tiger Regiment, Taking the Tiger Mountain by Strategy,* and *On the Docks.* It is noteworthy that these are the same plays that cluster together into three types in the terminal value analysis: salvation, national security, and sense of accomplishment. The relationship can be formulated as follows:

Loyal (instrumental values) → salvation, national security, sense of accomplishment (terminal values)

These findings can be summarized as follows: First of all, loyalty is a prevalent value not only in revolutionary opera but also in traditional opera. Second, loyalty, as portrayed in these plays, is instrumental to the causes of salvation, national security, and sense of accomplishment. Third, loyalty manifested in Chinese opera is given different interpretations according to the policies of the ruling classes. In the traditional plays, loyalty was directed to the royal courts, emperors, princes, or the nation; today, in Communist China, loyalty is directed to the proletariat class, the mass of people, the Party, and the leaders, particularly Chairman Mao.

SALVATION, NATIONAL SECURITY, AND ACCOMPLISHMENT

The clustering of four revolutionary operas,—*The Red Lantern*, *Shachiapang*, *The Raid on the White Tiger Regiment*, and *Taking the Tiger Mountain by Strategy*—indicates that salvation is closely identified with the Communist revolutionary cause for the liberation of the general masses, the proletariat, and the new society. The Chinese Communist Party, especially Chairman Mao, is invariably referred to as the source of salvation. Ordinary patriotic concepts, such as nation and country, are seldom used except in those circumstances which involve international strife.

The finding that only one traditional opera, *The Pass at Yu Meng*, but no revolutionary operas, fell within the national security type suggests that national security is not emphasized in revolutionary plays; this theme apparently has been replaced by security of the proletariat class, the people, or the Party. In most traditional operas, the value of national security is mentioned, but it often becomes obscured when emperors, princes, or the royal courts take the dominant roles on the stage.

The sense of accomplishment is accentuated in both traditional and revolutionary operas—in *The Feast at the Yellow Crane Tower* as well as *On the Docks*. As we have noted earlier, sense of accomplishment has often assumed a collective tenor for the Chinese. Our finding that sense of accomplishment and loyalty are both stressed in the same operas would suggest that not only is loyalty essential to accomplishment in Chinese culture, but accomlishment may be conceived as an expression of loyalty and gratitude offered by the lower classes to the ruling class. It was a common practice in the past for subjects to offer the fruits of their labor to the emperor, as a tribute and a symbol of gratitude. The Chinese term for this practice is *kui kung*, literally meaning "attribute accomplishment to." Such themes are frequently portrayed in traditional opera. Today, as exemplified in the revolutionary opera and similar accounts in the press, the gratitude in accomplishment belongs to communism, the Communist Party, and the Party leaders, especially Chairman Mao.

Under the careful design, planning, and supervision of the Chinese Communist authorities, revolutionary opera can serve as an effective socializing agent for political indoctrination. As long as the traditional opera is completely banned, such a dominant instrument as revolutionary opera would be in a position to function as a pervasive medium of communication. It is open to question, however, whether the revolutionary opera in its current form will continue to serve the Communist objectives effectively in the long run. Since the themes and plots of the revolutionary operas are limited to the Communist causes, these plays may lose their appeal to the audience sooner or later simply because of a lack of diversity, variety, and multiformity.

APPENDIX A

I. SIMPLE STRUCTURE FACTOR MATRIX FOR TERMINAL VALUES

Operas	1	2	3	4
1. *Brave King*	−0.044	0.348	0.588	−0.114
2. *White Snake*	0.002	−0.085	0.717	−0.052
3. *Fisherman*	−0.065	−0.265	0.778	0.221
4. *Yu Meng Pass*	0.060	0.834	−0.180	0.007
5. *Yellow Crane Tower*	−0.027	0.437	0.039	0.562
6. *Red Lantern*	0.735	0.067	0.301	−0.115
7. *Shachiapang*	0.857	0.064	−0.053	0.116
8. *White Tiger Raid*	0.903	0.004	−0.164	−0.037
9. *Tiger Mountain*	0.585	−0.138	0.011	0.067
10. *On the Docks*	0.031	−0.081	0.095	0.763

II. SIMPLE STRUCTURE FACTOR MATRIX FOR INSTRUMENTAL VALUES

Operas	I	II
1. *Brave King*	−0.017	*0.846*
2. *White Snake*	−0.080	*0.714*
3. *Fisherman*	*0.400*	*0.764*
4. *Yu Meng Pass*	*0.578*	−0.014
5. *Yellow Crane Tower*	*0.951*	0.046
6. *Red Lantern*	*0.790*	0.016
7. *Shachiapang*	*0.537*	0.141
8. *White Tiger Raid*	*0.857*	0.358
9. *Tiger Mountain*	*0.753*	0.364
10. *On the Docks*	*0.606*	−0.233

NOTES

1. Milton Rokeach, "The Role of Values in Public Opinion Research," *Public Opinion Quarterly* 32 (1968–69): 547–559.

2. Two major portions of the factor printout are analyzed. The first is the descending array of standard z-scores and descriptions for factors. This section shows how the factors are oriented to each value. Separate factor analyses were computed for the terminal values and the instrumental values. Based on a range of 3 to −3, with a mean of 0, the descending z-score array identifies the values that best describe the operas in a certain factor. For instance, if a factor has a significantly high and positive z-score on one value, say family security, it means that this value is prominent in those operatic plays represented by high factor loadings on this factor.

The number of cases in the analysis was nineteen for the terminal values and twenty-one for the instrumental values. The number of variables was ten (plays) in both analyses. Standard z-scores were calculated for each value in each type of play. All factor analyses were initially made by specifying a minimum eigen-value of 1.0 as a criterion for stopping factoring.

The second portion of the factor printout analyzed is the section on consensus items and average z-scores. The resulting factors are discussed in terms of hierarchies of value orientation for each factor and in terms of consensus items. When z-score differences across all factors are less than ±1.0, the values are considered consensus items. To establish a subjective criterion for determining patterns of operas on both z-score arrays and consensus items, a response greater than or equal to +1 will be considered a substantial acceptance; any response less than or equal to −1 will be considered substantial rejection. Positive scores of increasing magnitude indicate greater value orientation; and negative scores of decreasing magnitude denote that less orientation in certain values was detected.

Detailed information of the descending array of z-scores and item descriptions for the factors by the magnitude of their factor loadings and the consensus items is shown in Philip H. Cheng, "The Functions of Chinese Opera in Social Control and Change" (Ph.D. dissertation, Southern Illinois University, 1974).

3. Lois W. Snow, *China on Stage* (New York: Random House, 1972), p. 19.

CHAPTER 6   Short Stories in China:
Theory and Practice, 1973–1975

Ai-li Chin
Nien-ling Liu

INTRODUCTION

The short story in China today can be studied as a form of
popular media because it is expressly produced *for* the
masses and increasingly also *by* the masses. And, like other
forms of popular media, the short story in the People's
Republic is also an instrument of political communication.
These popular media, while differing in several important
respects, share the common functions of transmitting politically sanctioned norms, values, and beliefs, as well as other
cultural patterns, and of promoting an approved and integrated national culture.

The present approach, using the short story as source
material for the study of social-cultural patterns, stems from
a perspective that is more sociological than literary and
which views the short story more as a form of political education and persuasion than as an expression of the individual
creative impulse. While the relationship between fiction and
society can be examined from either perspective, the frame-
works and criteria for analysis are not the same. The sociological approach emphasizes the questions: "What groups do
the writers come from or have close relations with?" "Under
what circumstances or arrangements are the stories writ-

ten?" "Under whose influence, direction, or control do the writers work?" And finally, "With what kind of structured relationship to the audience?" The literary approach, however, usually focuses its analysis on the individual writer. It may trace social influences on the shaping of his content and style, or project the impact of his work on society; in the final analysis, it evaluates the work according to given sets of artistic criteria. When we study story content in the sociological manner, in contrast, we are seeking to understand the relationships between the stories and the society from which they come. Only then can we know what the "social reality" revealed in the stories actually represents, or what meaning and insight the findings can hold for this particular society.

The term "social reality" itself needs careful examination. What is the definition of "reality," and who defines it? Thus, a prior question is added to the dimensions of "who?" "what?" "how?" and "under what circumstances?" What is the epistemology behind this view of "reality," and in what way is it translated into the theory of fiction writing? When this theory is put into practice in short stories of the 1970s in the People's Republic, what principles can be said to govern short story writing? What are the revolutionary images contained therein? And how are we to interpret them?

The complete cycle of the study of the short story as a medium of communication would of course include the nature of the audience and the effects of this communication upon them. The present study does not touch upon this matter. What is learned from the first two sets of questions posed in this study, however, stands on its own ground: What is the social-political context for short story writing in China today, and what is the message being transmitted to the people who read these stories? And as we attempt to answer these questions, similarities and differences among stories and other forms of popular media will become apparent, and hopefully some general patterns of this realm of communications will emerge.

In this analysis, a total of 160 short stories from nineteen collected works of different authors published from 1973 through 1975 have been examined and their contents classified. These stories are about peasants and youths sent down to work in the countryside, urban factory workers and store clerks, shipbuilders and forest rangers, People's Liberation Army soldiers and local Party secretaries. The locales of the stories are geographically widespread, although a majority of the anthologies came from the larger publishing houses such as those in Shanghai, Peking, and Hupeh Province. The volumes included for study were those available in accessible libraries and bookstores during 1976. Before the Cultural Revolution, a few Chinese language literary or general magazines containing stories were available in the United States, but they have been difficult to locate since the late sixties.

In addition, for background and comparison, this study has drawn freely upon two previous analyses of short stories in the People's Republic by the senior author. One was a study of images of the local Party secretary and model citizen in a sample of forty-eight stories published in 1960,[1] and the second one was based on forty-seven family and kinship stories which appeared between 1962–1966.[2] Since a consistent theoretical framework and method of classifying content according to roles have been used, the results are generally comparable and a degree of continuity has been achieved.

THE SHORT STORY IN MODERN CHINA

The modern Chinese short story was a legacy of the intellectual ferment of the May Fourth era which spanned the first few decades of the twentieth century. It was a product of borrowings from the West and of the fervent spirit of collective self-examination and self-renewal that accompanied the social-political upheaval of the period. As an experimental form of writing in the beginning, it was an inseparable aspect of the language reform, in which the *pai-hua* or vernacular style supplanted the classical, *wen-yen* mold. As a vehicle of creative expression, it was an integral part of the New Literature Movement, which rejected the narrow, conventional subject matter of traditional literature and broke new ground for grappling with pressing national, social, and personal problems of the day. And as an outcry of a newly awakened collective consciousness, it embodied the agony, the fury, and the visions of a people faced with the prospects of external threat and internal disintegration.

The early practitioners of the modern short story were not only pioneers of a new craft but were personally embroiled in the process of breaking away from the confinement of their own traditional family and roots, and of carving out new, individual destinies and collective responsibilities. Originating mostly from gentry or urban middle class backgrounds, they took it upon themselves to shoulder the burden of rousing the populace to the dangers of national myopia and complacency. Targets of their attack included the Confucian family system, the tradition-encrusted, elite-dominated moral order, the corruption of the bureaucracy, and the greed of merchant groups old and new, as well as the avaricious encroachment of foreign powers. These new writers believed that if they could free their fellow men from the clutches of these evils, they could unleash a monumental force toward the creation of a new nation.

Among the new writers, some followed the humanistic line of literary development, while others gradually came to embrace Marxism as the political creed that best promised national salvation.[3] Thus, the styles and messages contained in short stories of this period began to be differentiated into "schools" of writing, each with its associated political orientation.[4] Both were serious commentaries on the social-political shape of China; both assumed the solemn mission of transforming man and society. In the main, except for minor developments such as the "Saturday" or "Butterfly" school of literature and the later proliferation of pulp magazine stories for popular entertainment, the modern short story in its first phase of development in China became a vehicle for individual outcries of the newly awakened national consciousness.

A study of short stories of the 1920s and 1930s in China in terms of changing roles uncovered the following themes: youth's defiance of paternal authority; protest against the crushing weight of tradition upon the individual; assertion of the right to fall in love and to choose one's own marriage mate; and the search for a personally fulfilling life, whether through exploration into the inner self, through love and friendship, or through dedication to some social or patriotic cause. Sometimes the struggle of the individual against overwhelming odds forms the drama of the stories; other times the strain and stress between competing goals provide tension and movement.[5] In any case, change and innovation touching on issues of massive dimensions were the main burden of short stories of this period.

POLITICAL CREED AND SHORT STORY WRITING IN THE PRC

The first phase of the modern short story on the mainland of China came to an end with the success of the Communist revolution in 1949 and the establishment of the People's Republic, although the fledgling tradition was carried on and developed in Hong Kong and in the Republic of China in Taiwan.

The discontinuity in short story writing on the mainland before and after 1949 was of course not sharp; the transition was not that abrupt. A political orientation in creative writing was already creeping in before the Long March by leftist writers and other Marxists in China. But it was Mao's enunciations in the much-quoted Yenan Forum on Literature and Art in 1942 (also known as the Yenan *Talks*) which elevated these orientations to a creed. All major discussions of literature and art in the People's Republic of China since then have taken the Forum as the point of departure. Thus short story development there since the 1940s is in some ways the un-folding of this creed. This was true for writers of the early seventies as well. As a visitor to China noted: "The 'Talks' are on the frontispiece of every publication and in every auditorium."[6]

By and large, the pre-PRC short stories in China were het-erogeneous in orientation and experimental in spirit. Writers were not governed by any uniform doctrine or authoritative guidelines. Although individual writers after 1949 did not in-variably conform to the theory and objectives as defined in the Forum, all literary products came to be weighed, at least periodically, in light of this creed. During the past three decades, characterization and story themes have in fact been more or less congruent with the creed and with major policy emphases of various periods.

For example, in the first three or four years of Communist literature, popular themes are land reform and the exploits of the Liberation Army. Parents, out of stupidity and ignorance, oppose land reform, refuse to join a cooperative, or choose the wrong kind of son-in-law or daughter-in-law, whereas the son or daughter falls in love with a progressive and joins in the vanguard of revolutionary change. Sometimes the old peasant, having suffered oppression, is given revolutionary stature. In the case of industrial workers, a frequent theme in these early stories is the ideological gap between husband and wife—with the backward or reactionary member finally being reformed.

Immediately before the Hundred Flowers movement of 1957, great diversification appears in the stories. In late 1956, we find a few unabashed love stories, with ideology playing a supportive role. During the Great Leap Forward and the start of the commune movement in 1958–1959, stories glorify production duties in preference to home duties. Differences in dedication to work and revolutionary enthusi-asm sometimes introduce tensions in the family, but these are mostly overcome in the course of the story.

Despite these temporal fluctuations, the main ideas contained in the *Talks* have had a dominant influence on the short stories of PRC.[7] Here we shall only summarize a few points from the *Talks* as a base for discussing specific policies and programs on the writing of short stories in the seventies:

1. *The correct stand of writers.* Under the United Front policy, Mao in 1942 was advocating the conversion of leftist intellectuals with a bourgeois past into revolutionary cultural workers. He admonished them to "shift their stand" and to "move their feet over to the side of the workers, peasants, and soldiers, to the side of the proletariat."

2. *The source for creative material.* The life of the masses, he pointed out, was a rich mine of raw material for literature and art. "They are the only source, for there can be no other." Cultural workers must "learn from the masses" by "going into their very midst and into the thick of practical struggles, and through the processes of studying Marxism and society." Other sources, such as works of the past, and even foreign works, should be "critically assimilated" and used as examples.

3. *The process of creative work.* The task of literary and artistic workers must be to transform ordinary, actual life onto a richer, higher, more intense and ideal level.

4. *The mission of literature and art.* Cultural workers must launch a campaign of enlightenment and education, for the masses were "illiterate and uneducated as a result of long years of rule by the feudal and bourgeois classes."

5. *The prime need of the masses for literature and art.* Mao likened this need to "fuel in the winter," and not "mere flowers on the brocade." Literature and art were as "cogs and wheels" to the revolution, and could help "transform the spirit" and "propel history forward."

6. *Audience.* Creative works should be produced for the masses and should "adopt the thoughts and feelings and language of the masses." Cultural workers must undertake

the task of "popularization," writing what the masses need and can readily accept.

7. *Standards.* The proper form for literature is "socialist realism," later called also "revolutionary romanticism": the portrayal of social reality primarily in terms of class struggle, and in the direction in which the workers, peasants, and soldiers are themselves advancing. There are two criteria for excellence, political and artistic, and in meeting these, literary and artistic criticism should also play a part.

Subsequently, various Party leaders and official spokes-men have quoted from or elaborated upon these points, and every ten years, anniversary commentators reaffirm them and reinterpret them. On the Tenth Anniversary, the *People's Daily* decried the presence of bourgeois ideas in literature and warned against the tendency toward "formularization" or "conceptualization"[8] (more on this later). On the Twen-tieth Anniversary, the same paper again commented on the role of cultural work in the revolution: "China's literature and art must bring into full play their militancy and inspire the whole people to strive for the nation's prosperity and make efforts to establish a new socialist life."[9]

The Constitution, promulgated in 1975, also contains ref-erences to the proper role of cultural workers. Article 12, Chapter I states: "The proletariat must exercise all-around dictatorship over the bourgeoisie in the superstructure, in-cluding all spheres of culture. Culture and education, litera-ture and art, physical education, health work, and scientific research work must all serve the workers, peasants, and sol-diers, and be combined with productive labor."

AN AMPLIFICATION ON THE THEORY OF KNOWLEDGE

To give a better understanding of the theory of short story writing as it has developed in China, let us pause a moment to consider the theory of knowledge in which it is embedded.

In Marxist-Leninist epistemology, a person's knowledge is based on the function of "reflection" in the human brain. What is reflected is the external world, that is, "objective reality" or "social reality." The product of this process of reflection is consciousness, of which the most important aspect is class consciousness. People differ in their consciousness, and that difference is due both to the nature of the reality and to the class background of the individual.

As this basic theory of knowledge is developed in China and tested and transformed through the Chinese experience, subtle modifications take place. One such modification can be detected in the development of psychology in China after 1949.[10] As Chinese psychologists began to grapple with the problem of conceptualizing mental phenomena, a particularly Chinese or Maoist slant emerged. The Marxist concept of consciousness becomes in Chinese *chu-kuan neng-tung-li*, or "active consciousness." In other words, as the Soviet-based psychology becomes sinicized, some of the motivating forces that are attributed to the objective historical process are moved within the individual's consciousness, making it an active agent rather than a passive object of the reflection process. Thus there is in Chinese thought a subjective counterpart to the objective motivating force. This activist slant in the Chinese conception of consciousness has been compared by one of the Chinese psychologists with man's "positive nature, creative nature, voluntary nature, spiritual nature, and predictive nature." It is said to be manifested in hard work, willful behavior, or in struggle.[11] In practical terms, much social and educational policy seems to be based on this theoretical position. An area of ambiguity remains, however, for Marxist-Leninist orthodoxy dictates that the ultimate or primary source of change still resides in the unfolding of objective reality.

Within the concept of active consciousness, Chinese psychologists specify three functions: recognition (or the act of recognizing), emotion, and will. Of the three, only the first is so far developed and studied in pre-Cultural Revolution experiments and field observations, indicating the importance it occupies in theoretical thinking and applied work in psychology. Knowledge is viewed primarily as the result of the process of recognition, in other words, of accurate perception and rational understanding. In the absence of other intervening variables, it would seem appropriate to interpret the theory as saying that the more the individual perceives his objective world fully and understands it adequately, the more he would *automatically* want to do the correct thing. Correct recognition, as a function of a well-developed active consciousness, is posited as the key to proper or socially desirable behavior. Attention to motivational factors was rudimentary and short lived.

This brief digression into the psychological theory of recognition, and concepts of active consciousness and recognition, provides the foundation to our understanding of why the educating function of literature and art is so important in China. "Personal experience" for writers in China takes on different meaning from its equivalent in Western culture, and the exercise of "imagination," that is, transformation of the writer's observations and experiences into a unique idiom of his own, the epitome of Western creativity, is far from being the essence of good writing in China.

INDIVIDUALITY, ESSENCE OF COLLECTIVITY, AND TYPIFICATION

The theoretical preoccupation in short story writing in the early seventies is framed in terms of three concepts: *ko-hsing*, *kung-hsing*, and *tien-hsing-hua*, for which the closest English equivalents would be "individuality," "the essence of collectivity," and "typification." *Ko-hsing* and *kung-hsing* are general philosophical concepts in Mao's writings. In terms of story writing, *ko-hsing* refers to the essence of the character or hero figure, and *kung-hsing* to the "social reality" as the writer is expected to experience it, or as the reader should experience it vicariously. *Tien-hsing-hua*, or "typification," is the process of endowing heroes and heroines with desirable qualities, "elevating" them to heroic proportions.

Let us explore the theoretical problems which these three concepts are attempting to deal with. On the surface, the first two, *ko-hsing* and *kung-hsing*, seem to point to the simple relationship between the particular and the general, the unique and the universal. But in terms of the theory of knowledge just outlined, the critical dilemma becomes this: The task of literature and art is to further the revolution. Heroes possess exemplary characteristics and these should be delineated sharply, vividly, and in the richest kind of detail so as to portray their struggles to the fullest. Yet the hero or heroine is one of the masses and should never be detached from them or become distant from *their* struggles. How is the writer to reconcile them?

A further dilemma, which the concept *tien-hsing-hua* addresses, is this: Since the writer "reflects" his external world, should he portray his heroes and heroines exactly as he finds them in actual life? Is his task one of selecting the best examples from what he can personally observe? Or should he represent his heroes and heroines in terms of ideal elements, models "advancing in the direction of the masses"?

These preoccupations find expression in the many commentaries or critical discussions which appear either as prefaces to short story anthologies or postscripts, or as articles in literary magazines. Statements such as the following are found in different versions: "The proletarian hero is the unification of individuality and the essence of collectivity," or "the essence of collectivity is embodied in all the individual characteristics—without individuality there is no essence of collectivity," or "the hero figure dramatizes the typical characteristics of a typical environment."

Thus writers are warned of the pitfalls of "formularization" or "conceptualization," the mechanical portrayal of a hero or heroine merely as an exemplification of a correct political idea—a "formula" or "concept." This was a tendency singled out for criticism at the Tenth Anniversary of the Yenan *Talks*, and now brought up again as a reminder. Writers are urged instead to bring out the "individuality" of heroes and heroines, to make them lifelike, and to utilize details to render their life circumstances rich and vital. Only by doing so, it is said, would they be expressing fully the "spirit of collectivism."

How, then, should the writer depict the hero or heroine? This is indeed the topic of central importance in discussions on short story writing in the early seventies. Since the lives of the masses, which are the only source for fiction, are full of struggles—class struggle, ideological struggle, and struggle between two "roads" or two lines of thinking—the heroes or heroines, being part of the masses, must also be engaged in the same struggles.

The other concern has to do with the danger of separating the hero from the masses, if the hero is shown with superior qualities. This problem is being met in part by having heroes and heroines engage in struggles of everyday activities, demonstrating the common life they share with the masses; and in part by highlighting the political meaning contained in ordinary attitudes and actions. The role of heroes and heroines is to show to the masses the correct road to take in everyday affairs in order to push ahead the course of the revolution.

Yet what is "real" in the hero image has no room for human defects. As an article on the story "Seeds of Yenan" states, "Someone mistakenly equates writing about the maturing of heroes with describing their defects. This is incorrect."[12] And when Hao Jan, foremost novelist in China today, was asked if he was ever concerned about making the hero "too perfect," his reply was that he would only worry if he "failed to make the heroic images real, that is, if they turned out to be mere abstractions."[13]

This takes us to the application to fiction writing of the

concept of "social reality" in Communist epistemology. "Reality" includes not only "what is" but also "what should be," and "what will be in the future." It is clear that Marxist Chinese theorists do not share the Western preoccupation in literary discussions with the dichotomy between "truth" and "fiction," but are rather concerned with socialist archetypes versus "products of the individual imagination."

NEW SHORT STORY WRITERS

The 1970s begin a new era for the worker-as-writer. A concerted effort seems to be made to search out new talent, to train them and to support them through periods of writing, and to help them publish their products. Much commentary is written, over and beyond the usual literary-political criticism, to discuss the mission of literature, techniques of short story writing, and the nature and function of building heroic models. The goal of having ordinary workers, peasants, and soldiers try their hands at writing is not a new one, but only in recent years does it appear to have been pursued explicitly and systematically. As a result, the position of the worker-writers has reached a new height. They originate from a wider geographic area than ever before, with a wider range of occupations, and they typically return, after completing a writing project, to their original jobs and previous localities. Now the principle of having writers come from the masses and remain part of the masses is being put into practice.

This situation has not always been so. In the years immediately following the Yenan Forum, it was the leftist writers of the May Fourth generation who dominated the literary scene in the Communist-controlled territory. They were familiar names with reputations established in prewar China, such as Ting Ling, Pa Chin, Mao Tun, Hsiao Chün, Ai Ching, and Feng Hsueh-feng. Although they were committed to the cause of the Communist revolution, their bourgeois background and generally humanistic orientation made them targets of periodic attack. The Yenan Forum can be interpreted as partly an effort to bring these writers closer to orthodox party lines in their work.

On January 15, 1956, a twelve-year plan to develop literature and art was announced. Kuo Mo-jo, as chairman of the All-China Federation of Literary and Art Circles, said that "cultural work must be led by amateurs who have mastered Marxism-Leninism."[14] An editorial in the *People's Daily* of March 27, 1956 declared:

> Party organizations in various localities should extend political guidance to their local writers' groups and other units in literature and art, and should appropriately send working personnel well versed in political and organizational ability to these bodies to work with them.[15]

Part of the plan was apparently to encourage and train new writers, for by the end of the year, newspapers and periodicals were claiming that most writers were "workers by profession." The Writers' Union opened its door to large numbers of new, amateur writers, so that its membership jumped from 889 in 1957 to 200,000 in 1958. During the Great Leap Forward in 1958, peasants and workers were encouraged to write poems and create songs, and the era of the worker-as-writer was launched. It was said that folk poems were produced "by the millions," some of them described as "group products." The stage was set for the workers and peasants to be the main producers of socialist literature. From 1960 until the Cultural Revolution, the great majority of the short stories published in the *Jen Min Wen Hsueh* (People's Literature) were by writers whose names seldom reappeared. Undoubtedly many of them were new, amateur writers, though not much was written about them—who they were and how they came to write.

During the Cultural Revolution, most publications ceased and production of short stories was interrupted along with many other intellectual and artistic activities. After the ex-

citement and confusion died down, cultural workers, like
many others, began slowly to redefine their work and to pick
up the thread again where they had left off. The biggest
casualty of the Cultural Revolution in the literary world was
undoubtedly the older generation of writers. In the words of
Hsu Kai-yü, "The Cultural Revolution just about erased the
last trace of the pre-Liberation intellectual writers, bringing
to a successful completion the program started by the Yenan
Talks."

One way to look at the shifting weight of writers of different backgrounds in recent years is to examine the composition of present-day writers. Hao Jan was quoted by Hsu as
having classified contemporary writers into four generations:

1. First generation—survivors of the May Fourth Movement, who are hardly producing at all today.

2. Second generation—those who emerged after the
Yenan *Talks*, most of whom have not published since the
ideological rectifications of the 1950s. A few are editing or
doing administrative work for government agencies.

3. Third generation—those who grew up during the war
of liberation. They have "lived enough in the revolution to
know what it means. Almost none of them originally intended to become professional writers; their careers started
because of their roles in the revolution. They are the
standard-bearers for the developing literature of the proletariat prescribed in the Yenan *Talks.*" And Hao Jan put
himself in this group.

4. Fourth generation—those born after 1949, presumably the new proletarian writers today.[16]

The stories covered in this study are indeed written by
"nonprofessional" writers—workers from all walks of life
who take short periods of time off to produce stories and
return to their original jobs. Many of the anthologies of short
stories provide some sketchy information on the writers.

A few examples will illustrate the background of the new
authors: Tuan Sui-hsia, writer of a story involving some tech-

nical problems in improving a recording device, is a worker
in an electric plant. Shih Han-fu, author of "Tsao-hsia," a
story about an agricultural commune, is an army medic. He
gathered his material from a woman intellectual whom he
met on a bus trip. Yao Ke-min is a political worker and wrote
a story about a party cadre. Chu Min-shen, a clerk in a retail
store in Shanghai, incorporated his experience in a story involving differences in management before and after 1949.
Yeh Mien, herself a textile worker from Shanghai, authored a
story about an older woman, a *shih-fu* or master craftsman,
in a textile manufacturing factory and her dedication to her
work.

There are also writers from provincial propaganda teams,
such as the Shantung Chinan Political Propaganda Team,
which published a collection of short stories called *Yi Meng
Shan Kao* (Yi Meng High Mountains). Others are former Red
Guards sent down to work in the oil mines in Chinghai, who
published a volume entitled *Yi-erh-wu tsan-ke* (One-Two-
Five Songs of Praise). Still others are medical workers from a
Shanghai hospital, precision instrument workers from a factory, dock workers, passenger train or steamboat workers, or
fishermen from a seaside commune.

It is apparent from these examples that writers now come
from diversified occupations and a wide geographic area.
Most of them are also new recruits, for many volumes are
designated as first attempts. The spread of the craft of short
story writing is not an accidental phenomenon but rather the
carrying out of a plan to create a massive corps of new
writers from among the ordinary masses.

WRITERS' WORKSHOPS

There is a pattern to the recruitment of new writers, their
training and support, and the publication of their stories.
From prefaces to various anthologies and essays in literary
magazines, we can discern the bare outlines of the pro-
cedures.

Anyone, it seems, who wants to write can submit an idea

or plan to "responsible members of his work unit," and upon the approval of the plan will be granted paid release time from work and assigned to a writing group or workshop. Many such groups originate from a factory or a commune, the army or some other work unit, from a school or the literature department of a university. Others may draw candidates from a wider geographic area. Some groups gather at a central place where their board and room are arranged for.

These workshops follow a plan called the *san chieh-ho*, or Three-in-One Union where three kinds of people are assigned to help the writers: party representatives, editors from newspapers and publishing houses, and experienced older writers.[17] These older writers seem to be attached to the Bureau of Cultural Affairs of each province and municipality and are sent out to work with the groups.[18] In addition, other "relevant work units" are consulted. For example, the Shanghai Medical Workers Writing Workshop had the support of the First Shanghai Medical College, the Shanghai Pharmaceutical Company, the Shanghai Medical Appliances and Supplies Company, and the Shanghai Medical Instruments Company. In another case, the Creative Writing Group of the Futan University Chinese Literature Department had the support of the leading cadres of the municipal government, schools, and related units. "Help and direction" was received from editors of the Shanghai People's Publishing Company, the *Liberation Daily*, and the *Wen-hui-pao*. The preface was contributed by the Literary Criticism Group of the same university department.[19]

As for authorship, most stories come under the signature of one name, sometimes two and occasionally more. The stories are therefore not written by teams in the strict sense, though some are said to be the result of cooperation between master worker and apprentice, or teacher and students, and all are in a sense the fruit of collective guidance and review.

When groups assemble, they discuss matters of two general kinds: one is the Party's policy toward literature and art, and the meaning of furthering the revolution via cultural work, and the other is techniques and principles of writing short stories. Contents of the first category can only be surmised from prefaces and other essays on story writing in general, much of which has already been discussed on other pages. It needs only to be added here that the stated goals of story writing include the representation of the post-Cultural Revolution society, the campaign against Liu Shao-ch'i, and the struggle between two roads and two lines of thought.

On techniques of short story writing, the following specifications are explicitly discussed:

1. There must be a moving story with appropriate situational detail.

2. There must be attention to form and structure, such as the use of a critical episode to represent a rich idea or complex situation.

3. There must be careful selection of main characters to represent positions and view, for example, the choice of a retired woman worker as a main character to represent the masses, and of an assistant in a unit as a minor character to represent someone with a "problem in his thinking."[20]

Other specific techniques mentioned here and there include skill in the use of descriptive passages and refinements in the use of the language. Care is apparently taken, as a later paragraph will demonstrate, to ensure that vivid folk sayings, regional colloquialisms, and even certain familiar semi-classical phrases are employed to enhance style.

The principles of story writing are identified as follows: *chi-chung, kai-kua, ti-lien*, or "concentration," "generalization," and "refinement."[21] From what we can piece together, "concentration" refers to the gathering and selecting of scattered material and their organization into the main characters or central situations. "Generalization" points to the use of specific characters or situations to represent broader ideas or policy directions. And "refinement" means the craft of writing: of "eliminating the rough and preserving the good, cutting out the false and keeping the true," and of maintaining unity and continuity in a piece of work.

A special technique or principle which has appeared in literary discussion of the seventies is called *san-tu-chu*,[22] the "three breakthroughs" or the "three ascents." This has to do with the gradual emergence of the hero model out of the story material depicting the life of the masses. The first "breakthrough" is to describe positive characters in a story and have them stand out among the rest. The second is to distinguish heroic figures from among the positive ones. The final step is to select and construct the main hero or heroine, the true hero model, *ying-hsiung tien-hsing*. This process seems to be the chief focus in contemporary story writing. Curiously, mention has been made of examples of hero models taken from traditional or foreign fiction to instruct new writers, such as Chu-ko Liang of *Romance of the Three Kingdoms*, or *The Count of Monte Cristo*.

The workshops meet for varying periods of time. It is not clear whether groups remain together for continuous sessions until all final drafts are completed, or whether they disperse after an initial stage. In any case, suggestions and criticisms from both political and literary standpoints are exchanged and progressive improvements are made. Sometimes groups will go to see a play or revolutionary opera in order to learn from it. The author of one story in the volume by medical workers writes that it took him five drafts and eight months to complete his story, while the author of the preface to an anthology entitled *Hsin Ko-tang* (The New Classroom) states that the entire volume was the fruit of three years' struggle.

PUBLISHING

All books for the general market are published by the central government press, *Jen-min chu-pan-she* (People's Press), while reference books and school texts are handled by two separate publishing houses. The People's Press has many provincial branches and the large Shanghai plant, as well as the subsidiary *Jen-min wen-hsueh* or People's Literature Press. Literary works can be published by all these branches or by the subsidiary.

One of the notable developments of the first half of the 1970s is the appearance of short story anthologies out of many of these provincial branches, presumably publishing stories written by local new writers. While most of the volumes available for this study come from the better-known places such as Shanghai, Peking, and Kuangtung Province, with the exception of an anthology from Chinghai, an examination of a few catalogues from Hong Kong and elsewhere reveal story collections from the following additional provinces: Kirin, Shantung, Hopei, Hunan, Hupei, Fukien, Kuanghsi, Shansi, and Tibet.

The number of copies printed for each anthology of stories we have seen ranges from 100,000 to 600,000, some titles having had a second or third printing. We would, however, be underestimating the reading audience based on the size of the printings, because of the probability of study groups sharing and discussing stories. Furthermore, some stories appear first in the daily press, such as the *People's Daily* or the *Wen-hui-pao*, or in literary magazines such as the new *Chao-hsia* and *Kan Chin-chao*. A few favorite stories are reprinted in several kinds of publications and in several anthologies. An outstanding one may even make the official journal *Hung Ch'i*. For these reasons, it is impossible to make a reasonable estimate of the total audience.

INSTRUCTIONS TO THE READER

From a slim volume intended for the junior middle school student or graduate and entitled *Tu-shu yü tso-wen* (How to Read and Write Stories), one gets interesting glimpses into the intended use of the recent crop of short stories. The junior middle school student may in fact be the typical reader in China today, since the educational career of many young people in recent years has been altered by changes in policy arising out of the Cultural Revolution.

In any case, detailed instructions are spelled out for the reader of short stories. (1) The chief assignment is to grasp the *chu-ti*, the main theme or political lesson of the story. (2) Of equal importance is the reader's emotional identification with the characters in the stories. The reader is asked to respond with love and admiration for the heroes. The idea is that if the stories are successful, the reader should "feel glad for his triumphs, and anxious for his setbacks and difficulties." Unless one's feelings are aroused, "it would be useless even if one read 100 or 1000 stories." (3) Short stories are to be used as a means of self-cultivation. They help one to understand one's own situations and problems. In other words, story characters are to be used as role models for emulation and identification. (4) Short stories are to be vehicles for learning better ways of using the language. Readers can adopt "special expressions, more elaborate ways of saying things, and more beautiful ways of writing descriptive passages." Young readers of this volume are also given a brief lesson in writing stories and are encouraged to try their hand at it, being told that there is nothing difficult or mysterious in the process.

Thus it can be seen that short stories are consciously and systematically used in the current plan of citizen education and of defining new values and new norms for correct behavior.

THE GENRES OF THE SHORT STORY

The literary magazines in China today publish, along with literary criticism and articles on the theory and practice of creative writing, short stories according to three categories: *ku-shih, pao-kao wen-hsueh,* and *tuan-pien hsiao-shuo,* that is, "storytelling," "reportorial," and "short fiction," or the short story proper. In addition, the short-short story is also gaining popularity. Anthologies of short stories are also fre-

quently collected according to genres. Yet we have been discussing short story writing and will continue to do so, as if
there were no internal distinctions. This is because Chinese
articles on its theory and practice speak of the subject in
general terms, and because we can detect no basic difference
in source of material or content. Certainly the three genres do
not differ along the dimension of "truth" and fiction. All
three can, and often do, originate from some observation or
personal experience and contact, and all are not bound to the
criterion of "strict, objective reporting" in the Western sense.
The criteria of "scientific objectivity" as it is defined in the
West simply does not interest or concern the Chinese—it is an
irrelevant question.

It is, however, of considerable interest to sort out the dis-
tinguishing characteristics of the types, and to note the simultaneous development of the separate genres. In light of Mao's
original goal of "popularization" of literature, it is obviously
advantageous to preserve variety, especially since storytelling comes from an old oral tradition and the reportorial is
a comparatively simple form of writing well suited to the
purposes of popular education.

First, some minor differences among the genres having
mostly to do with appearances. In general, storytelling and
reportorials are often illustrated, while short stories seldom
are. Short stories are sometimes divided into numbered sections, whereas storytelling and reportorials are usually presented in a single unit, though the latter occasionally appear
with titled sections. More substantial characteristics of each
are as follows:

1. Storytelling in its modern form has inherited some of the
historical features of its old Chinese oral tradition. To hold
audience attention, the storyteller had to develop skills in the
use of dramatic words and eloquent style. A rhythmic use of
language is one way, producing a lilting, singsong effect.
Contemporary storytelling in written form is similarly characterized by colorful words and a lively manner of presenta-

tion. Words are often earthy, robust, and ornamental, and onomatopoeia is sometimes employed. We give two illustrations from *Hai-ping-hsin-i-tai* (The New Generation on the Sea Coast): "Welcome, welcome—two boatfuls of watercress!" intones the old group leader. "New things newly done—very, very good!" Or, "As I was saying, that yellow-haired *ya-tou*—three years ago she was a student . . . looking pretty good, horizontally or vertically. . . ." The opening phrase of the latter example, "As I was saying," is borrowed from traditional storytelling and lends an old-fashioned flavor to contemporary storytelling. Other opening sentences for episodes still in use are: "This time," "Actually," "Let me repeat," or "Afterwards."

One of the unique features in storytelling is that it usually contains a verse, somewhat martial in tone and written in the colloquial style, in the manner of Yuan dynasty drama. The verse generally sums up the moral of the story.

2. Reportorials are usually action-packed accounts of some great construction or engineering feat involving the labor of the masses. It is usually written in a straightforward manner, with no deliberate attention to artistry or conscious effort at manipulation of structure. The well-known "Story of Ta-chai" belongs to this genre. Here, as in other reportorials, the tone is heroic, and the theme is the struggle of man against nature. Often, the weather is menacing or a storm is brewing, providing environmental obstacles to be overcome or a sense of urgency in the job to be done. Local color may be added, such as a particularly bleak landscape or cruel, menacing natural surroundings. The sense of urgency and momentum of work can even be incorporated in the language itself, aided by onomatopoeia: "Pong, pong, pong goes the hammer," "Chuh, chuh, chuh the whistle blows," or "Hua, hua the rain pours down." Sometimes slogans are inserted to suggest ways of rallying the workers, and other times, a chorus of two lines of verse is sung. And hyperbole abounds. "Yes, this is a miracle, a great revolutionary miracle!" "The ambition of our workers is high!" "Materials, blueprints, equipment,

timetable . . . a tremendous challenge lying in wait!" Or, "On target! Attack imperialism, counterrevolutionaries . . . fight, fight, fight!" Endings are especially rousing: "Long live Chairman Mao!" or "People may rest, but never the revolution!"

Reportorials have been in use since 1949 to celebrate the labor accomplishments of individual labor heroes or group efforts. Biographical material or eyewitness accounts are the factual base, and while the virtues of these labor heroes may be accented and faults omitted, the goal is not deliberately to fictionalize biography or history. The essential story behind a reportorial and a short story of a labor hero, however, can be very similar. Certainly for didactic purposes, the exemplar in a heroic story serves as role model just the same as in a reportorial.[23]

3. The short story is the most consciously developed modern form among the three genres. It is clearly in the literary tradition of the May Fourth period. While the revolutionary theme in one shape or another is the main focus, or at least one element, of the short story since 1949, a good deal of deliberate attention is paid to structure and technique, language and style. More complex similes are frequently employed, and more delicate and subtle sentiments are often evoked, much as they were in the May Fourth literature. Here are some examples, the first two of similes, the following of descriptive passages. The last one portrays mood and sentiment as well.

The revolution is like a speedboat advancing on top of the undulating waves of the vast sea.

The revolutionary opera is like the first blossom of spring.

The moon, climbing over the window sill, shone onto the faces of the people . . .

The drumbeat in the valley circulated through the star-filled fields . . .

Tung Ma-ma looked at the two rows of pine trees through tear-moistened eyes. The leaves are young and robust, and the trees themselves, deeply rooted in the soil, are heavy with dew crystals, glowing like tiny halos in the morning light . . .

Some of these sentences, ending in dots, suggest lingering sentiments, a device often found in May Fourth stories.

CONTENT OF STORIES: 1973–1975

The content of mass communications can be classified in a number of ways. Some of the most common classifications, as developed in the United States and applied to the analysis of mass media, are themes, symbols, and hero/villain types. In this study, a modified approach to the usual content analysis method is employed. The primary unit of analysis is the social role. The particular roles to be analyzed are emergent categories in these stories. Among possible symbols, linguistic expressions are examined with reference to cultural continuity and discontinuity as well as for their meaning in terms of social interaction and personal outlook. Themes, too, are seen in relation to changing patterns in the social fabric. In all these respects, the qualitative-descriptive approach is relied upon rather than a quantitative one, sacrificing precision for flexibility and nuance. And finally, all analysis of content is placed in the context of Marxist-Leninist-Maoist epistemology and revolutionary ideology.

SOME USES OF THE LANGUAGE

Linguistic Expressions. The presence of terms arising from the Communist revolution and Marxist-Leninist-Maoist ideology is of course to be expected. They are interspersed in the midst of customary idioms of the language. A few such terms will suffice. The more commonly found descriptive terms include "revolutionary struggle," "capitalist roader," "a question of thought," and "a question of standpoint." Other terms or concepts which have a deeper impact on characterization and plot development are "class brother" or "class enemies," "class love" or "class hatred," "contradictions" and "contrast with the past."

Still another kind is sloganlike phrases embodying political attitudes, such as "giving grain priority" *(yi-liang wei-kang)*, or "letting money take command" *(chao-piao kua-shuai)*. And a last category has to do with character building, still of the newly combined use of familiar words. *Tzu-ke-lao, pu-te-shu* is a pair of phrases referring to someone with much experience but no special airs. *Yu-ta-kung, pu-chiao-ao* counterpoises two other characteristics, "making great contributions without being conceited." And *chih-wei-kao, pu-li lao-tung* is a last example of the same order, meaning "occupying a high post without disdaining physical labor." This kind of new language use is naturally more integrated with the content and political point of view of the stories than are the more traditional phrases.

A surprising finding in language use is the sprinkling of traditional and colloquial expressions in the contemporary *Pai-hua* prose and revolutionary content. Some are regional in nature. This kind of linguistic usage seems more noticeable and more deliberate now than in earlier periods, as if it were part of a campaign to enrich the language and improve the style.

Traditional words and phrases are most frequently associated with descriptive passages, usually of nature and occasionally of people, while the use of colloquialisms can be found anywhere, including in dialogue. Sometimes the shifting of gear from modern, direct, down-to-earth prose to a formal or flowery turn of phrase can be startling. Yet on the whole, the admixture of language adds color and vigor to the style. We shall give examples of classical or semiclassical phrases, colloquialisms and folk sayings, and homely aphorisms.

The first examples are words of a literary nature, such as: *shen-tai* for "mien" and in a broader sense "demeanor," and *chien-yi chen-ching* for "strong and calm." Such phrases can add a soft and lilting rhythm to the prose.

The use of the traditional language can also be semiliterary and semicolloquial—more distillations of folk wisdom:

shang-chih hsia-yü means "extremely brilliant people and extremely foolish people;" *jen-pu-neng mao hsiang* means "one cannot judge a person by his appearance."

Other less literary and more traditional terms are *chao-hsia* and *chao-yang*, literally meaning "the brilliant glow of the morning," used metaphorically in these stories to represent the new spirit. Still other expressions are more cliché—they are formalistic and ornate, though they may be of literary origin: *se-tsai pin-fen* is used to describe something multicolored or colorful, *ching-hsin tung-po* stands for "being frightened" or "state of panic," and *leng-tou leng-nao* for being "block-headed" or "fat-headed."

The classical novel, *Romance of the Three Kingdoms*, is a specially favored source of literary borrowings, as it was for much of pre-1949 popular writing as well. We shall give these examples without the lengthy transliteration: "eight thousand miles of clouds and moons," "all is ready except the east wind," "fomenting the wind and the cloud," and "the brocade bag of clever schemes and tricks." Even an entire couplet may be quoted to suggest mood and lend style: "It is a day of the spring wind and peach and pear blossoms/ Green leaves form a shade and the branches are heavy with fruit."

A different kind of expressions is common sayings or homely aphorisms. *Yan shih-ai, sung-shih-hai* is equivalent to "spare the rod and spoil the child." *Yung ke ching-mien* is "leave a little face," and *jen-yuan* is "human affinity," two traditional concepts in human relationships. *Yi-pan kung-fu yi-pan-hsin* expresses the homely philosophy on getting things done: "part hard work, part spirit."

There are common sayings used for character descriptions. First is a pair of positive and negative characteristics: *Kung-szu pu-fen* and *kung-shih-kung pan*, meaning "mixing of private and public affairs" versus "handling public affairs strictly as public affairs." *Shuo-yi pu-erh* is "one who means what he says," and *shuo-yueh pu-kai* describes one who "keeps appointments and does not go back on his word." *Shou-pu-nao, chiao-pu-ting* is a ditty used to depict someone whose hands and feet are not idle, and *pan-shih kan-ching li-lo* is a phrase used to refer to one who does things crisply and cleanly. These obviously add up to old-fashioned virtues as well as desirable qualities of the socialist man: industriousness, dependability, and conscientiousness.

Expressions used to describe negative characteristics include: *tso mai-mai-te wei-tao,* "one who smacks of commercialism," and *hen-tieh pu-cheng-kang,* "regretting iron for not turning into steel." Two colorful expressions for what leaders should not be: *chiao jen hui-tou shu chiao-yin,* "looking backward to count footsteps," or "one who is preoccupied with the distribution of merit" (implying the capitalist way). *Pa pu-tui kuan-tsai wu-li, pi-kao ti, heng-shang-hsia* translates into "keeping troops indoors, contesting about rank and privilege." The final example illustrates the use of everyday language to create a new kind of imagery, having to do with flying a kite: *Yu pa fei-pu-kao, yu pa tuan le-hsien, fang-fang la-la-ti pu fang-hsin,* "worried they would not fly high enough, but afraid of breaking the string—pulling and releasing indecisively, not knowing what is best." In popular usage, this suggests a general state of indecisiveness. Here in the story context, it is applied specifically to men's attitudes toward women.

Terms of Address. The persistence of a few kinship terms of address and the appearance of certain affectionate and mock-derogatory nicknames are the second element of cultural continuity with the past to warrant brief attention. This phenomenon will be compared with similar situations in the 1962–1966 sample of stories and discussed in light of dominant themes in the current collection.

The proliferation of kinship ties and terms of address was a prominent feature of short stories during the first half of the sixties. Currently, attention to family and relatives, along with the use of kinship terms of address, has clearly diminished. The old-fashioned familiar terms remain, however, such as terms used by husband and wife about or to each other, *ta tieh*, *ta ma*, "his (the child's) father" or "her (the child's) mother," or "so-and-so's father (or mother)." The courtesy title of "uncle" or "aunt" can be found also. An elderly salesclerk in a department store is called "uncle" by a boy customer, an older worker on a transport team is called *ta pa*, "elder uncle" by fellow workers, and a village woman is known by her nickname of *ya shen* or "speechless aunt." A colloquial expression referring to "everyone in the village" is put in kinship terms: "Second Aunt Wang from the east end of the village, and Big Uncle Li from the north." These terms, as well as the practice itself, are understandable to everyone familiar with traditional society. Their appearance in revolutionary short stories of today is evidence of the persistence of some cultural practices and the selective adaptation of elements from the past in the design of the contemporary fabric of society.

A new group of folk terms for addressing people or referring to them has come to the fore, terms which were not noticeable in stories of the past decades. Most of these are used by elders to young people, although a few are from the younger to the older or among elders themselves. The majority imply a good measure of affection; one or two definitely with malice. Taken together, these terms clearly indicate the area of social relationships which now come in for critical attention or which contain hints of ambiguities, given the overall ideological emphasis or social policy in present-day society.

First, a few semiserious epithets of old vintage exchanged between an old peasant and his wife who nags on behalf of her public duties: The wife, vegetable production team leader, is annoyed and impatient at her husband, the agricultural brigade leader, for not acceding to her request for more supplies. She teasingly calls him *na szi-lao-tou tzu*, "that dead old man," and *lao-tung-hsi*, "old thing." He, in mild retaliation, only mocks her with *wo-te tzu-tung-chih*, "my own comrade team leader." Softened by further sweet words of reassurance from him, she changes her tactics. Now she calls him *hao wo-te yeh-yeh*, which loosely translated would be "my good old man."

A more significant group of new terms which have emerged in recent stories has to do with relationships between youth and elders, and is a subtle indication of nuances in the new normative guidelines for social interaction between these two recently ascendent groups. There are terms used by elders toward boys or young males who have just reached adulthood: *mao-hai-tzu*, *hsiao-huo-tzu*, and *hsiao-kui*. *Mao-hai-tzu* means literally "a child who is still hairy," in other words, "wet behind the ears"—"a mere lad." One example of its use: A young man is promoted despite his tender age to be "Number One," top man or captain in charge of a sizable fishing vessel. The uncle, fond of his nephew but uneasy about his lack of experience, refers to him as *mao-hai-tzu*, hardly ready for the heavy responsibility entrusted to him. The term is used with a hint of desperation but with even more of basic affection and regard. A variation of this term is *hsiao-huo-tzu*, "a kid," "a young lad." The emphasis in this term is also on youthfulness, but his lack of experience or competence is not specifically in question. Thus, an elderly master seaman refers to a new apprentice as *hsiao-huo-tzu*, a youth who comes with secret dreams of a glamorous occupation but who is assigned by the wise and humane master to perform some necessary drudgery.

A term with somewhat different meaning is *hsiao kui-tzu* or *hsiao-kui*, "little devil." This is a familiar and frequently heard folk term used with some affection for a young lad who serves someone in the capacity of an orderly or errand boy, but with annoyance and disapproval for a mischievous boy who happens to be around. When used with affection, "an impish kid" is a good synonym. An example in a story is the former messenger boy of the PLA who is sent to meet a newly assigned deputy party secretary to the work site and mistakes the stranger for an ordinary worker.

A term for a boy used with definite malice is *hsiao-chao-szu*, "the young one who is looking for trouble." One of the few real villains in these stories uses the term for a twelve- to thirteen-year-old boy who challenges the political correctness of the old man's behavior. The latter also applies the adjective *li-hai* to the boy's character: sharp and tactless, merciless and direct. What is especially interesting about this negative characteristic is that it is exactly the counterpart to the new feature being celebrated in youth. The young revolutionary, as we shall see, is admired for being self-confident, forward, and relentless.

A new affectionate term for girls or very young women is *ya-tou*, which is an old traditional term that has the literal meaning of "slave girl" or young "bond servant." Customarily, parents may call a beloved young daughter *ya-tou* or refer to her by that lowly name in the superstitious hope that evil spirits would not claim her, or simply as an inverse way of showing affection. Outside the intimate circle of the family, including perhaps a favored relative, the use of that name would imply a derogatory or insulting attitude.

Significantly, the term *ya-tou* is appearing in stories of the seventies, we believe for the first time. It is used in situations in which the girl is mischievously disobedient, or at least independent minded, but for lofty political reasons. The attitude of the adult using that name is a mixture of exasperation and love, disapproval and admiration. First, an example of a mother calling her own daughter *ya-tou:* A peasant woman discovers, to her surprise and delight, that her daughter, the young barefoot doctor, is quietly studying herb medicine at night, drawing different species and classifying them. One day the girl is late in returning from another village. Suspecting that she stopped at some relative's house to amuse herself, the mother is afraid that her suspicion of the daughter's immaturity is confirmed. Instead, the mother discovers that the girl had gone to her uncle for help in collecting and identifying herbs. In great delight at the girl's initiative and ingenuity, and chagrined at her own mistake, the mother exclaims, "Oh, you *ya-tou!*" or "You sneaky, worthless creature!"

More importantly, the term is now extended in stories to nonfamilial relationships, notably to that between a master worker and a young apprentice. A young girl and the older woman worker she is apprenticed to in a factory frequently find themselves locked in heated ideological arguments or "struggle discussions." Yet the apprentice admires the master worker and voluntarily seeks her help in a variety of matters. The relationship is volatile but also affectionately close. The older woman is shown to be constantly concerned about the girl's well-being and development. It is in a moment of exasperation and concern that the master worker calls the girl *ya-tou.*

In another story, the term *ya-tou* is used by an old peasant in speaking to an unrelated girl. The old man is described as being "old enough to be her grandfather," implying a kind of license. The young girl, newly sent down to the countryside to learn agricultural work, is willing enough to work and correct enough in her political attitudes, but shows just a hint of smugness about her farming techniques and advanced political ideas. The old man in calling her *ya-tou* is at the same time scolding her and showing affectionate concern.

A few variations of the name are found in these stories: *Mao ya-tou* means a young or "green" *ya-tou; kuei ya-tou* is "a little devil of a *ya-tou*"; and *hou ya-tou* is "a monkey of a *ya-tou.*"

The appearance of these folk terms in stories of the seventies signals the norm for a special kind of bond between youth and the older person, a bond that is born of the ambiguity and the tension between the exaltation of the prowess of youth and reverence for maturity and experience. The patterns of interaction portrayed in these stories point the way to reconciling the competing values and resolving inescapable differences if changing social policies are heeded by the people.

CHARACTERIZATION AND RELATIONSHIPS

Physical characteristics of heroes and heroines on the whole receive more attention in stories of the seventies than in previous periods, although the absolute amount is still very small.

The hero is usually portrayed as well-built and broad-shouldered, sometimes tall as well. When more details are given, heroes' faces are likely to be described as square jawed and thick browed, and eyes are always bright. Sometimes clothes are described as old and worn and made of coarse material, whether they are military uniforms or work clothes. A satchel may be carried over the shoulder, and pant legs may be rolled up. In short, whatever the occupation or rank, the hero is dressed ready for work and looks like a member of the toiling masses.

A secondary group of characteristics applies to the demeanor of heroes and heroines. Cadres are usually "serious and determined," "dignified," "crisp and decisive," or possess "boundless energy."

Heroines are even more often endowed with "bright," "lively," or even "burning" eyes. Their faces are either round or oval, sometimes of a dark or ruddy complexion. It is an unusual story that includes more refined descriptions, such as a straight nose or trim mouth, as if detailed features are of no interest in the revolutionary heroine. Hair is short, often braided, adding to their youthful, appearance.

There is a notable shift in the demeanor of young heroines in the past two decades. In the stories of the early sixties, the ideal girl was shy and demure, submissive to family elders though also competent and straightforward on suitable occasions. Now, in the seventies, shyness is rarely mentioned, except in the case of a village girl whose traditional sense of modesty prompts her to hide her face when she is praised in public. The favorite heroine type of the seventies is self-confident, direct, dauntless, and determined. She knows her own mind and knows how to go about accomplishing her goals. "Eyes of hot fire" are meant to convey this sense of resoluteness and impatience, and short hair suggests a matter of factness, a no-nonsense quality. She can be tactless and even brash, and she can be jaunty, *ting-shen-chi*. One girl, a young shipyard electrician new to the job, is said to run instead of walk. "And if she bumps into people, she does not bother to stop and apologize." With a flick of her braids backwards, she continues full speed ahead, preoccupied as she is with more pressing matters on her mind.

These characteristics of the hero and heroine form the beginnings of a new heroic image, the *ying hsiung hsing-hsiang* around which writers are to weave their stories. What these characters look like in action and how they relate to others will be taken up in following sections.

Family Relations. The emphasis on family relations in short stories since 1949 has shifted somewhat from one period to another both in degree and in content. A brief review of the patterns in pre-1970 stories will pave the way for the presentation of findings in the current sample.

Fiction in the People's Republic never went through a period of concerted attack upon the legal family or marriage as an institution as it did in the Soviet Union during the 1920s, when the free love theme or the "glass of water" theory of sex had a brief vogue. Chinese stories in the past two decades have indeed downplayed some family functions, portrayed weakened parental authority or family unity in some matters, and generally subordinated familial loyalty to loyalty to the Party, people, or state.

In the early 1950s, when the oppressed wife and daughter-in-law were urged to "speak their bitterness" publicly and to seek divorce, stories did not celebrate the "liberated" woman per se, freed from all family ties. Stories from the same period on land reform or later on collectivization often put family members on different sides of the political fence, but the plot would center on the enlightenment and thought conversion of the politically backward ones. Entire families may of course have been portrayed as villains, but stories focusing on political differences breaking up a family were relatively rare. On the eve of the short-lived Hundred Flowers movement, there was a brief flurry of story interest in the family itself. Even a few unabashed love themes appeared. But with the advent of the Great Leap Forward and the commune movement immediately following, family and love themes both receded and familial duties took a decided second place to the public responsibility of all family members to be productive members of society.

By the first half of the sixties, the family recaptured top place of interest in stories. Family and kin characters multiplied, and nuances of relationships were lovingly explored. Familial virtues rose to a new height, and the search for a proper mate, indeed even for the good daughter-in-law to fit harmoniously into the complex household, including the mother-in-law, became a recurrent theme in stories. And although the matter of ideological correctness was never neglected, it was often a minor focus compared to other themes such as the following: (1) closeness in the three-generational family or ties with wider kin; (2) respect for the older generation, especially for the father's authority; (3) the father as role model for his sons and daughters, as someone skilled in his work and devoted to it, progressive in political outlook, and in full and unquestioned charge of the family; (4) the mother as the good-natured meddler in the choice of a son-in-law or daughter-in-law, and even as the welcome addition to the married son's family; and the mother as the competitor in production with the daughter or daughter-in-law; (5) the younger generation as cooperative, even submissive members of the larger family unit, though still independent in mind and spirit.

During the Cultural Revolution, the publication of short

stories was curtailed. But the first part of the seventies has witnessed a substantial buildup of interest in short story writing. Now, family and politics have again reversed their relative positions of prominence. Family ties are present and are drawn in favorable light, but are not explored for their intrinsic interest and are not the pivotal points in story line. The preoccupation with relatives in stories of the last decade has dropped out, and the fascination with the semiarranged match and the in-law relationship has disappeared altogether. Courtship as a theme is virtually absent in current stories. Even the matter of authority itself within the family is now open to question; sometimes elders come out on top in story development, and other times youth is portrayed as more skillful, more politically correct, or generally more sympathetic. Yet the matter of family continuity is often given more than passing interest. What the family relationships do look like in current stories will be taken up in some detail, but first let us examine the same comparison expressed in numerical terms (see Table 6.1).

Major and minor family relationships are found to appear less than half as often in the 1973–1975 stories as in the 1962–1966 group. In stories of the sixties, 229 family relationships were counted in a total of the 182 stories examined (out of which 47 stories were selected for a detailed analysis because these contained family relationships.)[24] For the 1973–1975 period, a total of 160 stories have been studied and 55 family relationships counted. The average number is 1.29 family relationships per story in 1962–1966 as compared to 0.34 for the later period. While we are not primarily interested in detailed quantitative comparisons in this study, the marked shift in emphasis is nevertheless noteworthy.

Now for a discussion of some major relationships in the current stories.

The Father Figure. Though the father is usually painted in favorable light in this group of stories, he is often not around —either long dead or away at work. Yet his presence can be

TABLE 1. Comparison of Family and Kin Relationships in Short Stories of 1962–1966 and 1973–1975

| Relationship | Frequency Count[a] | | | |
| | (1962–1966) | | (1973–1975) | |
	Freq.	%	Freq.	%
Parent-child	62	27	35	65
Husband-wife	28	12	6	11
Grandparent-grandchild	9	4	1	1
Siblings	11	5	4	7
Aunts/uncles/nephews/nieces	0	0	5	9
Boy-girl	77	34	1	1
"Intended"	16	7	1	1
In-laws	26	12	1	2
Others	3		2	
Total	229		55	
Number of stories	182[b]		160	
Average mentions	1.29		0.34	

a. The frequency count is the number of times the relationship is present in a story. One story may contain more than one relationship.

b. More than twice the number of stories do not have any relationship mentioned. These are about war heroes and other themes.

felt or his memory invoked as an example for the younger generation. One of the favorite devices is to have a close friend or comrade from the father's younger days turn up unexpectedly when the grown son or daughter is now assigned to work. In one stroke, two lessons are driven home: a meaningful relationship in the older generation devoted to the revolution, and a family heritage of correct political thinking and attitude toward work. This is all done in a few economical lines, suggesting family continuity without going into details of the relationship between a father and his young adult children.

In a story called "Seeds from Yenan," the narrator of the story is asked by her dead father's old army friend of twenty years' standing to look up the daughter who is newly sent down to work in the village. The girl has been keeping a packet of seeds from Yenan, a memento from the narrator's father when he had to retreat from a village with his guerrilla unit, leaving his pregnant wife behind. His gifts to the unborn child, the narrator, carried by the mother in her own escape, were a Red Book, a family photograph, and a few seeds from Yenan.

A recently dead father is the inspiration for a seventeen- or eighteen-year-old farmer's daughter. Determined to carry on her father's agricultural work, the girl refuses other offers of jobs. She is elected a team leader despite her age, and receives this solemn charge by her mother: She must emulate her father, who never overlooked the smallest matter.

In another father-daughter story, the retired keeper of the key for the commune's production brigade warehouse is the model for his daughter, who aspires to the same job despite both parents' qualms. After proving herself in several difficult situations, she shows herself worthy of becoming her father's successor.

The last example of the father figure illustrates the rarer kind of story about actual ongoing interactions between the generations. A girl barely past twenty is determined to become a tractor driver in a commune. Father disapproves of this: "Whoever heard of a mere girl of twenty driving an iron monster all over the place?" The girl sweetly calls her father *tieh* and retorts that there are more girls than he realizes driving on the highways. "But," exclaims father, "they are not helter-skelter like you! Except for airplanes in the sky, I believe you would drive anything!" To this the girl replies, "*Aya*, father has become a rumor monger! Have I ever been in an accident?" Yet her father cannot hide his worry. Because the mother is dead, he feels the sole responsibility to bring up the daughter properly. "If people criticize, I would not be able to bear it. . . ." But the daughter silences her father with these words: "*Aya!* This day and age, you come forth with such old-fashioned talk. Girls are cultivated by the

Party now, and the commune. If it were not so, we would all be beggars still." With the support of villagers, the girl goes ahead to drive a tractor.

After another argument, the girl speaks sharply to her father and brings out this retreat on his part: "I am illiterate like a blind man. I cannot keep up this talk—I am no match for you in an argument. Go and look for your second uncle!" Then at the urging of Second Aunt, who happens to be nearby, the girl heats some food for her father while the latter sits on the brick bed glumly smoking. The girl goes to pull him over by his arm to eat, her big eyes flashing: "Father, are you still angry with me?" Father silently wipes off some mud from the girl's face and says, "Let us eat first."

This is an uncommon scene for a Chinese peasant family, even in modern times. The free and easy way in which the daughter talks to her father, or talks back, the impertinence and irreverence, and finally the physical contact initiated by both father and daughter at the end, are all highly unusual. This degree of familiarity and informality between father and daughter certainly did not conform to traditional standards of behavior, though it could have existed as a variant form in the transitional period of Westernization in China. During the first half of the sixties, while close cooperative living between parents and adult sons and daughters was stressed in stories, the father figure retained a measure of distance and stern quality, somewhat reminiscent of the traditional *yen* (strict) father.[25] The scenes in this story of a decade later represent a new model. It would seem reasonable to interpret the new pattern as a result of the simultaneous accent on youth and age in the post-Cultural Revolution years.

The Mother Figure. The mother in this group of stories can appear well meaning and meddlesome, or she can be reinforcer of the socialist conscience, transmitter of a sense of duty to the people. She can be unbendingly strict with her son or daughter, and she can be objective and rational in assessing the true capacity of a son or daughter. She can even surmount personal sentiments and rise above suspicions of favoritism. Here are some illustrations:

A peasant woman used to be oppressed by the landlord in the old society. She acquired the nickname of "Auntie Speechless" because she was intimidated into silent submission. Her husband, a farm laborer, was dismissed by his employer because grain was lost through a leaking sack. Now, even after liberation, she is meticulously careful about saving every grain. In her new job as keeper of the pigs for the production brigade, she is affectionately called "Auntie Manager." She frugally sweeps up all the loose grain from the ground and is particularly careful about grain bags. Her son makes light of her frugality, saying she is competing with the chicken for the few grains. Joking about her tendency to take charge over everything, he complains that living with her makes him feel like a daughter-in-law. To this the mother retorts, "If I did not interfere, the cracks of your teeth would become wider and wider," meaning he would become more and more conceited.

In this story, two otherwise favorable characteristics of the mother, frugality and managing ability, are treated humorously as objectionable by her son, introducing a note of ambiguity in the portrait of the mother. A mother's commendable habit based on past experience as the oppressed can become a source of irritation to her son's need for independence and decisive action. A possible type of strain between the generations might be indicated here.

Husband-Wife. The husband and wife relationship is decidedly of secondary importance in these stories. Where it is treated, the husband and wife are generally supportive of each other or portrayed as having minor ideological differences, to be resolved with joking, prodding, or friendly persuasion. The same basic relationship as equal partners that was found in stories of the early sixties also prevails here.

In one story where an older couple are minor characters,

the husband works in a commune hospital and is seldom at home except at mealtime, and the wife is the local keeper of pigs whose hours are long and irregular, requiring cooperation from the husband for the preparation of meals. As the wife puts it, "I put the dough to rise and he bakes. We cook the next meal while eating what we have prepared earlier." She finds dignity in her job and feels that although her work ties her down to the village, her outlook is not necessarily confined.

The husband-wife relationship in another story reveals the prodding manner in which the husband deals with the comparatively conservative-minded wife. While the husband merely doubts the maturity of their daughter to be keeper of the production brigade's warehouse, the wife still holds the old-fashioned view that it would be best to avoid involvement with officialdom. "Big or small, taking the job means being an official, *tsokuan*." "You are ordinarily an enlightened person. How is it you are suddenly so muddled?" he seems to be provoking her good-naturedly. The wife then explains her fear that the villagers might criticize their daughter and ridicule her for her mistakes. At this, the husband calls her an "old feudalistic brain," pointing out that there are girl secretaries nowadays, and even directors of communes. The wife puts up no more arguments. She can only say accusingly, "Oh, you father and daughter are in league with each other!"

Another kind of marital difference is that between two worthy goals. The agricultural brigade leader, known as "Uncle Chuang," and his wife, production team leader "Auntie Chuang," are constantly bickering about matters of work priority. She is worried about the water supply for the team's vegetable plots, about fertilizer and insecticides. He, as leader at a higher level, has to make decisions affecting the entire brigade. When she presses him for supplies and receives no satisfaction, she complains: "If you will not take charge, neither will I! Let the people look at our differences and decide who is right!" The husband laughingly replies, "Look at you. Are you not again guilty of thinking only of your own unit? As I explained before, managing this brigade is like playing a chess game. And you have already forgotten our theme song: 'All action must flow from above; victory comes only when everyone is in step.' " She says despairingly: "Do not talk to me about such things. I have had enough of this job—all responsibility and no power. Go and find someone else!"

But of course she does not quit. Instead, she redoubles her efforts and takes on the extra task of mending the work team's pig fence. At her husband's teasing, she throws a look at him and says gravely: "Hm! Differences are differences, work is work. We cadres are for the revolution. If we cast off our load midway, how can we account to Chairman Mao and the poor, middle peasants?" Her husband knows her all too well to be surprised.

Others. Even though sibling or in-law relations are rarely delineated in the 1973–1975 stories, the few that are found usually conform to thematic emphases of other stories, that is, younger persons may be more correct ideologically than elders, and women are often more advanced than men. The resolution of differences, however, presents greater difficulties.

A young boy and his little sister are on the same production team collecting grain. The brother worries that the sister might overtake him and make him a laughingstock among his schoolmates. The sister is concerned only with doing the job efficiently. While the one does a speedy but sloppy job, the other raises key ideological questions: "Brother, tell me the reason for collecting grain." "Why ask," he replies, "Everyone knows it is the directive of Chairman Mao." "Then, brother, how shall we do it?" "Who doesn't know?" he replies, "The more grain, the better." Before the sister can pursue with the next question, the brother hastily leaves. At home after supper, when the dispute is brought up, their father tells them their work is equally good. The brother feels the judgment is unfair since he has the fuller bag of grain, but the father drives the correct lesson home.

In another sibling story, the sister is again shown as wiser and more correct in political thinking. This case concerns work in the coal mines, and the sister criticizes the brother's proposal in a workers' meeting to slacken the production schedule because of the heavy workload. The brother, a young man of twenty-eight or twenty-nine, is dismayed that his own sister would attack him in public. They carry the quarrel home and argue about the merits of each other's cooking. The conflict is resolved when the Party directive arrives to prove the sister right.

An unusual story involving a daughter-in-law shows a young woman's correctness in all respects: ideological awareness, skill in work, and competency. The girl is the new woman representative of the commune's production team. The father-in-law is first skeptical about her ability to do the work, but when he is convinced, he openly expresses amazement and admiration.

Such are the ideal portraits in stories delineating normative standards for behavior for family relations. Family relations, it seems, are in a process of readjustment in these stories. They no longer occupy center stage, but neither are they relegated to a position of minor importance. Young and old, husband-wife, and others all have a responsibility to bring the misguided members into line. Such "help" can include open discussion, challenge and argument, and even public criticism and confrontation, but the preferred methods seem to be humor, reason and persuasion, and personal consideration.

The Party Secretary. The prominence of the local Party Branch Secretary or the Deputy Secretary rises and recedes in stories of the past two or three decades. His role may be pivotal or subsidiary, but he definitely occupies an assured place in fiction. In the 1960 sample, the local Party Secretary was the single most frequent role, appearing in half the stories. But in stories of 1962–1966, he took a definite second place to family and relatives, and where he did appear his role was minor. The 1973–1975 stories show a partial swing back, and he can be seen either as the main or secondary character.

The current role of the local Party Secretary can be seen in better perspective if we recall the nature of the role in the 1960 sample of stories. At that time, the local Party Secretary was characterized by equality and informality, near-omnipotence, and as someone able and willing to make decisions on the spot and take action without consulting higher authority. Sometimes he appeared to possess almost magical powers.

In the current group of stories, the local Party Secretary is still painted in favorable light but is no longer invested with such a wide scope of powers. Neither does he or she always stand out as a vivid person, but rather as a solemn and supportive figure often in the background, either taking or encouraging the correct political step.

We shall describe the present role in terms of three sub-roles: supporting role, decision-making or decision-sharing role, and hero or heroine role. A few examples of each type follow:

1. In the supporting role, the local Party Secretary participates in a variety of everyday activities of the people, calling attention to the fact that he shares the life of the masses and is ever ready to lend encouragement or point to a correct line of action. Thus he may read aloud to a master worker and the new apprentice not only the Party Declaration but also the "contract," the *yueh-ting* outlining their agreed-upon goals and mutual obligations. Another local Party Secretary praises a twelve-year-old boy for his effort in tracking down a duck thief, telling him that he is truly engaged in class struggle. The Party Secretary here relates a piece of everyday behavior to the larger social scene and gives it political meaning. This episode illustrates the principle of "elevation," one of the tasks in short story writing.

Another instance of encouragement and approval is extended by the local Party Secretary who meets and congratulates a transport team for volunteering to ship a load of fish for breeding to a village in Chairman Mao's own native district. A last example has to do with procuring a special hybrid wheat seedling for a seventeen-year-old girl newly sent down to the countryside. Some of the old peasants are skeptical that she could carry on the difficult experiment but she receives the support of the local Party Secretary. The experiment of course succeeds, resulting in a new production record for the production brigade.

2. In the second subrole, the local Party Secretary is responsible for making decisions, alone or with others, that directly affect the life of the masses. In one story, for example, he alone seems to decide to which work unit a new apprentice seaman should be assigned. In another, the local Party Secretary together with the master worker agrees to allow an apprentice girl to learn to operate the crane. A Branch Secretary can also approve or support the nomination of candidates for training, or approve a peasant woman's nomination of her own daughter to be trained as barefoot doctor.

3. Finally, the local Party Secretary may be the main character, the hero or heroine. A former staff member of the New Fourth Army, now assigned to a geological survey unit as the party's Deputy Branch Secretary, is such a hero. Years ago, during the Sino-Japanese war, when he was wounded in action, he was befriended by a peasant who nursed him back to health and shielded him at great personal sacrifice. Now, when challenged with the near-hopeless task of finding a source of water for the village, the Deputy Party Secretary recalls the information given him by the peasant and persists in his plan to drill the well despite orders to the contrary from the geology brigade headquarters. His faith in the knowledge of the peasant and his fidelity to an old encounter are virtues which sustain him in countermanding orders from above. This spirit typifies one kind of model for the contemporary cadre.

Another model in the person of a Party Branch Secretary is the younger man who finds his former coworker, an older man, slipping into the "spirit of commercialism" while managing a metal supply company. The new Branch Secretary soon institutes a priority system for meeting orders according to need, and justifies this move in terms of helping his older friend bring his thinking more in line with correct policy. "Political work is the lifeline of all economic work" is the principle for correct behavior.

A final example is a Deputy Party Secretary as heroine. A thirty-two-year-old former worker in a spinning and weaving factory and people's representative on the District Party Committee for the past three or four years is the subject of a story on her model behavior in her new capacity. Returning from another assignment one day, she is late for a mass meeting in the village. The young cadre who works in the office wants to request a postponement of the village meeting, but the Deputy Secretary explains that one must keep appointments and not allow the organization lightly to change the affairs of the masses. Later a letter arrives from a retired worker in the village asking why is it that the secretary is so busy and that "the people could no longer see her as originating from the masses?" The young cadre thinks of the letter as a minor matter, a routine piece of business, and acts on his own judgment that a district secretary would be too busy to deal with the masses directly, suggesting that the letter writer consult the local representative instead. And when the Deputy Secretary points out the error of this move, the young cadre explains the basis of his own erroneous thinking: He had assumed that since the Cultural Revolution is several years old and a new order is established, the interests of the masses are already being taken care of. The Deputy Secretary sets him straight on this: Contained in this polite but reproachful question in the letter from the people is criticism to be taken seriously. What the letter tells the Deputy Secretary is something which "cannot be heard at meetings and cannot be read in reports." Furthermore, for her to sit isolated in the office would be to "allow rules to take command."

In the office, rather than issuing orders for assistants to prepare reports, the Deputy Secretary herself works along with them, going over successive drafts, always being available for consultation. She also welcomes visits from people of the district and is known as someone who "puts on no airs." She says, "It is good that the masses want to look for us." While regarding praise as a sign of encouragement, she also invites them to criticize: "Wipe the dust off my face. Be my doctor and cure my illnesses." She quotes a common saying to the effect that to be stern is to show love, and to be lax is to bring on misfortune. It should be noted, however, that this popular saying traditionally applies to parental treatment of children. Now she is deliberately reversing the message: For the masses to be stern to leadership is to show love; to be lax with them is to bring on unfortunate results for everyone.

This is a much-anthologized story entitled *Chü-wei fu-shu-chi*, "Deputy Secretary of the District Committee." It first appeared in *Wen-hui-pao* (January 16,1972) and was reprinted in at least three anthologies. A preface in the volume *Tuan pian hsiao-shuo chuang-tso tan* (The Creation of Short Stories) explicitly states that stories such as this exemplify the general point: how cadres should maintain close relations with the masses. A special lesson in this story is how after moving up from being a representative of the masses, a Deputy Secretary can continue to maintain the perspective as one of the masses.

In short, the local Party Secretary in these stories seems to be faced with new ambiguities which his counterpart a decade ago did not have. In stories of the 1960 sample, he was called upon to exhibit near-superhuman efforts or to be almost omniscient about people's needs. The challenge was there and the direction for action was clearcut. Now, the correct road to action is not always self-evident: Alternatives are presented and conflicting demands have to be resolved. For example, should he follow the sentiments of the old peasants or even his former revolutionary comrades, or should he stand on the side of the eager young workers? Should he listen to the demands of the masses or should he obey rules and practices of the organization? These are possibly the dilemmas of the 1970s.

Youth as Hero. Age roles as a category cuts across familial and other roles. Two age groups receive a great deal of attention in these stories and show clearcut patterns: the role of youth and the role of mature age.

Perhaps the most striking single feature of this group of stories is the accent on the positive characteristics of youth on the threshhold of adulthood, especially young women about twenty years of age. One is reminded of the politically correct, progressive-minded youth of stories in the early fifties, yet youth in the current stories appear to receive more attention as character types per se rather than as primarily the embodiment of ideas or concepts. The contemporary portrait of youth has nuances of characteristics that are new and noteworthy, and its relationship with age contains special features as well. Both aspects can be seen to arise out of conditions in the post-Cultural Revolution decade.

We shall first consider stories in which youth is hero or heroine, in which older people are shown by comparison in less favorable light.

The first characteristic of youth is skill, maturity, and ability to undertake the responsibility entrusted to him or her, or even the eagerness to seek such responsibility. For example, twenty-eight-year-old Ah Hai is newly appointed as the "number one" man on a fishing vessel belonging to a fishing brigade on Dunghai. Ah Hai's remote paternal uncle, Ah Hsing, is worried that he is too young and inexperienced for such a responsible post, and confides in Party Secretary Chou, who points out that Ah Hai had already been the "number two" man on another boat, and that being "number one" really depends upon following Chairman Mao's thought and winning the cooperation of the masses. Chou adds that the Party Branch Committee had carried out a thorough investigation before appointing him. With this, Ah Hsing is reassured. In time, the young man proves his worth: He is resourceful in getting a bigger catch by experimenting with casting a deep net at night. The uncle is convinced and proud of his nephew.

The second characteristic has to do with youth's correct ideological attitudes and judgment. An example is the story about a young apprentice in a spinning and weaving factory. Although newly promoted to work independently of her master worker, Chüeh-tsun Mei still searches out the older woman for political discussions. The two often come to arguments, but "the more they argue, the fonder of each other they become." The young woman emerges as someone with a high sense of responsibility. She is not only chosen to demonstrate her work techniques to three different teams but also argues for exporting cloth to Africa as part of the workers' duty to world revolution. This wins the silent approval of the older woman.

The third characteristic is that despite the age gap, youth can nevertheless lead his elders in correct thinking and appropriate action.

In the first example, Ku, a new Party Branch Secretary, comes to work at the same metal supply depot as Chen, his former coworker, a somewhat older man. Before the Liberation, the two of them used to have a hard time with the old owner of a hardware store. Now, many years later, Ku finds that Chen himself, though educated by the Party for twenty years, has become commercially minded through his long years at this post. Ku proposes a priority system to meet metal supply orders according to need, not commercial considerations. This move does not meet with Chen's initial support. The younger man, feeling the responsibility to help out his friend and set his thinking along the right path, tells Chen that one must not be satisfied just with superficial changes in the matter of service to the people. "We must get rid of commercialism and treat the whole metal company as a battleground for warfare against capitalistic tendencies." Chen is persuaded and takes steps to correct his former mistakes.

Another story concerns a young girl of about twenty who refuses to leave the village for cadre training even though she is recommended by fellow villagers and approved by the Party. She is determined to carry on her father's work on the land. She disagrees with the belief that able young people should be sent out of the village and trained for higher posts because this would imply that those left behind have inferior ability. She therefore submits the name of a friend to take her place.

Another example is a story about a young man nicknamed *Hsiao Tou*. His name means "the Struggler" because he always challenges others on their correct ideological stand. He boldly decides not to send some steel to an army construction project but instead takes the initiative to divert supplies to a local smith shop which is in greater need.

The last story is about a young shipyard apprentice, Hsiao Ling, a representative of the Youth Shock Troop. She is dauntless, impatient, and self-assured. When a big welding job is called for and others hesitate, Hsiao Ling shows her determination to go ahead. To all those who oppose the idea, even when they are older and more experienced, she has a critical remark to make. She accuses the foreman of "not looking down below," meaning not soliciting the opinions and contributions of the younger, less experienced workers. The workers agree that he has not given them due consideration and give her their support. Another time Hsiao Ling challenges the inspector: "How come today you are so hesitant, so indecisive?" And to her foreman, she declares: "It must be that you do not dare to take on the job yourself, that is why you will not let others do it. This job is not insurmountable, if we rely on Chairman Mao's revolutionary doctrine." The foreman admits Hsiao Ling is correct in her thinking and that he himself is a victim of rightist conservatism. Henceforth, he is determined to support her revolutionary suggestions.

The skill, resourcefulness, and political awareness of youth in these stories is nothing new. These qualities were present in land reform and collectivization stories of the 1950s and, though not highlighted as much in stories of the following decade, were nevertheless present. Now, a new note can be detected: the celebration of the audacious, self-determined, sometimes brash quality of youth, willing to face or even provoke conflict, and ready to challenge the authority of age. A dedicated revolutionary youth can even be tactless and brazen in meddling with the activities of assorted coworkers, as did the young apprentice welder in the last story.

Strength and Wisdom of Mature Age. The older workers are often described as spartan, hardy, and physically robust, equal in strength and endurance to young people. This also means having suffered past oppression in the old society, having experienced revolutionary struggle, and therefore possessing sound judgment in present circumstances. In these current stories, there is additionally a new quality in the older people hitherto not found in fiction, a quality close to parental affection and solicitude for the young workers in their charge.

The following are some examples of the first kind of characteristics. An old brigade leader of a rural commune performs great feats of strength, rowing boats in rough, stormy weather. An old shipyard worker always saves the hardest chores for himself; it is said that "his hands and feet are never idle." He does not hesitate to venture out in a storm to save a young stranded on a reef. A retired woman worker, silver-haired but firm-bodied, twice walks to the district headquarters from her village to raise some questions with the Deputy Party Secretary. A fifty-year-old former commander of a brigade in the revolutionary army always walks, refusing to be met by car. Though suffering from an old back injury incurred in war, he refuses the use of a soft hemp bed borrowed for him by the young boy assistant from a storage room. He displays courage and strength by rushing out in a storm to rescue horses from a collapsing stall.

The next group of stories describe the older person as politically more correct than younger people. An old brigade leader returning from a commune meeting finds the young Deputy Brigade Leader leaving with the commune rowboat to hire it out to a neighboring village to transport grain for cash income for the commune. The older man opposes the young deputy in this policy, reminding him that the use of the boat should be determined by the priority of hauling grain and not by the opportunity for cash income.

The old Party Branch Secretary at a production brigade believes the brigade should devote more land to radish production because the consumer public likes them and because they are used as preventive medicine for a certain illness. He convinces the Deputy Brigade Leader and other peasants in the village that although this decision means a financial loss, it serves the people better.

The last example is about a retired, silver-haired woman who asks a penetrating question of a young, newly promoted Deputy District Party Secretary: "Why is it that the Secretary is no longer seen as originating from the people?" This question is taken to heart by the young Secretary, who now recognizes her obligation to keep in close touch with the masses. (This story was summarized more fully in the section "Party Secretary.")

The last characteristic of older people not matched by a corresponding one among the youth is a caring quality, an affectionate concern for the younger workers, serving a sort of parent surrogate function. This quality is somewhat reminiscent of the Party Secretary in the 1960 stories, someone who personally looks after the welfare of the people. In the stories of the seventies, however, this quality is both more pronounced and more personalized. There is a specifically as-

signed, contracted one-to-one relationship between an older
worker and his or her younger charge.

For example, young Hsiao Feng is a novice at operating
the crane. She is apprenticed to a master worker who teaches
her and watches over her work, mindful of her development
as a person. Out of eagerness, young Hsiao Feng drops her
first load at the dock, scattering the contents of a crate on the
ground. The master worker loudly scolds her about the accident and orders her to "come down immediately," and "go
inside and think carefully" about her mistakes. Yet the next
day, the old master worker demonstrates his confidence in
the girl by allowing her to operate the crane again, alone. His
affectionate treatment of the girl is likened by the writer to
that of a father for his daughter. The girl's own father, who
has witnessed the accident, comes at the end of the day's
work to talk to her, telling her to remember her responsibility
and to emulate Dr. Norman Bethune and other older workers. He equates a careless act to being irresponsible to the revolution and to the people. Next day, after she successfully
operates the crane, her father stands there smiling, pleased
with her accomplishment, while the master worker pours her
a cup of tea and the Party Secretary takes both her hands in a
gesture of great approval. The girl thus vindicates herself and
earns the warm support of her elders.

The surrogate father is matched by the substitute mother,
equally caring for the well-being of young workers in her
charge. Tan Shao is an older woman who is devoted to her
pig-keeping work. Two young women have been sent down
from the city to work in rural areas. They have been assigned
to help Tan Shao care for the pigs. Tan Shao has prepared a
welcome for one of the new girls by making her an apron and
a pair of sleeve guards, proudly saying, "I haven't guessed
too badly on size, have I?" And when the new girl has a surprise visitor, a former classmate, Tan Shao gives her the day
off. When the girl returns late from an afternoon walk to the
mountains with her friend, her coworker angrily complains

to Tan Shao, who calmly explains that one must patiently teach a newcomer.

This kind of emotional dimension in a work relationship is a noteworthy new model of behavior for an otherwise impersonal, instrumental relationship. Here in these stories, a protofamilial type of affection is added to those with age and responsibility—not only to train youth and show them the correct road but also to lavish care and concern on them.

It is thus still possible for older people in the post-Cultural Revolution stories to serve as role models for youth, though in a less unequivocal way than in stories of the years immediately preceding it. Now the position of the older people, though correct, may be openly challenged by youth. The new note of emotional maturity of the older people, however, with their capacity to lavish care and affection on the young workers in their charge, earn them new esteem as heroes and heroines in comtemporary stories.

SUMMARY AND CONCLUSION

As a medium of communication, the short story in China in the past half decade is more popularly based and geographically dispersed than before, both in its authorship and in the audience it tries to reach. The writing of short stories appears also to be a more organized and more politically guided activity.

The meaning of what is communicated via short stories is based on the Marxist-Leninist theory of knowledge and the role of literature within it, as well as in the context of Mao's activism and his special vision of the revolutionary process in China. In simplest terms, the premise is that knowledge is the "reflection" of social "reality" upon the human consciousness, and that the responsibility of writers is to further the cause of the revolution by depicting and highlighting this "reality." The key to understanding this theoretical position lies in the special meaning of the terms "reflection" and

"reality." "Reality," and the "socialist realism" which portrays it, focuses on the forward-moving element in human experiences, being oriented "in the direction in which the revolution is advancing." The process of "reflection" therefore
involves depicting characters and creating story situations to
exemplify this direction.

The explication of this theoretical orientation in short
story writing varies somewhat according to the developmen-
tal phases of the Chinese Communist society, with resulting
variations in the content of stories. In the first half of the
1970s, discussion has highlighted the role of the hero and
heroine. The rationale of this emphasis lies in the concept of
"typification," the process by which the hero and heroine,
who are described as coming from the masses and remaining
close to them, exemplify the revolutionary essence of the
masses and the socialist environment. The responsibility of
the writers, who are again said to be from the masses themselves, is continually observing and learning from them while
at the same time demonstrating, via the heroes and heroines,
the correct path to follow in the revolution.

The content of stories of the 1973–1975 period has been
described and analyzed according to language use and role
relationships. We have identified linguistic expressions from
a variety of origins: Some are contemporary and ideological,
others literary, popular, or colloquial. Traditional expressions, whether classical or vernacular, are of course links
with the past and promote a sense of linguistic continuity.
Contemporary slogans, and even phrases used for character-
izing heroes and heroines, all embody political meaning that
can serve an integrative function at the symbolic level.

Terms of address and other names by which people call
one another in these stories fulfill similar functions. Traditional kinship terms, or terms by which husbands and wives
refer to each other, for example, speak for the preservation of
aspects of popular culture. Affectionate epithets, or the application of old, familiar pet names in new situations, evoke

memories from the past and rouse sentiments of identification. The result is the preservation of cultural continuity in the midst of perpetual change.

Characterizations and role portrayals in these stories provide, above all else, current or future-oriented norms for behavior, values, and appropriate world outlook. The thoughts, actions, and the process of struggle of the heroes and heroines are intended to be models for emulation as object lessons, particularly for those with problems in political orientation or behavior.

Family roles, the local Party Secretary, and the relationship between youth and age are analyzed in stories of this period. With the ascendence of politics at the onset of the Cultural Revolution in the mid-1960s, interest in short stories surrounding the large kinship group receded, although attention to relationships in the nuclear family unit remains. Parental authority, which enjoyed a moderate rise in stories of the early sixties, is now more open to questioning by sons and daughters. The position of respect which fathers enjoyed a decade ago, partly by virtue of their family status, now rests more heavily on revolutionary achievements or wisdom gained from years of work experience. Thus, young men and women are portrayed not so much as adjusting to parental wishes and expectations as inheriting their revolutionary zeal and dedication. It is not surprising that the younger generation can at times criticize parents or joke at the latter's expense. Mothers in these stories can possess managerial abilities, although they can also appear well meaning but meddlesome. At her best, a mother can be strict but also rational and objective, and can triumph over the traditional weakness of favoritism toward her own child.

Between husband and wife, there can be differences of thinking and political understanding, but there can also be mutual support and mutual influence. As among siblings or occasional in-laws, the struggle is often between the truly revolutionary member and the somewhat misguided ones.

Persuasion and humor rather than accusation or condemnation describe the usual mode of interaction between family members.

The local Party Secretary is regaining prominence in stories of the 1970s after a partial eclipse just before the Cultural Revolution. His importance rests not so much on his limitless energy and simple foresight about the physical or material needs of the people, as it did earlier, but rather on the subtler and more demanding ability to see the deeper significance of surface contradictions and the courage to make the correct long-range choice. The local cadre is called upon in contemporary stories to strike the delicate balance between close identification with the masses on one hand and being the exemplar on the other. All the while, he is the local symbol of the Party hierarchy and national leadership; he is the embodiment of political authority. He not only serves as a model in the media for aspiring cadres, a measuring stick for the behavior of veteran Party representatives on the local scene, but also defines and integrates the relationship in a symbolic sense between leader and led, between Party orthodoxy and the masses.

A somewhat newly counterpoised pair of complementary roles is that of the young adult fresh to the labor scene and the older seasoned worker. The youthful worker, especially a girl barely reaching adulthood, is in these stories capable, self-confident, and full of revolutionary zeal, and can at times be more politically advanced than older workers. The young worker dares to undertake difficult tasks and to question authority in order to prove the correctness of the action. The mature worker, often depicted as robust and hardy, can be a stern taskmaster to youth but is also capable of warmth and affectionate concern for the young, inexperienced workers in his charge. The stories of the early 1970s thus reveal some ambivalence in the competing emphases on youth and age, perhaps a reflection of unresolved value polarities in the post-Cultural Revolution Chinese society. This value dilemma is succinctly expressed in the preface to the short story entitled "A Deliberate Question," in the volume of collected stories named *The Little General:*

> Some will think that this Li Chun-hua is mischievous and irreverent, that although she is only an assembly line inspector, she does not know what is respect for elders. The truth is that she has good reasons[26] [for acting that way]. Not only does she perform her own work well, she is also watchful of the revolution. In fact, she thinks of herself as an integral part of the revolution. Thus, even if her own leader or own father turns out to be self-satisfied and stagnant, she still has to rise up and struggle with him.

These roles, when interwoven, make up part of the fabric of the desirable society as it is communicated to the readers of the stories. It is a moral and social map for the masses in the seventies. For the masses themselves are the heroes and heroines. The ordinary worker-peasant-soldier is not a "mere bystander to life, but must be a master in proletariat literature."[27] And the lessons for life are all around us, as it is stated in the preface to the collected volume of stories called *The New Classroom:*

> The new classroom is everywhere: It is the spinning factory, the rural commune, the seaside dock, the fishery, the craft bench, the public transportation and the seafaring boat. . . . Otherwise, we writers would feel that we are letting down the Party and insufficiently cultivating our own class.

The short story as a form of popular media in China thus plays a distinct role in the transmission of norms, values, and beliefs with which to guide one's action. From an examination of the story content, we see more distinctly the desired shape of Chinese society as ideology evolves into social policy, and as the latter is explicated into the minutia of daily living. And from unresolved issues in values and norms, one gets glimpses of the shapes of things to come in the immediate future—tensions to be dealt with, policy options to be decided upon. In short, stories provide one among many compasses to point the way to the road ahead.

NOTES

1. A. S. Chen [Ai-li S. Chin], "The Ideal Local Party Secretary and the 'Model' Man," *China Quarterly* (January-March, 1964): 229-240.

2. Ai-li S. Chin, "Family Relations in Modern Chinese Fiction," in *Family and Kinship in Chinese Society*, ed. Maurice Freedman (Stanford, Ca.: Stanford University Press, 1970), pp. 87-120.

3. For a collection of the earliest stories written by young Chinese Marxists, see *Straw Sandals—Chinese Short Stories, 1918-1933*, ed. Harold Isaacs (Cambridge, Mass.: The M.I.T. Press, 1974). The introduction by the editor contains the tragic story of these young writers and the role of Lu Hsun, modern China's foremost writer, during that interlude.

4. C. T. Hsia, *A History of Modern Chinese Fiction, 1917-1957* (New Haven, Conn.: Yale University Press, 1961), and Merle Goldman, *Literary Dissent in Communist China* (Cambridge, Mass.: Harvard University Press, 1967) are two comprehensive studies of the history of modern Chinese literature and writers.

5. See Ai-li S. Chin, "Interdependence of Roles in Transitional China—A Structural Analysis of Attitudes in Contemporary Chinese Literature" (Ph.D. dissertation, Radcliffe College [Harvard University], 1951).

6. Hsu Kai-yu, *The Chinese Literary Scene—A Writer's Visit to the People's Republic* (New York: Random House, Inc., 1975), p. 85.

7. From Mao Tse-tung, *Selected Readings from the Works of Mao Tse-tung* (Peking: People's Press, 1971), pp. 250-285.

8. T. A. Hsia, "Twenty Years after the Yenan Forum," *China Quarterly* (January-March, 1963): 226-253.

9. Howard L. Boorman, "The Literary World of Mao Tse-tung," *China Quarterly* 13 (January-March, 1963): 32.

10. See Robert and Ai-li S. Chin, *Psychological Research in Communist China* (Cambridge, Mass.: The M.I.T. Press, 1969).

11. Ibid., p. 13.

12. *Shang-hai Tuan-pien Hsiao-shuo Hsuan* (Shanghai: Jen-min chu-pan she, 1974), p. 142.

13. Hsu Kai-yu, *Chinese Literary Scene*, p. 96.

14. A. S. Chen, "Ideal Local Party Secretary," p. 230.

15. Chao Chung, "On Literature and Art," in *Communist China, 1956* (Hong Kong: Union Research Institute, 1957), p. 153.

16. Hsu Kai-yu, *Chinese Literary Scene*, p. 87–88.

17. The best systematic statement on these writers' workshops is to be found in *Tuan-pien hsiao-shuo chuang-tso-tan* [Discussions on the Creative Writing of the Short Story], *Shang-hai shih-fan ta-hsueh chung-wen-hsi wen-yi ping-lun tsu* [Literary Criticism Committee, Department of Chinese Literature, Shanghai Teachers' University] (Shanghai: *Shang-hai jen-min chu-pan-she* [Shanghai People's Publishing House], 1974).

18. Hsu Kai-yu, *Chinese Literary Scene*, p. 8.

19. The prefaces or postscripts of many collected volumes of short stories give some information about the writing teams or other units involved in the workshops or the consultation process.

20. *Tuan-pien hsiao-shuo chuang-tso-tan*, introductory essay to story 6.

21. See, for example, ibid., introductory essay to story 7.

22. Ibid., introductory essay to story 3.

23. This point was discussed in Chen, "Ideal Local Party Secretary," p. 231.

24. Chin, "Family Relations." For a breakdown of family relationships, see Tables C-1, C-2, C-3 and C-4, pp. 106–107.

25. Ibid., pp. 108–111.

26. The Chinese term for good reason is *yu-li-yu*. It is intriguing to note that the same term has been used in justifying youthful rebelliousness against elders since China started on her road toward modernization. It was found in stories of the May Fourth period, it was heard from young college students in Taiwan explaining away the need for small filial acts, and it is now found in post-Cultural Revolution stories in the People's Republic.

27. *Tuan-pien hsiao-shuo chuang-tso-tan*, introductory essay to story 3.

CHAPTER 7   *Tatzepao:* **Its History**
and Significance as
a Communication Medium

David Jim-tat Poon

TATZEPAO: ITS HISTORICAL BACKGROUND AND FORMAT

Tatzepao, a term coined by the Chinese Communists,[1] literally means a "paper of big letters or bold characters." A *tatzepao* is simply a large sheet of paper posted at any convenient location for people to read. Although the *tatzepao* is an important medium in China's communication network, it was not invented by Communist propagandists. The appearance of *tatzepao* can be traced back to the days when imperial edicts were posted on the city walls.[2] In those days, the posting of *tatzepao* was the only practical method to transmit important messages to the people.

Since the Chinese Communist Party initially structured its new national communication system on the Marxist-Leninist philosophy of communication functions and on the lessons of the Soviet experience after it was adapted to Chinese traditions,[3] the widespread use of *tatzepao* was influenced to some extent by the Soviet experience. In Soviet Russia, the posters in hand- or typewritten form were tacked up on walls of clubs, factories, institutions, or collective farms. (It was a fundamental feature of the Soviet press system in the early

1920s.)⁴ Its significance was first proclaimed in the Party's Thirteenth Congress, whose resolution on the press stated:

> Wall newspapers are acquiring an ever greater significance in our press system, as a medium of influencing the masses and as a form of manifesting their activity.⁵

The Party's Central Committee in 1931 and 1932 decided to establish more factory journals and wall newspapers at the local level to stimulate fulfillment and over-fulfillment of five-year-plan production goals, to develop proper socialist attitudes toward work, and to further the Communist education of the masses.⁶ The wall newspapers, as a product of the "creative" initiative and "amateur" participation that developed simultaneously with the worker-peasant correspondent program, became a vital device for keeping the professional journals in touch with the masses and for utilizing and encouraging the aid of amateurs in operating the media.

In China, Mao Tse-tung was influenced by the Soviet experience and became a strong advocate of *tatzepao* as an important arm of the propaganda network. If his official biography is in any way reliable, Mao was extremely active in politics while he was a student at a normal school in Hunan. He also acquired valuable experience in propaganda and agitation during this time. Many of his activities became common practice in later periods—and one of the activities was the preparation of *tatzepao*.⁷ The following is an official account of Mao describing the writing of his first *tatzepao* at the age of seventeen:

> I began to go to Changsha, the great city, the capital of the province [Hunan]. . . . The country was on the eve of the First Revolution. I was agitated so much that I wrote an article, which I posted on the school wall. It was my first expression of political opinion, and it was somewhat muddled.⁸

In Mao's first *tatzepao*, he advocated that Sun Yat-sen be called back from Japan to become president of a new government, that Kang Yu-wei be made premier, and that Liang Chi-chao become minister of foreign affairs.[9]

Mao's belief in the value of *tatzepao* prevailed in the following years. In 1958, he called *tatzepao* "the best form of *tou cheng* [struggle], which is beneficial to the proletariat but damaging to the bourgeois."[10] He also publicly encouraged the writing of *tatzepao:*

> It is good to use *tatzepao* in our rectification campaign in factories. The more we use, the better. If you have 10,000 sheets of *tatzepao* in your plant, that is first class. If you have 5,000 sheets, that is second class. If you have only a few scattered sheets here and there, then you don't count at all.[11]

In China today, *tatzepao* are used on a scale dramatically greater than in the Soviet Union. This phenomenon came as a shock to one Soviet visitor who travelled in China in 1958. Mikhail A. Klochko, a chemist who was sent to Peking from Moscow to work with his Chinese counterparts, later wrote:

> In China, the wall press is somewhat different. . . . But imagine my amazement when, arriving one morning, I found every wall of the vestibule and corridor literally papered with these multicolored sheets. On the second day, the sea of paper has risen up to the staircase, and, on the third day, it was all over the second floor. Apparently, the walls of every corridor were not sufficient to carry everything the Chinese wanted to say, for I found a line stretched down the middle of the hall with *tatzepao* hung from it like wash hung out to dry.[12]

Despite the appearance of hundreds of thousands of *tatzepao*, Klochko doubted the usefulness of all that gaudy display of paper, "for each sheet, after being shown for a few days, yielded its place to a new one or was simply covered over."[13]

The following is a description of the use of *tatzepao* on a university campus by Max Snurderl, professor of law at Ljubljana University in Yugoslavia and a member of the

Yugoslav National Assembly, who visited Peking in 1958. At the National University of Peking, Snurderl was told, "the students there had twice broken the record for writing posters in 1957 and 1958 . . . they had recently drawn 500,000 posters attacking waste and intolerance."[14] He also found "the making of posters had become the first and foremost method of general education and political indoctrination."[15] He continued:

> I found the flood of posters at every university, faculty, high school, and institution I visted in Peiping [Peking], Shanghai, Nanking and Wuchang. I was told that such posters could also be found in offices, hospitals, and elsewhere. . . . All the walls of the numerous buildings of the university, inside and out, were hung with posters as high as a man could reach! In front of the building, there were racks on which posters hung. Every corridor was decorated with posters. Strings were stretched across the corridors from one wall to another, with posters hanging from them like laundry hung to dry. You had to stoop in order to pass under them as you walked along the corridors.[16]

It is not surprising that both the Russian and Yugoslav visitors were fascinated and amazed by the extensive use of *tatzepao* for political indoctrination. For at no time in the entire course of Chinese history—indeed, in the history of any nation in the world—had such a medium of communication been so widely and shrewdly used.[17]

The *tatzepao* has no fixed format, length, or style.[18] It may contain slogans, satirical prose, comic strips, cartoons, letters of accusation, news reports, tables, graphs, or songs. It may be a short political slogan, such as *Kung Tsan Tang Wan Sui! Mao Tsu Hi Wan Sui!* (Long Live the Communist Party! Long Live Chairman Mao!), or a long essay that would cover a whole wall. While most *tatzepao* are handwritten papers posted on the wall, many are produced on blackboards, and it is not uncommon for *tatzepao* to be written with chalk on any kind of surface, including cement or wooden floors.

THE GROWING SIGNIFICANCE OF *TATZEPAO*

The modern use of *tatzepao* as a medium of political indoctrination in China dates back to the early 1930s, when
they appeared in the form of wall newspapers in every camp
of the Red Army—the military force of the Communist Party.
According to Edgar Snow, who spent some time sharing the
life of the Red Army and who finally became acquainted
with the Communist leaders, *tatzepao* were found in every
Lenin Club (a recreational area in an army camp).[19] A committee of soldiers was responsible for keeping the *tatzepao* up
to date. At that time, *tatzepao* were produced under the principles of the Lenin Club, which were as follows:

> All the life and activity in them [the club] must be connected
> with the daily work and development of men. It must be done by
> the men themselves. It must be simple and easy to understand. It
> must combine recreational value with practical education about
> the immediate tasks of the army.[20]

Snow also stated that the wall newspapers in the Lenin
Clubs "gave you a real insight into the soldier's problems and
a measure of his development."[21] The use of *tatzepao* not
merely as a means of information dissemination and political
indoctrination, as in Russia, but also as an instrument of
criticism and struggle became quite clear in the early years,
as Snow explains:

> . . . daily and weekly notices of the Communist Party and the
> Communist Youth League, a couple of columns of crude con-
> tributions by the newly literate, mostly revolutionary exhorta-
> tions and slogans; radio bulletins of Red Army victories in South
> Kansu; new songs to be learned, political news from the White
> areas; and, perhaps most interesting of all, two sections called
> the red and black columns, devoted respectively to praise and
> criticism.
>
> Praises consisted of tributes to the courage, bravery, unselfish-
> ness, diligence or other virtues of individuals or groups. In the

black column comrades lashed into each other and their officers (by name) for such things as failure to keep a rifle clean, slackness in study, losing a hand grenade or bayonet, smoking on duty, "political backwardness," "individualism," "reactionary habit," etc. . . . On one black column I saw a cook denounced for his "half-done" millet; in another a cook denounced a man for always "complaining" about his productions.[22]

The Chinese Communists began to use *tatzepao* as a major communication medium in 1942 during the Party rectification campaign, although on a limited scale.[23] It was during the brief Hundred Flowers period and the subsequent antirightest campaign in 1957 that *tatzepao* were first used on a dramatically large scale. The posters were regarded, in the course of that campaign, as the "most effective medium for criticism and self-criticism."[24]

This campaign started after Mao Tse-tung pleaded with China's intellectuals to speak out. A "democratic wall" was erected at Peking University on which concerned intellectuals were to express themselves. The wall, to Mao's surprise, soon bristled with frank and severe attacks on both the government and the Party. When the free speech movements were abruptly ended, the "democratic wall" was covered instead with attacks on the rightists. *Tatzepao* on the wall revealed the rightists' personal histories and their antirevolutionary activities. Poems, caricatures, and essays were featured in the Party's *tatzepao* counterattack. As a result of the campaign, hundreds of well-known intellectuals were dismissed from their posts and later purged.[25] It was the first victory scored by the use of *tatzepao* in a massive propaganda campaign.

The value of *tatzepao* was stressed explicitly by Teng Hsiao-ping, then Secretary of the Central Committee of the Chinese Communist Party, when commenting on the progress of the campaign:

Tatzepao should be used for the full and frank expression of opinions among workers. Such papers are simple in form, lively in style, attract attention easily, and they are convenient for mobilizing the masses. They are sharp and clear, vivid and colorful in criticizing the shortcomings of the leading personnel and workers and in raising rationalization proposals. The posters can gradually be turned into an important form for constantly developing criticism and self-criticism in the factories, offices, or schools.[26]

The growing significance of *tatzepao* was sanctioned by an editorial in the *People's Daily* on November 1, 1957:

The posters of all government organizations, educational institutions, and enterprises may gradually be turned into a regular weapon in pursuing much contending and debating.[27]

During the antiextravagance and anticonservatism movement in 1958, Chung Min, a member of the Shanghai Municipal Committee of the Chinese Communist Party, reported:

. . . the broad masses and cadres in Shanghai have produced slightly more than 100 million sheets of *tatzepao*. . . .

The Shipbuilding Yard posted 538,000 sheets of *tatzepao* in a short period of six or seven days.

Experience has told us: When jointly used with discussion meetings, accusation meetings, and debate sessions, *tatzepao* is the most effective method for solving the problems of internal contradiction among the people. *Tatzepao* is a driving force to enable us to accomplish our tasks; it is a form of pressure to those cadres who are at a low level of class consciousness. . . .

Tatzepao is something unique in our country of socialist democracy. It is the best instrument to bring to the open the problems of internal contradiction among the people, to solve problems, and thus to push forward progress. We should follow Comrade Mao's direction to develop and keep this particular instrument and to keep it forever.[28]

After the commune system was enforced in 1958, Wan Ching-liang, the First Secretary of the Party Committee of Patung, a small city near Shanghai, saluted the new system and again praised the massive use of *tatzepao*:

After the news about the people's communes appeared in newspapers last year, the broad masses of peasants in Patung welcomed the ideas enthusiastically and demanded speedy establishment of the commune. When the authorities decided to have the commune established, the masses posted more than 30,000 sheets of *tatzepao* in a few days resolutely asking to join the people's commune.[29]

During the "Double-Anti" campaign in 1958, more than 280,000 sheets of *tatzepao* were put up in Peking University within one month.[30] In Shanghai, more than 30,000,000 sheets of *tatzepao* were posted within one week by the 885,000 employees of the more than 3,300 enterprises. Almost every employee was thrown into the massive *tatzepao* writing campaign.[31]

In the same year, when the Heart Surrender movement was initiated, even more *tatzepao* were seen. According to incomplete statistics, more than 145,000 persons of the commercial and industrial circles in the major cities throughout the country participated in this movement and more than 33,000,000 *tatzepao* were produced by them.[32]

In addition to stimulating the active participation of huge masses of people in the propaganda campaigns, *tatzepao* also proved to be an extremely effective medium for criticism and self-criticism. An example was cited in the *People's Daily*.[33] The target of the attack, an engineer named Li Kwang-lun, was accused of the unforgivable sin of "individualism" by a technician in a *tatzepao* entitled: "The Grey Engineer." *Tatzepao* appeared in his office. As a matter of self-defense, Li put up a *tatzepao* entitled: "My Difficulties." But his explanation was rejected by his colleagues and severe attacks continued. According to the *People's Daily* story, Li, after repeated exposure to the *tatzepao*, finally accepted the criticisms of his colleagues. He in turn wrote a few dozen *tatzepao* exposing the various aspects of "extravagance," "waste," and "undesirable behavior" in his plant.

After *tatzepao* successfully proved its significance in various propaganda campaigns in 1958, the Chinese Communist Party ordered every government department and bureau to establish a *tatzepao* publishing unit and put up *tatzepao* regularly.[34]

On July 17, 1958, the *People's Daily* printed almost a full page to publicize the use of *tatzepao*. Its editorial, entitled "Long Live the *Tatzepao*," stated:

> The Chairman says: "*Tatzepao* is an extremely powerful weapon . . . it has been widely used and should be used permanently." . . . As a weapon, the effectiveness of *tatzepao* had been fully displayed in the rectification and double-anti campaigns. But now that the rectification movement is coming to an end, should *tatzepao* be used in the forthcoming campaigns? This remains doubtful to certain comrades. As we all know, we use *tatzepao* as a method to solve certain ideological and working problems. Therefore, as long as we can use it appropriately, it is perfectly clear that *tatzepao* "could be used permanently."[35]

The following excerpt from an interview conducted by Frederick Yu with a Chinese refugee who fled China in 1964 may illustrate the *tatzepao*'s importance in the mass mobilization movement.[36]

The scene is a village in Kwangtung Province in the spring of 1964. The campaign is "Socialist Education in the Countryside." The refugee participated in the campaign as a teacher, local cadre, and captain of a production brigade. He states:

> Among the most important media used in this campaign were the *tatzepao*. They were all over the village. Illiterate persons were expected to ask others who could write to produce a few sheets of *tatzepao*. A number of school children helped write the posters for some of their relatives and other illiterate villagers. . . . The wall newspapers carried brief reports and occasional drawings depicting villagers in different teams carrying on the campaign.[37]

It was the Cultural Revolution of 1966, however, that brought *tatzepao* to worldwide attention.

THE PURGE BY *TATZEPAO*—THE CULTURAL REVOLUTION

After the abdication of Mao Tse-tung from the state chair-manship in 1958, daily affairs were handled by Liu Shao-chi and Teng Hsiao-ping—with Mao pushed back to the second line. This situation continued until mid-1966.[38]

With the ideological differences between Mao and Liu growing wider and deeper, both realized that a duel for ulti-mate control of the nation was inevitable.[39] The two leaders also realized that control of the press and radio stations was of central importance if the leadership was to be secured. In this respect, Mao faced an extremely difficult task in attempt-ing to reach the masses; at that time all the official media were controlled by Liu's faction. The monolithic structure of the Propaganda Department of the Party further frustrated the Maoists because the department functioned hierarchical-ly, from Peking down to the village level, through a tight communications network. The system oriented all provincial propaganda departments toward Peking, where every impor-tant message originated. The establishment of rival appara-tus to the existing Propaganda Department was therefore essential before the power seizure campaign could be carried out effectively by the Maoists. They finally selected the young Red Guards as the counterpart to the official pro-pagandists, and they also decided to use *tatzepao* as their primary medium to compete with other official media.

The writing of the first Cultural Revolution *tatzepao* in Peking on May 25, 1966 brought the power struggle between the two factions into a new phase. That *tatzepao*'s author was Nieh Yuan-tzu, a woman teaching assistant in the Philos-ophy Department of Peking University (Peita).[40] Nieh, ap-parently acting on Mao's instruction, attacked Lu Ping, the university president and secretary of the university's Party Committee. The same *tatzepao* also called other Party of-ficials of the university revisionists who were trying to suppress the Cultural Revolution. It further charged that university officials had discouraged the writing of *tatzepao*.

> To counterattack the sinister gang which has frantically attacked the Party, socialism and Mao Tse-tung's thought is a life-and-death class struggle. The revolutionary people must be fully aroused to vigorously and angrily denounce them, and to hold big meetings and put up *tatzepao* as one of the best ways to do battle. By "guiding" the masses not to hold big meetings, not to put up big-character posters and by creating all kinds of taboos, aren't you suppressing the masses' revolution, not allowing them to make revolution and opposing their revolution? We will never permit you to do this.[41]

Radio Peking later revealed that those under attack had counterattacked with *tatzepao* labeling Nieh and others "anti-Party elements." Many at the university apparently believed that Lu Ping did represent the "correct view" and supported him. The officials held struggle meetings; teachers and students made criticism and self-criticism; in the process, several persons were injured. On June 2, the Peking press published the Nieh Yuan-tzu *tatzepao* along with the *People's Daily* editorial attacking Lu Ping's group as an "anti-party group." The official blessing on the stand of Nieh's *tatzepao* finally resulted in the dismissal of Lu Ping and the reorganization of the University Party Committee.[42]

This clearly marked the first victory in the "purge by *tatzepao*" undertaken by the Maoists. It also indicated that the Maoists were ready to direct more attacks against the headquarters of Liu's faction—the Central Committee of the Party.

In praising the Peita *tatzepao*, Mao himself had written a *tatzepao* in August to express his full support. He described the *tatzepao* by Nieh as the first Marxist-Leninist big-character poster in the country and approved the publication of its text in newspapers throughout the nation.

The following is a portion of Mao's *tatzepao*, entitled "Bombard the Headquarters—*My* Big-Character Poster."

China's first Marxist-Leninist big-character poster and commentator's article on it in *People's Daily* are indeed superbly written. Comrades, please read them again. But in the last fifty days or so, some leading comrades from the central down to the local level have acted in a diametrically opposite way. Adopting the reactionary stand of the bourgeoisie, they have enforced a bourgeois dictatorship and struck down the surging movement of the great Cultural Revolution of the proletariat. They have stood facts on their heads and juggled black and white, encircled and suppressed revolutionaries, stifled opinions different from their own, imposed a white terror, and felt very pleased with themselves. They have puffed up the arrogance of the bourgeoisie and deflated the morals of the proletariat. How poisonous![43]

With the full blessing of Mao, *tatzepao* flourished throughout the country at a time when so many of the official propaganda organs—city and provincial newspapers and radio stations—were under attack by the Maoists. The mass production of *tatzepao* reflected Mao's urgent need to establish the unofficial propaganda organs so that attacks on the Party and some of its leaders could be carried on.

The *tatzepao* that appeared during this period carried different ideas and reports than the official media.[44] These *tatzepao* often gave the initial report disclosing a leading official was in trouble. They reported speeches never released in the press—including some by Mao. They insulted the offenders directly, such as calling Liu Shao-chi a "dog's head," while the Peking press was still using euphemisms. They reported in detail how former Peking Mayor Peng Chen was arrested at night by students who "scaled his house and found him trembling in his bed." And sometimes they carried stories that Peking probably would have preferred to keep secret.

Since the *tatzepao* was not an official organ, it could violate official restrictions without being hampered. For instance, the press rarely attacked an individual by name after a special decision on the subject was adopted by the CPP Central Committee on August 8, 1966. The decision reads:

In the course of the mass movement of the Cultural Revolution, the criticism of bourgeois and feudal ideology should be well combined with the dissemination of the proletarian world outlook and of Marxism-Leninism, Mao Tse-tung thought.

Criticism should be directed against typical bourgeois representatives who have wormed their way into the Party and typical reactionary bourgeois academic authorities and this should include criticism of various kinds of reactionary views in philosophy, history, political economy, and education, in works and theories of literature and art, in theories of natural science, and in other fields. Criticism of anyone by name in the press should be decided after discussion by the Party Committee at the same level, and in some cases submitted to the Party Committee at the higher level for approval.[45]

As indicated, criticizing an individual by name in the press was a serious matter and therefore to be conducted with care. *Tatzepao*, however, as long as it was not official, enjoyed a free hand in conducting severe and direct attacks on individuals or groups.

Tatzepao, albeit unofficial, were welcomed by the masses. This was revealed by the *People's Daily* when clarifying how pro-Maoist *tatzepao* were to be regarded by the masses:

The attitude towards these revolutionary posters is an important yardstick in the current Great Proletarian Cultural Revolution by which to differentiate genuine from sham revolutionaries and proletarian revolutionaries from bourgeois royalists.

Are you a revolutionary? Then you are bound to welcome these posters, stand up for them, take a lead in writing them and encourage the masses to write them freely and freely reveal the problems.

Are you a royalist? Then you are bound to be scared to death of such posters . . . .

. . . We encourage the masses to write big-character posters in order to facilitate our struggle against the enemy.[46]

In the course of the "purge by *tatzepao*" campaign, Maoists faced a temporary setback when *tatzepao* began appearing in support of the intended victims. The Maoists lost their grip and the proliferating posters virtually became everybody's weapon. Posters attacking groups or individuals were plastered over with posters defending them. As one Party cadre described the *tatzepao*, they are like "reconnaissance by artillery. You fire a salvo or two and problems are exposed one by one. After that you analyze the materials by different sources and you come up with all kinds of information . . . "[47]

The following is an elaboration on one instance of the *tatzepao* attack and counterattack between the Maoists and anti-Maoists. It took place in the Shanghai Foreign Language Institute in the city of Shanghai. There were 2,000 students and roughly three hundred Chinese teachers in the institute. In addition to the Chinese teaching staff, there were about forty foreign teachers.[48] The first *tatzepao* to criticize the Party Committee appeared on the wall of the institute on June 3, 1966. Entitled "A Few Questions for Our Party Secretary," the *tatzepao* ran as follows:

> Why doesn't the Party Committee get this Cultural Revolution really moving? The whole country has been howling for months about these writers who have been attacking the Party, yet we didn't have a mass rally until yesterday—and that was only after the Peking University wall posters were publicized. We feel our Party Committee has been lagging behind. . . .
>
> The Party Secretary says that we can't put up posters in the corridor, because the foreign teachers might read them. He says we can't put them up on the campus, because the foreign teachers might go for a walk and see them. He says the dining room is no good either, because the foreign teachers might go in there. Would you mind telling us just where can we put them? To say we can write *tatzepao*, and then to add that the foreigners must not see them, is equivalent to saying we cannot write posters.
>
> If the Party Secretary cares to wander around, he will see that the posters have gone up anyway. Does he now want us to take them down? We invite everybody to comment on these questions.[49]

The Party Secretary's response was fast and shrewd. He signed and put up a *tatzepao* in the institute on the same day. In his poster, however, he did not reply directly to the questions involved. He turned the challenge aside by calling for an all-out war on the "bourgeois academics." This is an example of how Maoists' political criticisms were sidetracked by anti-Maoists into a less dangerous field.[50] The significant role of *tatzepao* in the power struggle campaign was reiterated on two separate occasions:

In June 1966, an editorial in the *People's Daily* stated:

> The revolutionary big-character poster is a mirror to expose all kinds of ogres. It is an effective method of mobilizing the masses to attack the enemy violently. All anti-Party and antisocialism persons are afraid of big-character posters. All revolutionary masses like big-character posters.[51]

Two months later, the same kind of attitude was revealed in the *Red Flag*.

> The big-character poster is a powerful weapon which these young leaders use to attack those overt and covert factions in power who follow the capitalist road, and all demons and freaks. Their big-character posters, like sword and daggers, hit the vital part of the enemy and make his sore spot hurt.[52]

It took the Maoists almost three years before they could pronounce the completion of the power seizure. If the Maoists had had to struggle with their opponents without the aid of the *tatzepao*, the outcome might have been different.

THE *TATZEPAO* WRITING CRAZE IN CHINA

One may well call the Cultural Revolution the "poster revolution." Indeed, during the year when the power struggle between the two factions went on, millions of *tatzepao* appeared on the walls of the major cities in China—from Peking and Shanghai to some remote border cities.

In an article in the *Peking Review*, the mushrooming of

big-character wall newspapers was described as "a sea of revolutionary criticism":

> Big-character poster wall newspapers are mushrooming in the streets of Peking, Shanghai, and other cities. The revolutionary masses—workers, soldiers, young Red Guard fighters, and others—have written hundreds of thousands of big-character posters denouncing China's Khrushchev and his followers and a handful of Party people taking the capitalist road. Big-character posters are an effective weapon widely used in the Great Cultural Revolution by the revolutionary masses, who enjoy the right of extensive democracy in this medium as in the free airing of views in meetings and discussions and in great debates.
>
> At the start of the Cultural Revolution, the revolutionary masses wrote countless big-character posters putting forward their opinions and exposing contradictions from different angles.[53]

The appearance of wall newspapers was also described by the *Peking Review* as "written forms of creatively studying and applying Chairman Mao's works" and "mass criticism meetings without a meeting place."[54] To the Red Guards, the wall newspapers in the streets "are shells raining down on China's Khrushchev."[55] They *(tatzepao)* are classrooms propagating Mao Tse-tung's thought. They have made clear to the masses "the heinous crimes of China's Khrushchev in opposing Chairman Mao's proletarian revolution line, in plotting to usurp the Party, army, and government leadership and in bringing about an all-round capitalist restoration."[56]

Mao himself had reiterated the importance of *tatzepao* on several occasions. Here is one example:

> The big-character poster is an extremely useful new type of weapon. It can be used in cities and the countryside, government and other organizations, army units and streets, in short, wherever the masses are. Now that it has been widely used, people should go on using it constantly.[57]

How did the Chinese people react to the posting of these *tatzepao?* A Chinese interpreter had the following to say when he was interviewed by Louis Barcata, a French writer who traveled in China during the Cultural Revolution:

> The wall newspapers had achieved an extraordinary significance in China's domestic politics. It was the first time for many years that internal political movement had not been launched by the Communist Party leadership, but had sprung from the depth of the people.[58]

Then he continued to discuss why the people picked the *tatzepao* as the medium to express themselves:

> The regular newspapers do not have enough space to include criticism. We needed tens of thousands of square kilometers in the papers to air our problems and then, also in writing, to let our readers have their say. The answer can differ from province to province, from city to city, even from street to street. Only when we gather all these responses, shall we be able to develop a reliable picture of what the nation is thinking. In addition, the people desired to be in control. They wanted to find their voice; they do not want to be regimented.[59]

Did the leadership then follow the demands of the wall newspapers? The interpreter answered:

> In local affairs, yes. It's rather simple to do this on the local level, of course. It is easier to decide whether a court was just in its verdict, whether a policeman was brutal, whether a chair factory was sensibly organized, than it is to work out new guidelines for our national economic policy. Similarly, changes in our social structure cannot be accomplished overnight. It will take years before the ideas being bandied about in the wall newspapers can be applied and ideologically scrutinized ... You must remember that the Cultural Revolution not only has to fight the class struggle at home, it has to prepare our great country for the confrontation with foreign enemies.[60]

The study of *tatzepao* by the masses was again elaborated by Louis Barcata. The account was written during his stay in the city of Canton in Kwangtung province.

In one respect, the center of Canton was just like its suburbs. Wall newspapers supplanted other wall newspapers. Some of these were works of art, executed with traditional refinement of masters of caligraphical art. Others were coarse and loud, with Chinese characters the size of a book. A few hung from apartment or office windows in streamers. In one of the downtown squares, some Red Guards were in the process of mounting a new edition to the walls. They ordered the people who pressed forward to step back, and everyone obeyed the order—without a single demurrer . . . They allowed themselves to be arrayed in long columns until they were close enough to read the news. They did their reading attentively, without hurry.[61]

The writer, however, pointed out that all those reading were young people. He said the workers passed by the wall newspapers in silence and did not take part in the study. Nevertheless, one may conclude that this was the period when millions of Chinese were engaged in either writing or studying the posters. Indeed, the Maoists, with the help of the Red Guards, had skillfully converted the writing, reading, and studying of *tatzepao* into a political obligation. Anyone who resisted this obligation would be viewed as a reactionary element. The suppression of the writing of *tatzepao*, to the Maoists, was an unforgivable sin.

THE PRODUCTION OF *TATZEPAO*

Long before the Cultural Revolution, the masses were frequently encouraged to participate in the *tatzepao*-writing campaigns in which criticism and self-criticism were made known. The masses were allowed to criticize Party members who had committed errors. Sometimes the target of a *tatzepao* attack could even be one's next-door neighbor.

As mentioned previously, *tatzepao* have no standard format. A *tatzepao* is a large sheet of cheap paper, sometimes a used newspaper, with words more than an inch high written on it, pasted on the walls of an office building or on bamboo mats especially erected for the purpose. The *tatzepao* may be signed, by a person or by a group, or it may be unsigned. (Figures 7–1 and 7–2.)

For years, normal procedure has been that after a *tatzepao* is prepared, it is handed to the committee of Party members, who put it up according to the order in which it is received.[62]

It would be wrong to think that the writing of *tatzepao* is spontaneous. In some cities, the writing of *tatzepao* has become a formalized affair run almost like a newspaper, complete with "editorial board, production center, correspondent network and distribution center."[63] Those who cannot write could seek help from the special "*tatzepao* writing stations."[64]

One of the main functions of those specially picked propagandists of the Party is the preparation of posters or other materials, and editing *tatzepao*.[65]

FIGURE 7–1. Sketch in the *People's Daily* (November 22, 1976) shows a group of Chinese writing *tatzepao* to condemn the "Gang of Four."

FIGURE 7-2. A group of Chinese are shown discussing what to put down in their *tatzepao* while the person designated to be the writer (holding a brush) waits. At this moment, their *tatzepao* has only a headline: "Down with the anti-Party faction of the Gang of Four!" (*People's Daily*, November 29, 1976)

During the Cultural Revolution, the production of *tatzepao* became totally institutionalized by the Maoists. Since most of the *tatzepao* were produced by the Red Guards and the "revolutionary masses," the main theme of *tatzepao* was thus controlled by the Maoist faction. According to the official releases, all *tatzepao* were produced under the inspiration of "Mao's thought, support, concern and encouragement."[66]

In practice, the Red Guard communications network originated from its leadership—the Maoists. Directives were issued by the faction to the various Red Guard organizations, and the strategically located groups transmitted this policy statement downward to the publication team and also to the mass of the Red Guards. Then both the publication team and members of the Red Guards swung into operation. They produced *tatzepao* based on the direction from above. This completed the chain of information from the Maoist leadership to the Chinese population. In response to the Maoist *tatzepao*, the mass of people then produced *tatzepao* to voice their reaction, which served the valuable purpose of feedback.[67]

From this, one can see that the *tatzepao*-writing campaign during the Cultural Revolution was conducted in the form of mass communication. Not only was opinion voiced from above, the masses could also respond to the contents of the posters by putting up their own *tatzepao*. A single-lined communication had become a two-way street. Therefore, the Chinese authorities had not only skillfully used *tatzepao* as a propaganda machine but had also converted it into a form of mass communication.

THE RELIABILITY OF *TATZEPAO*

Churo Nishimura, a Japanese correspondent of *Yomiuri Shimbun*, after his return to his home base from China in 1967, remarked that all foreign correspondents residing in Peking were observing the Cultural Revolution "through the peephole of wall newspapers."[68]

Indeed, at the early stage of the revolution, the main sources of information to all foreign correspondents dried up completely. All newspapers and broadcasting stations repeated day after day the country's enthusiasm in learning and applying the sayings of Mao according to the instruction of Lin Piao.[69] The Propaganda Department had been purged after most of its senior officials were dismissed and many of its communication organs dissolved. The two major news organs of China, the New China News Agency and the *People's Daily*, remained silent for months on all events that were rocking China and arousing the curiosity of the entire world. The whole country, to most of the foreigners, was in a state of great confusion. Thus, *tatzepao* became the principal source of information available to outsiders on the events and progress of the Cultural Revolution.[70] For many months, newspapers from all parts of the world relied heavily on the reports dispatched by the Japanese correspondents. Those correspondents, in turn, were totally dependent on what was appearing from day to day in the wall posters that appeared by the hundreds and thousands on the walls of streets and buildings.

However, even to some Chinese, *tatzepao* seemed unreliable and confused. A Japanese correspondent, Takeo Takagi, had the following experience in 1966 when he was copying *tatzepao* in Peking:

> One day when he [Takagi] was engrossed in one of the wall posters, a kindly-looking man came up to him and offered some service:
>
> "Don't believe it! It's all a rumor."
>
> "It is?" asked the reporter.
>
> "Yes. It's got to be a rumor. Tomorrow there will probably be another poster criticizing this," he said.
>
> "But I still think it is interesting," answered Takagi.
>
> "It might be interesting to foreigners, but these reports are either groundless or exaggerated. If one of the Red Guards cuts his finger in a minor clash, they will report the fracas the next day as a bloody tragedy," the man said.[71]

The reliability of *tatzepao*, however, depends on the purposes for which the posters are used. When used in a power struggle such as the Cultural Revolution, in which two factions contended for political supremacy, the *tatzepao* would reflect the many accusations and counteraccusations which may or may not have a factual basis. The Chinese people probably have learned to recognize this possibility, as suggested by the man who talked with correspondent Takagi, and take the poster content with a grain of salt.

In an officially proclaimed campaign, on the other hand, such as the one in 1974 and 1975 to criticize Confucius and Lin Piao, people write *tatzepao* to voice their support by denouncing the Party-designated targets. The content of the *tatzepao* would probably reflect the writers' varying degrees of individual creativity in interpreting the Party policy, and the question of reliability normally does not arise.

Occasionally, the *tatzepao* has been used by individuals to air a minor grievance or to expose the errors of local cadre. Such a complaint would most likely be made on a factual basis. For instance, the *New York Times* had this report in 1972:

> In Shanghai, glued to a shop window, was the following: "I brought a watch here to be repaired. The people in this shop told me that the watch was in such a bad state that it could not be repaired. I then took the watch to another shop where it was repaired in two days. How does one explain this? Obviously, this shop does not serve the people."[72]

If the practice of submitting a *tatzepao* to a responsible Party cadre for prior approval is widely followed, posters of this nature would most probably be quite reliable.

More recently, the Chinese authorities seem to be experimenting with the use of *tatzepao* as an oblique instrument for revealing important political events. The purge of Chiang Ching and her followers in October, 1976 preceding the appointment of Hua Kuo-feng as the new Party chairman provides an example. Following the announcement on October 9, 1976 that the "task of publishing Chairman Mao's works would be carried out by the Central Politburo directly under the leadership of Hua," many wall posters soon appeared in Peking, Shanghai, and Canton to welcome this decision. This was the first indication that Hua had been chosen the Party's new leader.[73] Two days later, stories began to circulate in Peking that Chiang Ching and her allies had been put under house arrest. But the official announcement of their arrest and Hua's new appointment did not come until more than a week later. In this case, the *tatzepao* were accurate indicators of an important political decision.

CONTENTS OF THE CULTURAL REVOLUTION
TATZEPAO

The Chinese Communist leaders have prescribed various responsibilities for *tatzepao* on different occasions. After examining most of the *tatzepao* that are available, this writer divides them into three categories: news reports; directives, orders, and proposals; and criticism. The following is an analysis of the contents of the *tatzepao* posted during the Cultural Revolution.

TATZEPAO AS NEWS REPORTS

As the power struggle between the two factions intensified in 1966, many newspapers were reorganized or else simply ceased publication.[74] The *People's Daily* was no exception. It was seized and finally reorganized by military personnel. The same situation prevailed at the radio stations. It was at this time that the *tatzepao* began to emerge as a news medium and fed the information-hungry Chinese with news the Red Guards wanted to make known. Therefore, most of the items publicized were records or remarks of Red Guard meetings.

For instance, *tatzepao* appearing in Peking reported the brief minutes of a forum in People's Hall in Peking on December 18, at which representatatives of the First and Second Revolutionary Rebel Liaison Center General Headquarters, the Third Headquarters, the Capital Corps, and revolutionary groups of some capital colleges and universities were in attendance. The major speaker of the forum was Chiang Ching, wife of Mao Tse-tung, who warned Red Guards of their abuses in Peking. The *tatzepao*, devoted primarily to the comments, quotes:

> These days I have heard that you [groups represented at the forum] had arrested many persons. I am very afraid that you have made mistakes in doing this. . . . Those you have arrested should be handed over to the Ministry of Public Security for detention and question. . . . You could not hold persons privately and limit any person's freedom without suffering the consequences for such actions.
>
> Some may ask: What kind of person could be arrested? The Central Cultural Revolution Committee answers: Those who put up *tatzepao* attacking Chairman Mao and Vice-Chairman Lin

Piao should be arrested. When there is a *tatzepao* attacking
Chiang Ching, we must consider its motives. We should arrest
the one who wrote it if it was a malicious attack. Besides, all
those who used violence should be arrested.[75]

Regardless of the accuracy of the reports carried by the
tatzepao, the significant point is that these *tatzepao* had successfully taken up the function of a news medium, although
their contents were still limited if compared with a standard
newspaper.

TATZEPAO AS DIRECTIVES, ORDERS, AND PROPOSALS

As described earlier, the communications system in China
collapsed after the Maoists began their power seizure campaign. And before the new system could be established by
either of the factions, *tatzepao* served as a substitute medium
to transmit directives and orders from above and proposals
and requests from below. Here are a few such examples.

After the Red Guards were officially formed in Peking in
August, 1966, students from all parts of China were encouraged to make trips to Peking to "study the revolutionary
spirit." The following *tatzepao* was one such plea to the Party Central by some students from a Shanghai school that they
be allowed to go to Peking. The poster, entitled "We Ask to
Be Allowed to Go to Peking," was signed by the senior
graduating class students of the Resistance to U.S. Military-
Political Middle School, Shanghai, on September 2, 1966.
The poster reads:

> It is our great desire and dream to go to Peking to see Chairman
> Mao. The sight of him would give us infinite strength. We are
> graduating students, the generation that counts in the Chinese
> and the world revolution. It is for us to guarantee that the
> bloody sacrifice for the country of the old revolutionaries was
> not in vain. . . . [76]

During the Cultural Revolution, major industrial cities

such as Shanghai were almost paralyzed when most of the factory workers left their posts to participate in the movement. Industrial production was brought to a standstill. In early 1967, workers were told to return to the factories to resume their work; at the same time, students were "encouraged" to go to the countryside to take part in the agricultural production. A Peking *tatzepao* entitled "To Worker Comrades Who Have Left Their Production Posts" was a message urging the workers to return to their posts.[77]

The official communication organs, as mentioned earlier, did not criticize or attack Liu Shao-chi and his followers by name. Even some of the Red Guard posters held by this rule. Instead, they used terms such as "the powerful scoundrels who walk the captialist path," "handful of power holders within the Party," and "a bunch of old bourgeois individuals" to indicate the targets. The following *tatzepao*, however, is an exception. It contained an order that all photographs of Liu Shao-chi and Teng Hsiao-ping be destroyed. The *tatzepao* of January 4, 1967 was signed by the *Tung Fang Hung* (East is Red) Commune of Hsin Hua Book Store Storage and Transportation Company.

> To all Hsin Hua Book Stores, industrial and mining enterprises, government organs, and schools: For the sake of thoroughly toppling the bourgeois reactionary line represented by Liu Shao-chi and Teng Hsiao-ping and defending the proletarian revolutionary line represented by Chairman Mao, all Hsin Hua Book Stores, industrial and mining enterprises, schools, government organs, and residents are ordered to smash and destroy all photographs of Liu and Teng which they have kept or hung up. . . .[78]

One interesting point of this poster was that the Chinese characters of Liu Shao-chi and Teng Hsiao-ping were all written in a reversed (upside-down) style. Later in the revolution, this became a common practice for humiliating the target figure of the *tatzepao*.

TATZEPAO AS CRITICISM

The use of *tatzepao* as an instrument of mass criticism and struggle is a unique Chinese phenomenon. Most of the *tatzepao* appearing during the Cultural Revolution belonged to this category. Those were the most vivid and earthy posters of this particular period. They criticized the ideology of the anti-Maoists and gave in addition lengthy and descriptive accounts of their daily lives. (Figures 7–3, 7–4.) The following are typical examples from this category.

Tao Chu, the short-termed director of the Propaganda Department, who rose to prominence at the early stage of the movement, was described by Red Guards in 1967 in this way:

> Tao Chu belongs to the landlord class by origin. . . . He thinks all the time of his dog-ancestors. When his mother died, he asked the Kwangtung Provincial Committee to send on his behalf a telegram saying: "I am unfilial because I could not pay for your upkeep when you were alive [referring to his mother] nor could I come to attend your funeral. . . . " What was especially serious was that he made use of his functions and powers to send his dog-mother a wreath in the name of the Central South Bureau.[79]

An undated poster exposed an affair between Tao Chu and a Cantonese opera actress, Hung Hsien-nui.[80]

One of the main targets of the Red Guards was Teng Hsiao-ping. On February 18, 1967, the Red Guards published the following exposé on Teng:

> Through playing bridge together, Teng Hsiao-ping formed an unbreakable friendship with these counterrevolutionaries and demons and monsters. In those several years, when they were not gone to other areas on official business, they always gathered together every Wednesday and Saturday night and every Sunday afternoon and evening, and there played games to their heart's content. In addition, during office hours Teng and Wan would ask their secretaries to invite the henchmen of the black gang to report for duty [slang used by Teng and his "gang" meaning to play bridge or other games]. While they enjoyed

FIGURE 7–3. Chinese peasants shown posting *tatzepao* to criticize the Gang of Four for their sin of sabotaging the movement to learn from Tachai in agriculture." (*People's Daily*, November 21, 1976)

themselves, they were served high-class food and hors d'oeuvres from Peking Restaurant. They often played for five to six or seven to eight hours at a stretch, carrying on till one or two o'clock in the morning. . . . [81]

Not only were members of Liu's faction attacked, their relatives also received the same treatment from the Red

FIGURE 7–4. In a rally in Canton, a poster depicts Chiang Ching and her followers impaled on a bayonet. (*Time*, November 8, 1976, p. 52)

Guards. For example, several posters carefully examined the in-laws of Liu Shao-chi and found his father-in-law to be a "bureaucrat-bourgeois" and his brother-in-law a capitalist. Liu was accused of helping his brother-in-law to rise in the Federation of Industry and Commerce. As one poster explained: "Liu Shao-chi chose to establish ties with this wicked family by marriage. It can be seen that he had long ago ceased to be a Communist cadre and a true Communist." What is worse, when Liu's father-in-law died in 1956, Liu was brazen enough to attend his memorial service and send a wreath. The poster pointed out that this "fully exposed the ugly bourgeois soul of Liu Shao-chi."[82]

CONCLUSION

Why is *tatzepao* so extensively used in China? As a communication medium, how efficient and powerful is it? What
is its impact on the masses? These are some of the questions
this study attempts to answer.

First, the *tatzepao* is widely used because it is an inexpensive medium. Because most of the *tatzepao* are handwritten
on inexpensive paper, sometimes even on used newsprint, the
Chinese authorities need not invest much capital in this
medium, as compared to the operational costs of newspapers
and radio stations. Second, a *tatzepao* is usually written by
and about local people whom its readers know. Even when it
concerns a particular national campaign or movement, the
readers will more likely become interested when its main
theme is given a local angle. It is because of this local appeal
that the Chinese authorities have used *tatzepao* for agitation
and criticism. Third, of all the media employed in China, only *tatzepao* can involve the audience as active participants,
both as readers and producers.

As to the target of *tatzepao* attack, the impact is severe and
immediate; above all, it cannot be ignored or dismissed. In a
campaign of criticism, *tatzepao* could appear on the wall of
one's office or even the door of one's house. In short,
wherever there are walls, there are likely to be *tatzepao*
pointing to the "crimes" and "sins" of the target figure. The
local community will most likely be influenced by the opinions expressed in the *tatzepao*. This is one aspect a newspaper
could not accomplish in such an efficient manner, for it is
physically impossible to involve both itself and most of its
readers directly in the campaign. A newspaper can print only
a limited number of stories attacking an individual or group,
and usually cannot employ local appeals effectively because
of its heterogeneous audience. A *tatzepao* assault, however,
once started, is direct and personal. As one scholar on the
Chinese communication system has pointed out, virtually

everyone in China today is within the reach of *tatzepao* and is in one way or another involved in this particular form of persuasion.[83]

What has actually inspired the Communist leaders to use the *tatzepao* with such vigor and confidence? To answer this, one must refer to the communication theory of the Chinese Communist Party. For years, the Chinese propagandists have stressed two aspects of communication theory: the "mass line" and the "unity of theory and practice." The *People's Daily* once editorialized: "The fundamental policy of the Party is the policy of the mass line."[84] This means that every policy enforced by the Party should be desired and demanded by the masses. In more contemporary terms, the Party's policy should be a "popular choice," to be enforced on "popular demand." The whole process could be outlined in a simple formula: The policy and practices of the Party must originate from the masses and go back to the masses,[85] even though not all the suggestions, opinions, and ideas will be accepted by the Party.

The *tatzepao* is a medium tailor-made to comply with the "mass line" theory. As Mao pointed out earlier on the principle of "from the masses, to the masses," the *tatzepao* as a medium is used in almost every "to and from" process. In the first half of the process—from the masses—*tatzepao* can reflect the desires and demands of the masses. Although most of these demands and desires are either inspired or influenced by the Party propagandists, the emergence of these opinions does give the readers an impression that such expressions are spontaneous. When these messages are transmitted to the Party organs, and after a decision is reached by the Party, the same medium, together with other media such as newspapers and radio stations, will then be used to disseminate the decision of the Party back to the masses and the whole process is completed.

The "unity of theory and practice"—the application of theory to one's work—is another main emphasis in the com-

munication theory of the Chinese Communist Party. In today's China, the leadership would allow neither opposition to
the Party's policy nor the passive acceptance of its doctrine
from the masses. In other words, the Party leaders expect
everyone in the nation to engage in the active practice of
Communist ideology.

To achieve this aim, the Peking government since 1949
has initiated numerous mass movements in which the whole
nation was engaged. In the progress of these movements,
large-scale campaigns for different sections of the population
were conducted. During these movements and campaigns,
the *tatzepao* has been constantly used as the medium to involve the masses in an active participation. As illustrated
earlier, the Chinese are told by Party officials to hand in a
certain number of *tatzepao* before a certain deadline so as to
demonstrate their support for the campaign. This virtually
puts everybody into action—and almost no one in the nation
can avoid this obligation.

Indeed, Chinese Communism is a "working ideology" that
requires everyone under its rule to demonstrate his adherence
to the ideology through action. For years, the use of *tatzepao*
has effectively called up the masses to participate actively
and vigorously in the movements designed by the Party.

It would be impossible to calculate the power and efficiency of *tatzepao* as a communication medium. No medium in
the huge and tightly controlled communication network of
China could be singled out for a measure of its efficiency
because the various media are jointly used and closely coordinated. It would be possible, however, to discuss the effects
of *tatzepao* according to its objectives. When the *tatzepao* is
used for disseminating news reports, as during the Cultural
Revolution when there was an information vacuum, we have
reason to believe that the effects can be considerable. During
the chaotic months of 1966, it was from the *tatzepao* that the
Chinese learned what was going on. When the posters are
used as a carrier of political attack on a national scale, cer-

tain results can be expected. During the Cultural Revolution, for instance, the Maoist groups were able to use the *tatzepao* as one of their weapons to disrupt the Party organization under Liu Shao-chi, and to involve the Red Guards in a mass movement that eventually paved the way for the seizure of power by the radicals. In small local groups, when tens of hundreds of *tatzepao* zero in on a target figure, the effects of group pressure can be overwhelming, as we have illustrated earlier. It is in the area of persuasion—when the Party uses the *tatzepao* for such purposes as trying to convince the Chinese that Confucius was an evil or that Teng Hsiao-ping was a capitalist follower—that the effectiveness of the wall posters becomes uncertain. It seems that in this respect the posters have no particular advantage over any of the other mass media such as newspapers and radio.

Tatzepao seem to have certain latent effects that are unintended by the Party. Because it is often a group activity, producing *tatzepao* can have the effect of promoting group integration among those who work as a team. This phenomenon seems to be more pronounced when people need the support of a group at a time of social disintegration, as during the Cultural Revolution.[86] Another unintended effect, one that may have long-term significance, is the role of *tatzepao* in fomenting activism among the Chinese. It seems that after the Chinese have been repeatedly urged to participate in Party-organized *tatzepao* campaigns, they may have acquired both the skill and the propensity to engage in such activities more or less for their own purposes. Such an instance took place during the campaign against Lin Piao and Confucius. Taking advantage of the opportunity of criticism, some people in Peking, including a worker who employed the pseudonym "Golden Monkey," posted *tatzepao* that proved to be embarrassing to the Party authorities.[87]

Indeed, the *tatzepao* has become a new social institution guaranteed by the Constitution.[88] Although initially directed and organized by the Party authorities, the posters seem to have acquired a tenure of their own that is quite distinctively part of the new Chinese cultural patterns.

NOTES

1. See Frederick Yu, *Mass Persuasion in Communist China* (New York: Praeger Publishers, 1964), p. 137.

2. Barry M. Broman, "Tatzepao: Medium of Conflict in China's 'Cultural Revolution,' " *Journalism Quarterly* 46:1 (Spring, 1969): 100.

3. James W. Markham, *Voices of the Red Giants* (Ames: Iowa State University Press, 1967), p. 350.

4. Ibid., p. 75.

5. Ibid.

6. Ibid.

7. Yu, *Mass Persuasion*, p. 40.

8. Edgar Snow, *Red Star over China* (New York: Random House, 1938), p. 135.

9. Ibid.

10. *Hsueh Hsi* 12 (June 18, 1958): 20–21.

11. Ibid., p. 21.

12. Mikhail A. Klochko, *Soviet Scientist in China* (New York: Praeger Publishers, 1962), p. 70.

13. Ibid., p. 73.

14. Yu, *Mass Persuasion*, p. 138.

15. Ibid.

16. Ibid.

17. Ibid.

18. For a description on the format of *tatzepao*, see Yu, *Mass Persuasion*, p. 140 and Markham, *Voices*, p. 114.

19. Snow, *Red Star*, p. 309.

20. Ibid.

21. Ibid., p. 310.

22. Ibid.

23. Vincent King, *Propaganda Campaigns in Communist China* (Cambridge, Mass.: The M.I.T. Press, 1966), p. 79.

24. *Chinese Literature* 6 (November-December, 1958): 14.

25. For discussions on the antirightist campaign, see Jack Gray and Patrick Cavendish, *Chinese Communism in Crisis* (New York: Praeger Publishers, 1968), pp. 30, 78. Also see Roderick MacFarquhar, *The Hundred Flowers Campaign and the Chinese Intellectuals* (New York: Praeger Publishers, 1960).

26. *People's Daily*, October 19, 1957.

27. *People's Daily*, November 1, 1957.

28. *Hsueh Hsi* 12 (June 18, 1958): 20–21.

29. *People's Daily*, November 23, 1957.

30. *People's Daily*, March 28, 1958.

31. *New China Semi-Monthly* 9 (1958): 12.

32. *New China Semi-Monthly* 10 (1958): 30.

33. *New China Semi-Monthly* 12 (1958): 22.

34. *Jen Min Chiao Yu* 93:6 (1958): 19.

35. *People's Daily*, March 27, 1958.

36. The interview was published in Yu, *Mass Persuasion*, pp. 7–9.

37. Ibid., p. 8.

38. See Mao's speech on October 26, 1966.

39. Gray and Cavendish, *Chinese Communism*, pp. 114–152.

40. Franklin W. Houn, *A Short History of Chinese Communism* (Englewood Cliffs, N.J.: Prentice-Hall, 1967), p. 125.

41. *Peking Review*, September 9, 1966.

42. Details of the incident were broadcast in the New China News Agency domestic service from Peking on June 5, 1966.

43. *Peking Review*, August 11, 1966.

44. *Current Scene* (Hong Kong), May 31, 1967, p. 4.

45. The decision "The Question of Criticising by Name in the Press" was quoted from *The Great Cultural Revolution in China*, compiled and edited by the Asia Research Centre (Rutland, Vt.: Charles E. Tuttle Co., 1968), p. 402.

46. New China News Agency, June 20, 1966.

47. *Wen Wei Pao* (Hong Kong), October 31, 1966.

48. Neale Hunter, *Shanghai Journal* (New York: Praeger Publishers, 1969), p. 44.

49. Ibid., pp. 44–45.

50. Ibid.

51. *People's Daily*, June 16, 1966.

52. *Red Flag* 11 (August, 1966).

53. *Peking Review*, September 15, 1967, p. 22.

54. Ibid., p. 23.

55. Liu Shao-chi was nicknamed China's Khrushchev by the Maoists during the Cultural Revolution.

56. *Peking Review*, September 15, 1967.

57. *Peking Review*, September 11, 1967.

58. Louis Barcata, *China in the Throes of the Cultural Revolution* (New York: Hart Publishing Co., 1968), pp. 101–103.

59. Ibid.

60. Ibid.

61. Barcata, *China in the Throes*, pp. 48–49.

62. Mu Fu-sheng, *The Wilting of the Hundred Flowers* (New York: Praeger Publishers, 1962), p. 159.

63. Yu, *Mass Persuasion*, p. 149.

64. Ibid., p. 140.

65. Ibid., p. 80.

66. New China News Agency (Shanghai), March 5, 1967.

67. Barry M. Broman, "Tatzepao: Medium of Conflict in China's 'Cultural Revolution,' " *Journalism Quarterly* 46:1 (Spring, 1969): 104, 127.

68. Robert Trumbull, ed., *This is Communist China* (New York: David McKay Co., 1968), p. 56.

69. *China News Analysis* (Hong Kong), January 6, 1967, p. 1.

70. Ibid., p. 2.

71. Trumbull, *Communist China*, p. 65.

72. James Chace, "The Five-Power World of Richard Nixon," *New York Times Magazine*, February 20, 1972, p. 34.

73. "Great Purge in the Forbidden City," *Time*, October 25, 1976, pp. 25–32.

74. The mass media in China received the severest blow in the revolution. When the revolution began to gain momentum in early 1966, Mao personally directed attacks on newspapers and journals. In May, the *People's Daily*, the official organ of the Central Committee and the most authoritative newspaper in the nation, was severely criticized by the Maoist *Liberation Army Daily*. The former was consequently taken over and reorganized by the military personnel. In June, Chen Po-ta, Mao's secretary, seized the editorship of the paper.

Among the seven national newspapers published before the Cultural Revolution, four were suspended in 1966. The *China Youth Daily* of the Young Communist League and the *Chinese Workers' Daily* of the All-China Labor Union Federation both ceased publication after the associated mass organization was dissolved. *Ta Kung Pao*, a nonpartisan newspaper, folded up on September 10 after adopting "demands and suggestions from the Red Guards, the revolutionary masses, and the majority readers, and receiving approval from the superior." Another newspaper, *Progressive Daily*, was printed in the same printing press after that date. However, the new daily did not last long enough to survive throughout the revolution. The fourth, *Sports News*, was suspended in November.

By the end of 1966, the "revolutionary masses" took over or suspended the following local newspapers: *Peking Morning News*, *Peking Evening News*, *Ta Chung Pao* (Public Daily), *Hupei Daily*, *Hunan Daily*, *Kwangsi Daily*, *Nan Fong Daily* (Southern Daily) of Kwangtung Province, *Canton*

Daily, Yang Chen Daily of Canton, *Kwei Chow Daily, Kongsi Daily, Liberation Daily, Wen Wei Pao* and *Sun Wen Man Pao* (New Citizen Evening News) of Shanghai. More than forty-two journals, including both national and provincial, were suspended before the end of 1966.

In the spring of 1966, Lu Ting-i, director of the Propaganda Department, was arrested by Red Guards and tried before a mass meeting in Peking. Consequently, Lu and four of his deputy directors—Chou Yang, Lin Mu-han, Wu Lan-si, and She Li-chuan—were dismissed. The propaganda chief of the Central-South Bureau, Wang Kuang, who supervised propaganda campaigns in five provinces, was also purged after a series of *tatzepao* attacks was launched against him. In the following months, the propaganda departments of eight provincial Party Committees were purged.

With the aid of *tatzepao*, more than two hundred fifty leading newspaper editors, propagandists, and leaders of arts had been removed from their posts. Other major national, provincial, and municipal newspapers and journals were either suspended or reorganized.

In early 1967, when the purge of the senior propagandists in the Party's Propaganda Department was carried out successfully, Maoists finally claimed total control over the major mass media in the country. (See Ting Wong, *Commentaries on the Cultural Revolution* [Hong Kong: Contemporary China Research Center, 1967], pp. 12–13, 57, 186–187, 190–194).

75. Original text of the poster appeared in *Samples of Red Guard Publication* (Washington, D.C.: Joint Publication Research Services, 1967), pp. 14–16.

76. The translation of the poster was quoted from *China News Analysis*, November 11, 1966, p. 7.

77. The text and translation of the poster appeared in *Samples*, pp. 20–21.

78. Ibid., pp. 34–35.

79. The poster was printed by the "Canton Liaison Center of the Wuhan Revolutionary Rebel Headquarters of the Red Guards for the Thought of Mao Tse-tung." It was dated Janury 14, 1967.

80. The text and translation of the *tatzepao* appeared in *Samples*, pp. 6–7.

81. The *tatzepao* was put up by the Revolutionary Rebel Liaison Center of Red Guards of Universities and Colleges of Peking on February 18, 1967. The translation of the text appeared in *Current Scene*, May 31, 1967, pp. 15–16.

82. *Current Scene*, May 31, 1967, p. 16.

83. Yu, *Mass Persuasion*, p. 142.

84. *People's Daily*, December 11, 1958.

85. Yu, *Mass Persuasion*, p. 15.

86. For a more detailed analysis of some of the latent functions of *tatzepao*, see Godwin C. Chu, Philip H. Cheng, and Leonard L. Chu, *The Roles of Tatzepao in the Cultural Revolution—A Structural Functional Analysis* (Carbondale, Ill.: Southern Illinois University, 1972).

87. For some of the press reports on the *tatzepao* campaign in Peking, see Reuters (Peking, June 13, 1974) "Posters in Peking Cite Shortcomings of City's Leaders," in *New York Times*, June 14, 1974; AFP (Peking, June 16, 1974) "Posters Attack Hua Kuo-feng," in Foreign Broadcast Information Service, FBIS-CHI-74-117, p. E10; "Largest Wall Posters in Peking Attack Factory Chiefs," *New York Times*, June 23, 1974; Reuters (Peking, June 23, 1974) "Posters in Peking Tell of Bloodshed in Rightist Uprising," in *New York Times*, June 24, 1974. Also see Shih Chih, "Briefly Discuss the Latest Tatzepao Campaign," *China Monthly*, August, 1974, pp. 31–32.

88. Article 13 of the Constitution of the People's Republic of China specifies *tatzepao* as a constitutional right of the "mass of people" to express their views. The Constitution was adopted by the Fourth People's Congress on January 17, 1975. See *People's Daily*, January 20, 1975.

CHAPTER 8   Cultural Processes in China:
             Continuity and Change
             Godwin C. Chu
             Ai-li Chin

FUNCTIONS OF POPULAR MEDIA
COGNITIVE FUNCTIONS

A major function of the Chinese popular media is to provide
the people with a clearly delineated cognitive mapping. If we
assume that human beings tend to seek order in their cognitive environment, then this function will be vital to their
psychological well-being. The anxiety we experience when
elements in our perceptual field get out of balance, as shown
in research generated by the theory of cognitive dissonance,
is illustrative of our tendency to seek cognitive clarity.[1] This
function seems to be particularly important in a culture that
is undergoing drastic changes. In China, the people can become reassured by learning the current values and beliefs
from the popular media.

The cognitive function is important not merely for psychological reassurance. It is also important because of the
necessity of adapting to a changing social-cultural environment, of knowing what the moral and social standards are,
for the purpose of adequate functioning. The new Chinese

society has two distinctive characteristics in this respect. It is a society in which everybody is urged to participate and to perform. No one is allowed to stay out of the momentous drama of social tranformation. It is also a society in which the people live and work under a degree of inspection not usually found elsewhere. Because of the need for performance and because deviance is likely to be detected and corrected, it is essential that the people fully understand the new values, beliefs, and goals. The popular media help fulfill this cognitive function. Revolutionary operas, serial picture books, short stories, and even children's songs all serve this purpose.

Of the five media we have analyzed, one medium needs to be mentioned in particular. This is the *tatzepao*. Like the other media, the big-character posters help keep the people informed on current campaigns, and on what is right and what is wrong according to the latest development. The denunciation of the "Gang of Four" in late 1976 provides an example. The change of targets of criticism from Teng Hsiao-ping to Chiang Ching was so swift and abrupt that one had to be alert to stay abreast of the new direction. In this context the *tatzepao*, along with other media, becomes important because it helps the people to survey their environment for the changing trend.[2] This is close to the kind of surveillance function Harold Lasswell speaks of, the function of knowing what is going on.[3]

The *tatzepao* has an additional surveillance function not shared by the other popular media. The widespread and intensive use of the posters—particularly since the Cultural Revolution—has created in China a new institution of using posters as a mechanism of open criticism against cadres.[4] Misdeeds and erroneous ideological inclinations can be and indeed are exposed in the posters. Even though the accusations are not always true, the possiblity of public exposure in posters will tend to keep the cadres, particularly those at the lower level, under surveillance and restraint.

INTEGRATIVE FUNCTION

Another function of communication suggested by Lasswell can be identified for the popular media of China.[5] This is the function of integrating the various parts of society in responding to the environment, particularly one that is undergoing radical changes. This function is perhaps more important from the group perspective than from the individual perspective.

Any society contains different interests that pull its members in different directions. Yet for a society to survive, these diverse elements must be coordinated and their conflicting interests resolved.[6] The correlation of the various parts can be facilitated by a few widely accepted, unifying themes that serve as a basis of unity as well as a common ground for resolving differences. For traditional China, the unifying themes were embodied in such cardinal values as loyalty to the emperor, filial piety to parents and elders, a spirit of brotherhood toward fellow men, and a close adherence to traditions.

From the contemporary popular media we have analyzed, we see a different set of unifying themes that bear some resemblance to the old values. There is the absolute loyalty to the Party, instead of the emperor. There is an almost pious devotion to Party leaders, particularly to Chairman Mao. There is a spirit of comradeship among the proletariat, instead of universal brotherhood. And, strongly emphasized now but missing in the past, there is the commitment to an active ideology, reflected in part in a sense of national purpose for building a socialist China.

These unifying themes are being conveyed to the mass of people through the popular media with a conviction that makes the outcome sound almost inevitable. The finale in *The Red Lantern* illustrates this point:

> The bright sun shines on the red flag, and sabers and rifles are waving amid a song of victory. As Tieh Mei lifts high the red

lantern, it radiates Marxism, Leninism, and the Mao Tse-tung thought. They [the comrades] march on more vigorously.[7]

It may be noted that the unifying themes are built not only on Party loyalty and a resolute national purpose. They also rest on a foundation of hatred, hatred against the Japanese invaders and Chinese traitors, but most prominently, hatred against class enemies—the landlords, the capitalists, and the oppressors. In this sense, the correlating forces are both ideological and emotional.

CULTURAL TRANSMISSION

Surveillance and correlation imply external pressure and direction. They relate to social control and coordination. For a new social system to become established, there must be genuine internalization of the new values and beliefs. The popular media, we suggest, have the function of transmitting the new cultural values to the Chinese people, particularly to the younger generation, so that in time they will accept these new values as the guidelines of their behavior.

We recognize that the popular media are not the only instrument used by the Party for the purpose of transmitting the new values. The Party also relies on many other channels —the schools, the mass media, the small group study sessions, the *hsia fang* rustication programs—for propagating the new values. While these other channels have occasionally provided an arena for debates on different means and goals, the popular media speak with a voice of unanimity. Indeed, it is an extraordinary kind of unanimity, maintained in the absence of contending external influence and overt internal dissent. Unlike many developing countries in Asia and elsewhere, which have been exposed to Western culture through the mass media and various channels of interpersonal contacts, China has pursued a self-contained communication policy. Ideas and values from the outside have thus far been effectively kept at a distance. If there is serious latent dissent among the Chinese writers, the present social system has

revealed only occasional manifestations. Under these circumstances, children's songs, serial pictures, short stories,
and revolutionary operas all deliver the same uniform messages, creating, as it were, a perception of consensus. This
perception, to the extent that it is not openly contested, is expected to facilitate the process of cultural transmission. The
Chinese popular media thus represent a unique case in which
what the American anthropologist Robert Redfield called the
"great tradition"—ideas and values that belong to a reflec-
tive elite, the Party—is consciously employed to redirect and
modify, on a massive scale, the "little traditions" which are
the ways of life of the common people.[8]

The popular media have several other characteristics that
are not shared by the other channels. First, the popular
media appear to be the only channels that provide both entertainment and ideological admonishment. The messages come
in songs, pictures, and stories that offer some variety and
relief from the routine life of work and study for the people of
China. These media are intended to entertain as well as to
educate, not to criticize or condemn members of the audience. With the exception of *tatzepao*, these popular media
are not nearly as threatening as the criticism sessions in small
groups. Two of these media, children's songs and revolutionary opera, are combined with music, making it possible
for the people to rehearse the messages in singing. If the Peking opera and folk songs were important channels for the
transmission of traditional values in the past, then we can expect their current revolutionary versions to contribute to the
propagation of new values while the old is being pushed more
and more to the past.

The popular media seek to transmit the new values not by
ordering the people to do this and not do that, but rather by
setting new behavioral examples in place of the old in a social
context that ordinary people can understand. The significance of this approach can be appreciated in two different
perspectives. First, the people cannot be expected to incul-
cate the new values unless they know what these values mean

and understand when and in what circumstances they should be followed. For instance, simply telling the people to support the proletarian dictatorship, without showing them what that means, cannot be effective. The popular media make it more likely that the new values will be clearly understood. Furthermore, through the trials and triumphs of the characters in the popular media, the people can gain insight into their own problems and find the correct solutions according to the Party's criteria. Second, the learning of values is usually facilitated when there is a basis of identification. A child learns the values of his cultural group by identifying first with his parents and later with his peers. The popular media, by arousing hatred against a variety of villains—the Japanese invaders, oppressive landlords, and so on—provide for the audience a basis of identification in the Party, the Liberation Army heroes, the model workers, and the poor and lower middle-class peasants. When presented in contrast with the hateful misdeeds of the villains, these horoes and heroines could become the objects of positive emotional catharsis. The people feel happy for the accomplishments of the heroes. They are saddened by their sufferings and temporary setbacks. Eventually a basis of identification will be established to foment the learning of new values.

Even the big-character posters, seemingly unrelated to cultural transmission, can be seen as an important channel for that purpose when we fully appreciate its function of emotional catharsis. The *tatzepao* has mostly been used as a means of involving the mass of people in criticism campaigns. The rectification campaign of 1958, the Cultural Revolution, and the more recent movements against Lin Piao and Confucius and the latest condemnation of the "Gang of Four" all illustrate this manifest characteristic of the *tatzepao*. But the posters have an important latent function beyond their role in mass campaigns. They have been used by the ordinary people to criticize local cadres for their errors and to air petty grievances of various sorts. This particular use of the posters, generally allowed by the Party authorities as long as the criticism stays within the bounds of ideological conformity, tends to give the people a sense of satisfaction, a release of frustration, if you will. Because of this latent function of the *tatzepao*, one would expect the Chinese to be more receptive to the other uses of the posters directed by the Party. In other words, *tatzepao* as a new cultural process thereby becomes more readily transmitted to the Chinese.

POPULAR MEDIA AS NEW CULTURAL PROCESSES

CULTURAL VALUES IN POPULAR MEDIA

What are some of the new values, basic as well as instrumental, that are being communicated to the people of China through the popular media?[9] What specific themes can be identified out of the general talks on class consciousness and proletarian ideology that are considered important and desirable as behavioral guidelines for the Chinese today?

For basic values, liberation (or salvation, in Rokeach's conceptualization) stands out among the supreme goals the Chinese are directed to seek. This is the most prominent theme that emerges in the analysis of five revolutionary operas. Top priority for the Chinese is to liberate and uplift the life of the common people, the proletariat and peasants. For the masses, that seems to take precedence over national security as a basic value, which is not given nearly as much emphasis as the supremacy and spiritedness of the proletariat, either in the revolutionary operas, short stories, or serial pictures.

Another important value that comes out clearly is the bond of comradeship in the common cause of revolution. This comradeship is advocated for peasants, workers as well as soldiers, whether young or old. It is apparently meant to replace the traditional family and kinship ties which have been the foundation of Chinese society for centuries. We can illustrate this point with the story of *The Red Lantern*, in which three generations—the grandmother, the father, and the granddaughter—fight together for Communism against the Japanese. Tieh Mei, the young girl, is close to her father and grandmother, but the relationships among the three are primarily demonstrated in their dedicated struggle against the same enemy.

For instance, after Tieh Mei's father Li Yu-ho has been arrested by the Japanese, Tieh Mei bursts out crying. Her grandmother consoles her calmly: "Tears will not save your father. Don't cry. Now is the time to let you in on what our family is." Then the grandmother tells Tieh Mei the background of their family. As it turned out, Tieh Mei's real parents died in an uprising, in which the grandmother's husband also participated and died. Tieh Mei, then a baby, was saved by her father's closest friend, Li, who was himself wounded and sought refuge in the grandmother's home because he was her husband's pupil. Thus they were from three different families, united only through revolution. Upon hearing the story, Tieh Mei stops crying, and vows to carry on the fight for her "father." It is significant to note that in this sole opera in which three generations of the same family fight the same cause, there are in fact no consanguine ties. What binds them together are their dedication and common suffering—the "grandmother" lost her husband, the "father" lost his closest friend, and Tieh Mei lost her parents, all in the same uprising.

Another scene in *The Red Lantern* may be noted. Before Li is going to be executed, the Japanese captors allow Tieh Mei to see him once. He starts to tell her about their true relations, but she says she already knows. Li then holds Tieh Mei in his hands, and says:

> People say that the blood ties between parents and children are the strongest. I say the attachment arising from class background is even stronger, weightier than the Mount of Tai.[10]

This scene emphatically demonstrates the spirit of comradeship as the new foundation of the Chinese family.

Achievement is another value espoused in the Chinese popular media. What the Chinese are urged to strive for is not individual achievement, which in a Western society is usually measured by means of personal accomplishment, prestige, and material well-being. For the Chinese the important thing is accomplishment in a collective sense, as demonstrated in the revolutionary opera *On the Docks*. It is the fulfillment of a mission assigned by the Party authorities, in this case to provide supplies for an international ally, that gives the workers a sense of accomplishment. Similar examples abound in the short stories and picture books.

For the Chinese today, the sense of accomplishment should not be egoistic, but rather altruistic. This theme is closely related to the value of liberation, in the sense that one's ultimate goal is to accomplish the victory of the proletariat, to work for the proletariat, or in Mao's phraseology, "to serve the people." Accomplishment is actually gained in self-sacrifice. This general concept is being taught even the small children. For instance, one revolutionary folk song asks the children to learn skills in their vast land so that everyone will be eager to be the "people's old yellow cattle"—that is, to sweat and toil for the proletariat.

Another basic value—one that we sense more vividly from the revolutionary children's songs than from the other popular media—is the negation of individualism. While people in the West are often heard to complain of a loss of individual identity, of being merely cogs in a wheel, the opposite is now being emphasized in China. Chinese children are being presented in revolutionary children's songs as being anxious to become "revolutionary screws," that is, cogs in the wheels of revolution. Also, while the fictitious characters in operas, serial picture books, and short stories must have names, the models in children's songs are mostly nameless, except those who are already deceased. Individual recognition is not to be sought as a valued end. Rather, one is encouraged to derive a sense of satisfaction from individual anonymity.

What personal qualities and behavioral standards are considered important and desirable? What are the important instrumental values that should guide the efforts of the Chinese in reaching their goals of liberation, comradeship, and collective accomplishment?

The foremost requirement is loyalty—loyalty to the revolutionary cause, to the Party, and above all to Chairman Mao.[11] This theme receives prominent treatment in all five revolutionary operas, as well as in the short stories, serial picture books, and revolutionary children's songs. This is to be an unquestioning loyalty that should remain firm and unswerving regardless of any setbacks or hardships in the pursuit of the revolutionary cause. For instance, when Tieh Mei's "father" Li is going to be executed by the Japanese because he refuses to reveal the Communist guerillas' secret code despite severe tortures, he lifts up his head and envisions a bright future for the Chinese people:

> At that time, the red flags will be planted all over China. . . . He saw a bright, glorious tomorrow when red flags are fluttering in the wind, he saw a beautiful prospect for Communism. The Torches of proletarian revolution are irresistible. The flames of Chairman Mao Tse-tung will definitely shine all over the Chinese territories. A new world with no exploitation and oppression will come into being. Thinking of this, Li felt his confidence and willpower even more positively strengthened.[12]

This loyalty is to be buttressed by an unyielding courage, a spirit of no fear. Again, *The Red Lantern* provides an apt illustration. Before Li's execution, he is allowed to talk to his "mother." There is no expression of grief when mother and son see each other for the last time.

> "Torture means nothing to me even if they broke every one of my bones," Li told his mother. "Nor am I afraid of imprisonment even if I had to be confined till the prison floor collapses." In the face of the cruel misdeeds of the [Japanese] imperialists, Li Yu-ho demonstrated the dauntless revolutionary spirit of the proletariat.[13]

Grandmother shows the same courage. She refuses to tell the Japanese any secret and calmly walks to her own execution. In other instances, this courage is demonstrated by a resolute spirit to overcome enormous difficulties in task performance, as illustrated in some of the short stories.

It is not a blind, pointless courage that is being praised and advocated, however. It is rather a courage to be supported by intelligence and ability, which make possible the accomplishment of the Party's assignment. This idea is clear in all the revolutionary operas, serial pictures, and short stories we have analyzed. In the end, despite incredible odds, the Communist heroes will triumph over their enemies. Intelligence and ability, however, are not meant to be just individual qualities. In theory at least, they appear to be the outcome of inspiration when one follows the teachings of Chairman Mao. This thinking is clearly illustrated in *Taking the Tiger Mountain by Strategy*, in which the Communist detachment commander drew courage and wisdom from Mao's teachings whenever he faced a seemingly impossible obstacle. In practice, it means that one must not depend on one's intelligence and ability alone, but above all must follow Chairman Mao's teachings.

Another value, which in other societies may be largely instrumental in nature, has become almost an important end in itself in China. This is the new value of activism, of participation, which we sense in the short stories, children's songs, and particularly the medium of *tatzepao*. These Chinese children have been urged to participate in every campaign, from the criticism of Lin Piao and Confucius to the denunciation of the "Gang of Four." In short stories, we see the characters, young and old, eager to express themselves. There is enough evidence to suggest that in an organized *tatzepao* campaign, practically everybody, except the very young and the very old, is asked to take part. Most people not only do so but also seem to have been impressed with the idea that outstanding performance in a *tatzepao* campaign is one way of earning recognition and promotion in the Chinese Communist social system.[14]

FORM AND STYLE OF COMMUNICATION

In what general form are social messages—values, beliefs, and goals—being communicated to the Chinese people? While in some societies, such as America, a large variety of message forms is used, we find only one predominant form in present-day China. There is little humor, except an occasional teasing among close comrades or members of a proletarian family, primarily as a political instrument for correcting minor ideological deviance. For those Western critics who are bothered by the fantasy materials in television soap operas, the ordinary fare presented to the Chinese audience would be an odd relief. One does not find in the Chinese popular media the slightest hint of fantasy, in the sense of individual indulgence in a world of imagined excitement. The Chinese in the past, like their ancient Greek counterparts, enjoyed mythologies of various sorts, in which supernatural powers usually sided with the good against evil. That has also changed. The gods, goddesses, and ghosts have been swept off the stage of Peking opera since the days of the Cultural Revolution, and they have never existed from the very beginning in the Communist-inspired literature.

The only form, which is prevalent in opera, short stories, serial picture books, and even in children's songs, is one of down-to-earth realism. The characters may be fictitious, with an occasional exception like the story of Liu Hu-lan, the revolutionary heroine, or the little hero, shepherd Chang Kao-chien. But the context, the flow of events, and even the climax are presented with a lifelike quality that is intended to be real. Even in the revolutionary children's songs, the aspirations (eager to be the people's yellow cow) and condemnations (down with traitor Lin Piao) are phrased with a conviction that approaches reality.

It is indeed an extraordinary realism, because the average

person would be disappointed if he should try to look around him for real people who are like the heroes or heroines in the Chinese popular media. Most real people have defects; the question is who has more and of what kinds. The Chinese heroes and heroines, however, are faultless. Most people have some degree of self-concern. These heroes and heroines are totally selfless. Most people experience fear in the face of imminent danger. These heroes and heroines demonstrate a dauntless courage that borders on the superhuman. Most people have limits to their wisdom and capability. These heroes and heroines are capable of overcoming seemingly insurmountable difficulties. When their own resources are not adequate, they rely successfully on the teachings of Chairman Mao. Thus, in a sense, the predominant form of communication in the Chinese popular media is not one of realism, as we usually understand that term. It portrays not necessarily "what is," but rather "what should be." It is thus a form of idealism or modelism. Neither of these terms, however, fully conveys the true meaning, because the term used by the Chinese Communist authorities is almost beyond translation. It is called *yang pan*, which is literally a mold or a plate which can be used to cast everything, and in this case everybody, into exactly the same shape. We shall call it "socialist realism."

Given this overriding *form* of communication, what are the *styles* in which the messages are organized and presented? This is a question apparently related to the form of communication. When one strives for realism or modelism, a satirical style for instance would not be readily adaptable for his purpose. An allegorical style would not be suitable, either, when one's objective is to present a clear model, because the full image of the model may be lost in an allegory. Nor is the popular media content presented primarily for entertainment, although that is recognized to have a place. To the Party authorities, entertainment without a purpose is pointless, and that purpose is to advance the cause of proletarian dictatorship. Mao has made this clear in his much-quoted Yenan *Talks* on the roles of literature in the Chinese Communist revolution. Because of this emphasis, the two predominant styles of presentation we have found in the Chinese popular media are moralistic and instructive: moralistic in the sense that the message always clearly distinguishes what is right from what is wrong, in the Party's perspective; instructive in the sense that the people are clearly told what to do in order to accomplish what is right and to renounce what is wrong.

Another important feature in the Chinese style of presentation must be noted. The distinction between right and wrong is considered self-evident, so that no empirical demonstration is called for; it has a sort of face validity that is beyond doubt. For instance, when Chinese children sing that they want to be screws in the gigantic machine of revolution, there is no need to demonstrate whether that is indeed a desirable end. The desirability is taken for granted because this song is inspired by the Communist ideology and must therefore be right. Or when a cadre is told to work for revolution, not commercialism, this statement is considered sufficient. No further explanation will be necessary. This style of presentation relies for validity on the repeated assertions by an authoritative source. It is a style that will probably sound alien to most Westerners, who are brought up in a cultural environment which values empirical verification as a means of establishing the validity of behavioral choices.

PROCESSES OF COMMUNICATION

The communication processes through the popular media in China today are different from the patterns in the past. Traditional Chinese opera, folk songs, and popular stories in the past generally followed a cumulative, nondirected process of creation and dissemination. The origin and authorship were usually unknown. A distinguished artist, such as Dr. Mei Lan-fang, would occasionally have a play adapted to suit his talents, but this was done infrequently. By and large, it was the popular demand and taste of the people that shaped the content and dissemination of the folk media in China, as in any other traditional societies.

The processes today represent a remarkable departure. The initial impetus usually begins with a policy decision reached in the Party hierarchy. The motivating force could be the Party's desire to support a particular movement, such as the criticism of Lin Piao and Confucius, or to correct a general trend that is considered ideologically undesirable, such as the romantic scholars and their beautiful ladies in traditional opera. Somewhere along the line, usually high in the leadership, a basic decision has to be made on what revolutionary operas or stories or serial pictures to produce.

Depending on the particular media involved, once a decision is made, one of two approaches can be pursued. For revolutionary children's songs, apparently the Party has encouraged school children in general to participate by writing their own songs. The better ones are selected and widely disseminated through publication in the *People's Daily* and, we suspect, in provincial newspapers as well. Not much is known about how the children are told what to write, whether they get help from their teachers and parents, and what criteria are employed by the official press to select certain songs for nationwide circulation. From our general knowledge about communication in China, we tend to believe that both the teachers and, perhaps more prominently, the small study groups among the children themselves play major roles.

For other popular media that require a high level of artistic achievement, such as the revolutionary opera and short stories, we have seen the rather elaborate process of cooperation involving the Party leadership, the artists, and some of the audience groups for producing the final work. In a process known as Three-in-One Union that has become prevalent in the last decade—as in the writers' workshops—the ideological requirements, artistic accomplishments, and audience evaluations are closely coordinated through constant communication, both vertically and horizontally. This process has been discussed in the chapters on short stories and revolutionary opera.

After that, the product is released for nationwide viewing or reading. At this stage the product can still be subject to meticulous criticism. This happened to a Hunan dialect opera, *A Song of Gardeners*. This opera was first staged in 1972 in Hunan, Chairman Mao's home province, and apparently the chairman saw it and liked it. But it was rather harshly criticized in 1974, as it has now been revealed, by the leftist group of Mao's wife, Chiang Ching.[15] The opera was about two model teachers who tried to reform a neglected boy by giving him loving care and by setting him a good example with their own behavior. The leftist group denounced this approach because of its lack of revolutionary fervor and ambiguity of the Party's role in the plot.

The popular media in China are closely linked with mass media of communication as well as communication in small groups. Both the *People's Daily* and the Party magazine *Red Flag* publish articles on revolutionary opera, short stories, and other forms of what in the West would be called entertainment arts. Radio has been used, apparently quite effectively, as a channel to teach the people how to sing revolutionary opera. At Hsiao Chin Chuang outside Tientsin, for instance, commune members learned to sing arias from the revolutionary opera from the radio. Those who had learned well then taught others.[16] Singing revolutionary opera was very popular in the villages, according to an account in the *People's Daily*:

> After the evening meal, neighbors from left and right gather together in front of their houses. I sing one part, and you sing another. It becomes a natural evening party of revolutionary opera.[17]

Revolutionary operas also feed into storytelling in local groups. At Chin Shan Commune outside Shanghai, the small group storytellers generally took advantage of the time before or after a study meeting, or political evening class, or rice paddy demonstration, to tell stories from revolutionary operas. An opera was usually broken into brief sections of storytelling lasting about twenty minutes each. The peasants' reception was described as enthusiastic.[18]

China's popular media are thus built on the basis of well-organized processes of communication involving the Party's policy makers, the artists in the various fields, and the general audience. These popular media as instruments of cultural change do not function by themselves but are closely tied in with China's overall communication networks, using both the mass media and small groups for intensified exposure and mutual reinforcement.

CULTURAL CONTINUITY AND CHANGE
CULTURAL CONTINUITY

When one takes a cursory look at China's popular media, what stands out is the emphasis on revolutionary spirit and radical change. Through our analysis, however, we found rather surprising links of cultural continuity with the past, in terms of prolonged manifestations of traditional values and linguistic expressions as well as forms and styles of communication.

Loyalty, primarily of a personal nature, has always been important to the Chinese for centuries. This basic value has had a particular significance to the functioning of the Chinese society because it permeates many shades of self-other relations. While these relations are capable of expression in a variety of forms, in any cultural groups we can identify two general categories. They are referred to by Francis Hsu as "role" and "affect."[19] The former refers to relations that are oriented toward role performance, characterized by specific rights and obligations. The latter refers to relations that are personal in nature and maintained for their intrinsic, affiliative qualities. One major characteristic of traditional

Chinese society was the extent to which affect relations prevailed over role relations. Personal loyalty, in particular, was the predominant factor in superior-subordinate relations so that other role-specific considerations were often ignored. There is the traditional saying that if an emperor wanted a subject to die, the subject must die willingly. In the current popular media one finds the same emphasis on personal loyalty as a basic value, reflecting as it were a continuation of the traditional self-other relations of this particular nature. It may be noted that this loyalty is now directed to Chairman Mao and the Party, rather than to the emperor and his royal dynasty.

Courage is another value which has been important to the Chinese now as well as in the past. In a sense, courage is a necessary concomitant of loyalty because the behavioral enactment of loyalty often requires courage. The heroes and heroines in the revolutionary operas, for instance, are portrayed as individuals of extraordinary courage and determination in demonstrating their dedication to Chairman Mao and the Party. One is reminded of the many heroes and the few heroines in traditional Chinese operas and novels who were undaunted by either torture or death in defending their emperor or master. Both loyalty and courage now find their expression in the new comradeship, the spirit of which can be traced to the traditional Chinese bond of sworn brotherhood that once held many secret societies together.

For many Westerners who have been able to visit China in the last few years, a common impression is the deemphasis on individualism. Our analysis revealed the same finding. The Chinese people, young and old, are being taught not to seek individual distinction of any kind but to work merely as members of a collectivity. Although this strong negation of individualism appears to be new, its root can be found in traditional Chinese culture. Individualism has never been prominent in the Chinese mind. The educated Chinese in fact avoided the use of "I" in both oral and written communica-

tion outside the circle of close relatives and friends. The term
hsiao ti (your younger brother), or *hsiao chih* (your little
nephew) was used instead, depending on the nature of the
relationship. One's achievement, too, was not perceived as
an individual distinction, but rather as a reflection on the
honor and glory of the extended family. In a sense, there was
among the Chinese a form of collectivism existing within the
bounds of kinship ties. The transformation of the old collectivism to its new form has been neither easy nor complete,
because it requires a change from personal to impersonal
relations. We suspect, however, that because individualism
has never been part of the Chinese culture, its denial is probably somewhat more acceptable to the Chinese than to people brought up in a Western cultural environment.

In the short stories, Ai-li Chin has found recurring
evidence of cultural continuity in linguistic uses and terms of
address. There are sprinklings of traditional phrases here and
there, particularly those borrowed from *Romance of the
Three Kingdoms*, said to be a favorite of Chiarman Mao.
Some of the writers have imitated a historical feature of the
old Chinese tradition by using a verse format from the Yuan
Dynasty drama to sum up the morals of the story. Use of
simulated kinship terms of address has diminished in the
stories of the seventies but is still practiced. Older men and
women are called "uncles" and "aunts." The term "PLA
uncles," referring to soldiers of the People's Liberation Army, appears frequently in revolutionary children's folk
songs.

In forms and styles of communication, the continuity with
the cultural past is even more pronounced. In the contemporary Chinese popular media one sees the same blend of modelism and realism that has distinguished much of China's
popular literature and drama in the past. Many traditional
Chinese operas were intended to teach a moral lesson, by pre-
senting both positive and negative behavioral models in a
context of reality. A very popular brand of Chinese novels in

the past followed the same pattern. Known as *ching shih* (social warning) novels, these were morality stories that told the Chinese what to do and what not to do. This basic concept of teaching moral standards through entertainment has essentially been followed by the Communist Party authorities, although the standards now are partly new. The moralistic, instructive style that one finds in the Chinese popular media today sounds highly similar to the tones of such Chinese folk stories as *Twenty-Four Legends of Filial Piety*.

Another evidence of cultural continuity is the use of hyperbole as a method of moral instruction. We have seen examples from the new revolutionary operas, for instance, *The Red Lantern*, and from some of the short stories and reportorials, such as *The Story of Taching People*, or *Learn from Iron Man Wang Chin-hsi*.[20] The determination and courage of the heroes and heroines sound almost superhuman. If these instances of supreme sacrifice and sufferings seem to be unreal to the Western mind, one needs to recall only the stories in *Twenty-Four Legends*. There was a pious son who cut a piece of flesh from his leg in order to cook a soup for his ailing mother. Miraculously, the mother was cured after eating the soup. There was another young man who did not know what to do when his mother wanted fresh fish for dinner on a freezing winter day. He went out to the lake, laid his warm body on the ice till it melted, and got his fish. Another pious man was bothered because mosquitoes kept his old father from sleep. So every night before his father went to bed, he would go in first and let the mosquitoes feed on him till they were full so that they would not disturb his father during the night. Seen in these historical-cultural contexts, the superhuman deeds of the Chinese Communist heroes and heroines will begin to sound plausible.

Even the use of *tatzepao* is not totally new. It has been customary for the Chinese to write posters for a variety of purposes, including the airing of petty grievances and anonymous accusations. This custom was particularly prevalent in the rural villages, where an anonymous poster would readily attract attention. Sometimes, such a poster resulted in remedial actions by the village elders. Even if no actions were initiated, the writer of the poster would have the satisfaction of knowing that his case was brought to the public attention, in a Chinese phrase known as "letting out one's breath" *(chu kou chi)*. One sees a subtle similarity between the traditional form of anonymous posters and the current version of *tatze-pao*.

CULTURAL CHANGE

While the indicators of cultural continuity appear to be remarkable, the changes are no less profound. The new value of liberation is something one does not readily find in China's old cultural traditions. Following the Confucian teachings, the Chinese were very much concerned with the perfection of the self as well as of those in their immediate environment. There was never, however, anything in Chinese cultural traditions that approaches the Christian spirit of evangelism, of reaching out to save the multitude of nonbelievers. Nor does one find in traditional China, until the inroad of Western influence, any massive attempt to uplift and improve the life of the common people. The central theme of liberation in the Chinese popular media is therefore a major indication of change, even though the liberation is to be selectively applied to the peasants, workers, and soldiers, and not to the "enemies" of the people, whose parents happened to be landlords, capitalists, or rightists.

We have noticed the current emphasis on loyalty as evidence of cultural continuity. It must be noted, however, that the Chinese in the past regarded as important not just loyalty *(chung)*, but also forgiveness *(shu)*. These were two of the cardinal values that supported Chinese society for centuries. Forgiveness, a prominent theme in the teachings of Confucius, was reinforced by the spirit of Buddhism. There is the popular Chinese saying: "Once you lay down your bloodied

knife, you can become a Buddha right on where you stand."
In this sense, the traditional Chinese culture had a strong
forgiving, reforming quality. That quality is conspicuously
missing in the popular media today. There is not the slightest
hint that evildoers may be reformed and forgiven. On the
contrary, one senses the urge to pursue relentlessly the class
enemies, who are presented as being incapable of reform.
There can be no forgiveness.

Traditional Chinese society was built on the foundation of
harmony in interpersonal relations. This is not to say that the
Chinese had no conflicts. The point is that the Chinese traditionally viewed conflicts generally in the perspective of their
eventual outcome in harmony. Conflicts, though inevitable,
were to be minimized, if not totally avoided, by restraint and
moderation. Conflicts were hardly to be recommended as a
means, and certainly not as an end. The impression one gains
from the Communist-inspired popular media, however, is
quite the opposite. Class struggle and conflict seem to be a
way of life. This dominating theme comes up again and
again, in the revolutionary operas, in the serial picture books,
and even in the children's songs. Life is a continual struggle,
against the Japanese invaders, against the Nationalists,
against the landlords, against Lin Piao, and against Confucius. (The list of class enemies has now been expanded
following the purge of the "Gang of Four.") Neither harmony nor forgiveness, which is essential to maintaining harmony, is even mentioned.

This departure from the traditional culture is also manifest
in two other related aspects. The Chinese in the past attached
great importance to family love. This love was expressed not
so much in the overt behavior of hugging and kissing, but
rather in the more subtle, covert emotional attachment of
caring and devotion, by the filial children as well as the
benevolent parents. If this kind of family love is still encouraged by the Communist authorities today, we do not see
much demonstration of it in the popular media we have

analyzed. Caring and devotion are now expressed among comrades fighting for the same cause, or among coworkers toiling together for the revolution. Even among the members of a proletarian family, the affection and concern are carefully phrased within the context of parents and children performing some collective duties. It is a *class* love, instead of family love or personal love. In this connection, it is interesting to note that family members who belong to the "enemy" class are shown to care a lot about each other on a personal basis. For instance, in one of the serial picture books, when an ailing ex-landlord is gravely ill and does not have enough to eat, his grandson, a young boy, goes out to catch frogs from the commune's paddy fields for food (and is subsequently caught by other boys who are children of the revolutionary classes). When the old man learns about it, he is upset and begins to cough badly. Upon seeing this, his son begins to massage the old man's back in order to relieve his cough.[21] While family love hardly receives a prominent treatment, hatred (against the class enemies) is strongly emphasized, another instance of change.

The absence of harmony, moderation, and family love as prominent themes is accompanied by a value in a different direction, the value of physical accomplishment to be pursued in an extreme degree. Time and again, the heroes and heroines in the popular media show the people of China how to fight against impossible odds to achieve what may otherwise be impossible objectives. The environment must, and can, be conquered. Nothing should stand in the way of this kind of accomplishment, which is for the benefit of the collectivity, not individuals. Conflicts are often employed as a means to achieve this end. Moderation has no place in this resolute task. And it is comradeship, not family love, that binds the people who work toward the same goal.

It is in this new spirit of comradeship that we can understand the changing relations between the older and younger people in China. Traditionally, the Chinese followed the old

cultural value of submission to authority.[22] They were expected to obey not only those individuals who had influence
and wealth but also elders within their kinship relations.
Even to an old person outside the kinship networks, one was
supposed to show respect and deference. This pattern of behavior appears to be changing. From the content of the
popular media, particularly the short stories, we see age as no
longer an important factor in social relations. A person,
whether male or female, is expected to be capable, resolute,
ideologically sound, and dedicated to the revolution. If the
person possesses these attributes, he or she will be respected
regardless of age. The young people are no longer submissive
to their older countrymen. In fact, they are shown in the
stories as sharp, tactless (li-hai), and ready to challenge their
elders, including their parents, although sometimes teasingly.

There is apparently one intended limitation to this spirit of
independence and boldness. The people are not encouraged
to criticize the policies of the Party. Rather, the Chinese,
young and old alike, are expected to follow the direction of
the Party, particularly of Chairman Mao. Repeatedly, the
revolutionary folk songs tell the Chinese children that they
must be *ting hua*, that is, show unquestioning obedience to
the Chairman as a child used to obey his parents.

Finally, we shall note the possibility of a rather fundamental change. This has to do with the traditional Chinese attitude of noninvolvement, an attitude that is related to submis-
siveness. Several traditional Chinese sayings can be cited to
illustrate this attitude. For instance, the Chinese used to
believe that "all troubles begin when you try to be involved
in other people's business." Therefore, "let's each sweep the
snow in front of our doors, and never mind the frost on other
people's roofs." This is because "rather than have one more
headache, it's much better to have one less headache." Now
that activism is promoted, as in the *tatzepao* campaigns, this
kind of noninvolvement becomes no longer tenable. Through
these campaigns, the Chinese have learned to express them-

selves and to criticize the condemned target, whether it is Lin Piao, Confucius, Teng Hsiao-ping, or the "Gang of Four." In so doing, they necessarily become involved. It is no longer possible merely to sweep the snow in front of one's door.

There is some evidence to suggest that, having been required to mind the frost on other people's roofs, the Chinese have departed from their reticent past and have begun to speak out on matters with which they are concerned, for instance, by exposing erring cadres in posters. A more dramatic example was a lengthy *tatzepao* posted in Canton in 1974 that pointedly criticized some of the basic policies and practices of the Party. The authors were later identified as a group of college students who grew up in the era of Mao Tse-tung.[23] It seems that the spirit of independence and criticism, once cultivated, cannot be selectively applied only to minor issues. If so, then perhaps a new page in Chinese culture has been turned.

NOTES

1. See Leon Festinger, *A Theory of Cognitive Dissonance* (Stanford, Ca.: Stanford University Press, 1962), and Jack W. Brehm and Arthur R. Cohen, *Explorations in Cognitive Dissonance* (New York: John Wiley & Sons, 1962).

2. How the Chinese learned about the changed trend from the posters is illustrated in "New Helmsman with an Old Crew," *Time*, November 8, 1976, p. 52.

3. Harold D. Lasswell, "The Structure and Function of Communication in Society," in *The Communication of Ideas*, ed. Lyman Bryson (New York: Institute for Religious and Social Studies, 1948).

4. The new institution of *tatzepao* as a mechanism for criticism is discussed by Godwin C. Chu, Philip H. Cheng, and Leonard Chu, *The Roles of Tatzepao in the Cultural Revolution—A Structural-Functional Analysis* (Carbondale,Ill.: Southern Illinois University, 1972).

5. Lasswell, "Structure and Function of Communication." Lasswell refers to this as the correlation function.

6. See Georg Simmel, *Conflict* and *The Web of Group-Affiliations* (New York: The Free Press, 1955).

7. *The Red Lantern* (Peking: Hsin Hua Book Publishers, 1972), p. 138.

8. Robert Redfield, *Peasant Society and Culture, An Anthropological Approach to Civilization* (Chicago: University of Chicago Press, 1956), pp. 68–71, 91–96, 155. The application of these concepts to the traditional Chinese society has been discussed in Hui-chen Wang Liu, "An Analysis of Chinese Clan Rules: Confucian Theories in Action," in *Confucianism in Action*, ed. David S. Nivison and Arthur F. Wright (Stanford, Ca.: Stanford University Press, 1959), pp. 63–96.

9. What we refer to as "basic values" are called "terminal values" by Rokeach. Although Philip Cheng has followed Rokeach's terminology in his paper, we have used the more common term of "basic values" to apply to all the popular media we have analyzed.

10. *The Red Lantern*, p. 172.

11. The media content we have analyzed was from the period before Mao's death. Mao is now being praised as the founding father of the People's Republic, although no longer as the Party's chairman.

12. *The Red Lantern*, pp. 124–125.

13. Ibid., p. 131.

14. See Chu, Cheng, and Chu, *Roles of Tatzepao*.

15. The criticism of "A Song of Gardeners" was first voiced in an article in the *People's Daily*. See Hsiang Hui, "Hunan Opera 'A Song of Gardeners' Reviewed," *People's Daily*, August 2, 1974. Hsiang Hui, meaning "the bright light of Hunan," was apparently a pseudonym. During the campaign against the "Gang of Four" in late 1976, it was revealed that this critical review was ordered by Mao's wife, Chiang Ching. The revelation was made public in an article entitled "Strangling 'A Song of Gardeners' Was a Plot to Usurp Party Power," in *People's Daily*, November 29, 1976.

16. "Revolutionary Model Opera at Hsiao Chin Chuang," *People's Daily*, October 10, 1974.

17. Ibid.

18. "A Desirable Way of Popularizing Model Opera," *People's Daily*, August 30, 1974.

19. Francis L. K. Hsu, "Psychosocial Homeostasis and *Jen*: Conceptual Tools for Advancing Psychological Anthropology," *American Anthropologist* 73:1 (February, 1971): 23–44.

20. See *Story of Taching People* (Shanghai: People's Publishing Press, 1971), and *Learn from Iron Man Wang Chin-hsi* (Peking: People's Publishing Press, 1972). These are about the heroic deeds of oil workers at the Taching oil field, particularly those of Iron Man Wang Chin-hsi. Wang died in 1970.

21. These scenes are from a serial picture book, *A Hand Gun*, which

describes how two peasant boys discover that the ailing ex-landlord has concealed a hand gun under his bed. Massaging the back of an elder by gentle tapping *(chui pei)* is a traditional Chinese gesture showing love and respect. It is interesting to note that the two little heroes, Ma Tuan-tuan and Ma Chuan-chuan (no relation), are shown to seek advice from an old poor peasant and the production team leader, but not from their parents (who do not even appear in the story). See *A Hand Gun* (Shanghai: Hsin Hua Book Publishers, 1972).

22. See Francis L. K. Hsu, *Under the Ancestors' Shadow* (Stanford, Ca.: Stanford University Press, 1971).

23. The *tatzepao*, signed by Li I-che, was posted in a street in Canton in November, 1974 and addressed to Chairman Mao and the Fourth National People's Congress. Its preface and text, about 23,000 words long, were later carried in full in *Ming Pao Monthly* (Hong Kong) 10:12 (December, 1975): 53–60. Li I-che, in reality, was three persons: *Li* Cheng-tien, a 1966 graduate from the Canton Art Institute, Chen *I*-yang, and Huang Hsi-*che*, both offspring of Party cadres. All active Red Guards during the Cultural Revolution, they criticized the Party for what they considered to be the major shortcomings of the Communist system. For a brief summary of the criticisms, see "Lee's Tatzepao: To Mao with Dissent," *The Asian Messenger* (Spring, 1976): 27.

Bibliography

Aberle, David. "The Psychological Analysis of a Hopi Life-History." *Comparative Psychology Monographs* 21:1. Berkeley: University of California Press, 1951.

Arlington, L. C. *The Chinese Drama*. New York: Benjamin Blom, 1966.

Association of Chinese Folk Art and Literature, ed. *Materials of Chinese Songs and Ballads*. Peking: Writers' Press, 1959.

Barcata, Louis. *China in the Throes of the Cultural Revolution*. New York: Hart Publishing Co., 1968.

Benedict, Ruth. *The Chrysanthemum and the Sword*. Boston: Houghton Mifflin Company, 1946.

Bennett, Gordon A. and Ronald N. Montaperto. *Red Guard: The Political Diary of Dai Hsiao-ai*. Garden City, N.Y.: Doubleday & Company, 1971.

Boorman, Howard L. "The Literary World of Mao Tse-tung." *China Quarterly* 13 (January-March, 1963): 15–38.

Brehm, Jack W. and Arthur R. Cohen. *Explorations in Cognitive Dissonance*. New York: John Wiley & Sons, 1962.

Broman, Barry M. "Tatzepao: Medium of Conflict in China's Cultural Revolution." *Journalism Quarterly* (Winter, 1970): 100–104, 127.

Chace, James. "The Five-Power World of Richard Nixon." *New York Times Magazine*, February 20, 1972.

Chang, Yu-fa. *Communication and Its Cultural and Political Impacts During the Pre-Chin Period.* Taipei, Taiwan: Chia Hsin Foundation, 1966.

Chao, Chung. "On Literature and Art." In *Communist China, 1956* (Hong Kong: Union Research, 1957).

Chen, A. S. [Ai-li S. Chin] "The Ideal Local Party Secretary and the 'Model' Man." *China Quarterly* (January-March, 1964): 229–240.

Chen, Po-tsui, ed. *Essays on Children's Literature.* Wuhan: Yangtze River Library and Art Press, 1959.

Cheng, Philip H. "The Functions of Chinese Opera in Social Control and Change." Ph.D. dissertation, Southern Illinois University, 1974.

Chi, J. S. *History of the Chinese Theater.* Taipei, Taiwan: Chung Kuang Literature Publishing Co., 1962.

Chiang, Ching. *On the Revolution of Peking Opera.* Peking: Foreign Languages Press, 1968.

Chin, Ai-li S. "Family Relations in Modern Chinese Fiction." In *Family and Kinship in Chinese Society,* edited by Maurice Freedman. Stanford, Ca.: Stanford University Press, 1970.

_____. "Interdependence of Roles in Transitional China—A Structural Analysis of Attitudes in Contemporary Chinese Literature." Ph.D. dissertation, Radcliffe College (Harvard University), 1951.

Chin, Robert and Ai-li S. Chin. *Psychological Research in Communist China: 1949–1966.* Cambridge, Mass.: The M.I.T. Press, 1969.

Chu, Chieh-fan. *Treatises on Chinese Songs and Ballads.* Taipei: Chung Hua Bookstore, 1974.

Chu, Godwin C. *Radical Change through Communication in Mao's China.* Honolulu, Hawaii: University Press of Hawaii, 1977.

Chu, Godwin C., Philip Cheng, and Leonard Chu. *The Roles of Tatzepao in the Cultural Revolution: A Structural- Functional Analysis.* Carbondale, Ill.: Southern Illinois University, 1972.

Eble, Kenneth. "Our Serious Comic." In *The Funnies: An American Idiom,* edited by David Manning White and Robert Abel. New York: The Free Press of Glencoe, 1963.

Festinger, Leon. *A Theory of Cognitive Dissonance*. Stanford, Ca.: Stanford University Press, 1962.

Goldman, Merle. *Literacy Dissent in Communist China*. Cambridge: Harvard University Press, 1967.

Gray, Jack, and Patrick Cavendish. *Chinese Communism in Crisis*. New York: Praeger Publishers, 1968.

Henry, William E. "Projective Tests in Cross-Cultural Research." In *Studying Personality Cross-Culturally*, edited by Bert Kaplan. Evanston, Ill.: Row, Peterson and Co., 1961.

————. "The Thematic Apperception Technique in the Study of Culture-Personality Relations." *Genetic Psychology Monographs* 35: 1947.

Houn, Franklin W. *A Short History of Chinese Communism*. Englewood Cliffs, N.J.: Prentice-Hall, 1967.

————. *To Change a Nation*. New York: The Free Press, 1961.

Hsia, C. T. *A History of Modern Chinese Fiction, 1917–1957*. New Haven, Conn.: Yale University Press, 1961.

Hsia, T. A. "Twenty Years after the Yenan Forum." *China Quarterly* (January-March, 1963): 226–253.

Hsu, Francis L. K. *American and Chinese: Reflections on Two Cultures and Their People*, 2nd ed. Garden City, N.Y.: Doubleday & Company, 1970.

————, ed. *Aspects of Culture and Personality*. New York: Abelard-Schuman, 1954.

————. "Psychosocial Homeostasis and *Jen:* Conceptual Tools for Advancing Psychological Anthropology." *American Anthropologist* 73:1 (February, 1971): 23–44.

————. *Under the Ancestors' Shadow*. Stanford, Ca.: Stanford University Press, 1971.

Hsu, Kai-yu. *The Chinese Literary Scene—A Writer's Visit to the People's Republic*. New York: Random House, 1975.

Hsu, Mou-yun. *History of Chinese Theater*. Shanghai: Commercial Press, 1937.

Hu, Hwai-sheng. *A Study of Chinese Folk Songs*. Hong Kong: Pai Lin Bookstore. Photo edition of a 1925 publication.

Huang, C. C., trans. *Hai Jui Dismissed from Office*. Honolulu, Hawaii: University Press of Hawaii, 1972.

Huang, Joe. *Heroes and Villains in Communist China*. New York: PICA Press, 1973.

Hung, Josephine Huang. *Classic Chinese Plays*. Taipei, Taiwan: Mei Ya Publications, Inc., 1971.

Hunter, Neale. *Shanghai Journal*. New York: Praeger Publishers, 1969.

Inkeles, Alex. "Some Sociological Observations on Culture and Personality Studies." In *Personality: In Nature, Society, and Culture*, edited by Clyde Kluckhohn, Henry A. Murray, and David M. Schneider. New York: Alfred A. Knopf, 1965.

Isaacs, Harold, ed. *Straw Sandals—Chinese Short Stories, 1918–1933*. Cambridge, Mass.: The M.I.T. Press, 1974.

King, Vincent. *Propaganda Campaigns in Communist China*. Cambridge, Mass.: The M.I.T. Press, 1966.

Klochko, Mikhail A. *Soviet Scientist in Red China*. New York: Praeger Publishers, 1964.

Kluckhohn, Clyde. "The Personal Documents in Anthropological Science." In L. Gottschalk et al., *The Use of Personal Documents in History, Anthropology and Sociology*. New York: Social Science Research Council Bulletin 53.

Kroeber, A. L. and Clyde Kluckhohn. *Culture, A Critical Review of Concepts and Definitions*. New York: Random House, 1963.

Kunzle, David. *The Early Comic Strip*. Berkeley, Ca.: University of California Press, 1973.

LaBarre, Weston. "Folklore and Psychology." *Journal of American Folklore* 61 (1948): 382–390.

Lasswell, Harold D. "The Structure and Function of Communication in Society." In *The Communication of Ideas*, edited by Lyman Bryson. New York: Institute for Religious and Social Studies, 1948.

Li, Chin-hui, Wu Chi-jui, and Li Shih, eds. *Children's Folk Songs from 20 Provinces in China*. Peking: National Peking University, 1925. Reprinted 1970 by Orient Cultural Service, Taipei, Taiwan.

Liu, Alan P. L. *Communication and National Integration in Communist China*. Berkeley, Ca.: University of California Press, 1971.

———. *The Use of Traditional Media for Modernization in Communist China*. Cambridge, Mass.: The M.I.T. Press, 1965.

Liu, Hui-chen Wang. "An Analysis of Chinese Clan Rules: Confucian Theories in Action." In *Confucianism in Action*, edited by David S. Nivison and Arthur F. Wright. Stanford, Ca.: Stanford University Press, 1959.

Liu, Hung-tou. *History of Chinese Drama in Sung Dynasty.* Taipei: World Books, 1960.

Liu, Wan-chang. *Children's Folk Songs in Canton.* Canton: Sun Yat-sen University, 1928.

Maccoby, Eleanor E. and Nathan Maccoby. "The Interview: A Tool of Social Science." In *Handbook of Social Psychology,* vol. 1, edited by Gardener Lindzey. Reading, Mass.: Addison-Wesley Publishing Co., 1954.

MacFarquhar, Roderick. *The Hundred Flowers Campaign and the Chinese Intellectuals.* New York: Praeger Publishers, 1960.

Mao, Tse-tung. *On Literature and Art.* Peking: Foreign Languages Press, 1967.

————. *Selected Readings from the Works of Mao Tse-tung.* Peking: People's Publishing House, 1971.

————. *Talks at the Yenan Forum on Literature and Art.* Peking: Foreign Languages Press, 1967.

Mehnert, Klaus. *Peking and the New Left: At Home and Abroad.* Berkeley, Ca.: University of California Press, 1969.

Meserve, Walter and Ruth Meserve. *Modern Drama from Communist China.* New York: New York University Press, 1970.

Moravia, Alberto. *The Red Book and the Great Wall.* New York: Farrar, Strauss & Giroux, 1968.

Mu, Fu-sheng. *The Wilting of the Hundred Flowers.* New York: Praeger Publishers, 1963.

Nebiolo, Gino. *The People's Comic Book,* translated by E. Wilkinson. Garden City, N.Y.: Doubleday & Company, 1973.

Nivison, David S. and Arthur F. Wright, eds. *Confucianism in Action.* Stanford, Ca.: Stanford University Press, 1959.

Pan, Stephen C. Y. and Rev. Raymond J. de Jaegher. *Peking's Red Guard.* New York: Twin Circle Publishing Co., Inc., 1968.

Redfield, Robert. *Peasant Society and Culture, and Anthropological Approach to Civilization.* Chicago: University of Chicago Press, 1956.

Rokeach, Milton. "The Role of Values in Public Opinion Research." *Public Opinion Quarterly* 32 (1968–69): 547–559.

Salisbury, Harrison E. *To Peking—And Beyond.* New York: Quadrangle/The New York Times Book Co., 1973.

Schurmann, Franz. *Ideology and Organization in Communist China*. Berkeley, Ca.: University of California Press, 1968.

Simmel, Georg. *Conflict* and *The Web of Group-Affiliations*. New York: The Free Press, 1955.

Snow, Edgar. *Red Star Over China*. New York: Random House, 1938.

Snow, Lois W. *China on Stage*. New York: Random House, 1972.

Soloman, Richard H. *Mao's Revolution and the Chinese Political Culture*. Berkeley, Ca.: University of California Press, 1971.

Trumbull, Robert, ed. *This is Communist China*. New York: David McKay Co., 1968.

Tung, Chi-ping and Humphrey Evans. *The Thought Revolution*. New York: Coward-McCann, 1966.

Yu, Frederick T. C. *Mass Persuasion in Communist China*. New York: Praeger Publishers, 1964.

――――. *The Strategy and Tactics of Chinese Communist Propaganda as of 1952*. Texas: Air Force Personnel and Training Research Center, 1955.

Yu, Siao. *Remembering My Boyhood*. Taipei, Taiwan: Yih Wen Chih Monthly Publications, 1969.

Wallace, Anthony F. C. *Culture and Personality*. New York: Random House, 1961.

Wang, Hsiao-yu. *Songs and Ballads from Shensi*. Taipei: Tien I Press, 1974. Reprint of a 1935 edition.

Wang, Kuo-wei. *History of Chinese Drama in Sung and Yuan*. Shanghai: Six Arts, 1938.

Contributors

A. DOAK BARNETT, born in China, received his doctorate from Franklin and Marshall College. A leading scholar in China studies, Dr. Barnett was professor of political science at Columbia University before he joined the Brookings Institution, where he is now a Senior Fellow. He has published numerous books on China, including *Communist China in Perspective*; *Cadres, Bureaucracy, and Political Power in Communist China*; *Uncertain Passage: China's Transition to the Post-Mao Era*; and most recently, *China and the Major Powers in East Asia*. He was a Senior Fellow at the East-West Center in 1976–1977.

PHILIP H. CHENG, born in China, received his Ph.D. in journalism from Southern Illinois University. He served as director of journalism, department of communicating arts, University of Wisconsin-Superior, from 1973 to 1975, and is currently an assistant professor in the department of communication, Washington State University. He was formerly a Chinese opera actor and is now doing research on opera as a medium of intercultural communication.

AI-LI S. CHIN, born in China, received her Ph.D. in sociology at Harvard University. She is the coauthor of *Psychological Research in Communist China, 1949–1966* and a contributor to academic journals and volumes on China and Chinese-Americans. Her main research interests are: role changes in modern Chinese society and Chinese-American identity and community affairs. She is an assistant professor at the University of Massachusetts.

GODWIN C. CHU, born in China, is a research associate with the East-West Center in Hawaii. He did his undergraduate work in China and received his Ph.D. in communication research from Stanford University. His articles have appeared in numerous journals. He is the author of *Radical Change through Communication in Mao's China*, senior author of *The Role of Tatzepao in Cultural Revolution—A Structural-Functional Analysis*, and co-editor of *Communication and Development in China* and *Communication for Group Transformation and Development*.

LEONARD L. CHU, born in China, is the editor of *The Asian Messenger* and a research specialist at the Centre for Communication Studies, Chinese University of Hong Kong. He is the author of *Planned Birth Campaigns in China: 1949-1976* and co-editor of *Women and Media in Asia*. He received his M.A. from Southern Illinois University, where he is a Ph.D. candidate in journalism.

JOHN C. HWANG, born in China, is an associate professor of Communication Studies at California State University, Sacramento. He received his doctoral degree from the University of Oregon. His research interests are in intercultural communication.

NIEN-LING LIU, born in China, received her education at the University of California at Berkeley, Columbia University, Harvard University, and Cambridge University, England. She works as an author and publisher. She is a frequent contributor to major magazines and journals in Hong Kong.

DAVID JIM-TAT POON received his master's degree in journalism from the University of California at Berkeley. He is currently information and public relations officer with the Hong Kong Polytechnic Institute. His research has been on China's *tatzepao*.

Index

⚒ Production Notes

This book was designed by Roger J. Eggers and typeset on the Unified Composing System by the design and production staff of The University Press of Hawaii.

The text and display typeface is California.

Offset presswork and binding were done by Halliday Lithograph. Text paper is Glatfelter P & S Offset, basis 55.